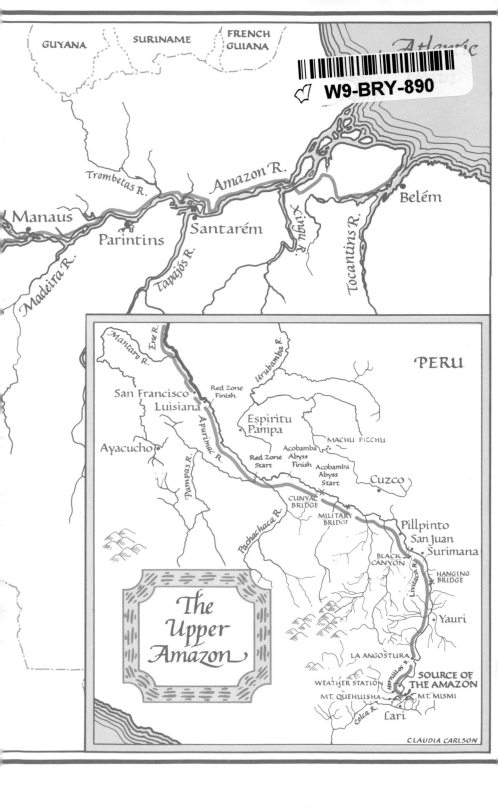

GUYANA SURINAME FRENCH GUIANA

Atlantic

Trombetas R. Amazon R. Belém

Manaus Santarém

Parintins

Madeira R. Tapajós R. Xingu R. Tocantins R.

Ene R.

Mantaro R. PERU

San Francisco Red Zone Uribamba R.
Luisiana Finish

Espiritu MACHU PICCHU
Pampa

Ayacucho Pampas R. Apurímac R. Acobamba
Red Zone Abyss
Start Finish
Acobamba
Abyss Cuzco
Start

CUNYAC
BRIDGE

MILITARY
BRIDGE

Pachachaca R. Pillpinto
San Juan
Surimana

BLACK
CANYON Liviac R. HANGING
BRIDGE

The
Upper Yauri
Amazon

LA ANGOSTURA

WEATHER STATION Hornillos R. SOURCE OF
THE AMAZON
MT. QUEHUISHA MT. MISMI

Colca R. Lari

CLAUDIA CARLSON

RUNNING THE AMAZON

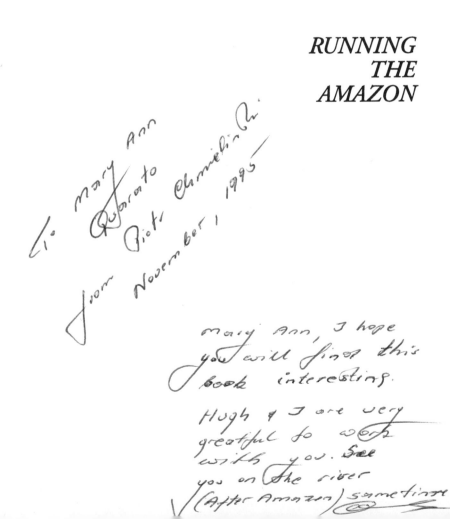

To Mary Ann
Quborato
from Piotr Chmielin...
November 1 1995

Mary Ann, I hope
you will find this
book interesting.

Hugh & I are very
greatful to work
with you. See
you on the river
(After Amazon) sometime.

RUNNING

THE AMAZON

BY JOE KANE

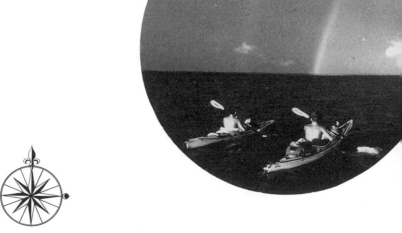

THE ADVENTURE LIBRARY

FOR ELYSE

Contents

	Illustrations	ix
	Acknowledgments	xi
	Introduction	xiii
	ONE • HIGH COUNTRY	
1	The Pacific	3
2	The Colca	13
3	Headwaters	27
4	The Upper Apurimac	47
5	The Black Canyon	67
6	Trail's End	85
	TWO • WHITE WATER	
7	Meeting the Great Speaker	103
8	The Acobamba Abyss	117
9	The Middle Apurimac	141
10	The Lower Apurimac (The Red Zone)	157
11	The Ene	177
12	The Tambo	191
	THREE • THE RIVER SEA	
13	The Upper Ucayali	207
14	The Lower Ucayali	225
15	The Marañón	239
16	The Solimões	261
17	The Amazon	281
18	The Pará	299
19	The Atlantic	313
	Afterword	319

Illustrations

Following page 158:

Seven members of the expedition.

"El Condorito."

At 15,000 feet on the approach to the source: François Odendaal, Tim Biggs, Pastor.

Portaging the upper Apurimac: Piotr Chmielinski, Tim Biggs, François Odendaal, Jerome Truran.

Dr. Kate Durrant and the author in San Juan.

The last Inca hanging bridge, woven entirely of hammered grass.

Kate Durrant consulting patients near the Hanging Bridge.

Jerome Truran on the upper Apurimac.

Tim Biggs executing an Eskimo roll.

Tim Biggs on the upper Apurimac.

Piotr Chmielinski, Jerome Truran, Tim Biggs.

Jerome Truran in the Acobamba Abyss.

Quechua man and son.

Shakedown run on the Apurimac: Piotr Chmielinski, the author, Sergio Leon, Kate Durrant.

In the Acobamba Abyss (note high-water mark).

Lining the raft through the Acobamba Abyss.

Jerome Truran in the Acobamba Abyss.

Cloud Forest in the Red Zone: Jerome Truran, Tim Biggs, François Odendaal.

Asháninka man.

In the Red Zone: Jerome Truran, the author, Kate Durrant.

On the lower Tambo: Kate Durrant and Jerome Truran on native raft; Piotr Chmielinski and the author on *gringo* equivalent.

Piotr Chmielinski, Kate Durrant, and the author with sea kayaks and the *Jhuliana* in Pucallpa.

Following page 254:

Sea kayak with Christmas tree, Iquitos.

On the River Sea: Piotr Chmielinski and the author near the Brazilian border, two thousand miles from the Atlantic.

Friends in Tabatinga.

Piotr Chmielinski and *caboclo* fisherman with the author's birthday dinner.

In storm's wake on the Solimões.

Piotr Chmielinski (foreground) and the author.

Sea kayak with bushmaster.

The author and Piotr Chmielinski in sea kayaks; Kate Durrant aboard the *Roberto II.*

Downtown Gurupá.

The author, Piotr Chmielinski, and *caboclo* fishermen near Marajó Bay.

Oz: the author and Piotr Chmielinski at Belém.

The author and Piotr Chmielinski at the mouth of the Amazon.

All photographs by Zbigniew Bzdak/Canoandes, Inc.

Acknowledgments

The experiences on which this book is based reflect a shared effort by the members of the Amazon Source to Sea Expedition: Tim Biggs, Zbyszek Bzdak, Piotr Chmielinski, Kate Durrant, Jack Jourgensen, Sergio Leon, François Odendaal, Jerome Truran, Fanie Van der Merwe, and Pierre Van Heerden. That they would commit themselves not only to running the Amazon but to being observed and written about by me, a stranger to all of them when I arrived in Peru, bespeaks a profound collective courage, one from which I continue to draw inspiration.

Without the encouragement, guidance, hard work, and friendship of my agent, Joe Spieler, I would have had neither the wherewithal to embark on such a journey nor the confidence to write about it; to him I extend my deepest thanks. My editor, Ashbel Green, patiently guided me out of the disaster area that is a first draft into the Promised Land of a finished book; without him this story would not have been told. Of the many people who also read and commented on the manuscript, I wish especially to thank K. Patrick Conner and Daniel Ben-Horin, who waded through several swampy drafts with keen eyes and unflagging pencils. I am eternally in their debt.

The expedition itself would not have succeeded without the off-the-water support—financial, logistical, and emotional—of Bryce Anderson, Patricia Moore, Jim Allison, Jacek and Teresa Bogucki, Kaye Reed and the people of Casper, Wyoming, Canoandes, Inc. and Michael and Selma Kon, Jerzy Majcherczyk, and Andrzej Pietowski of Canoandes Expeditions, Jerzy Dylski and Polonia of New York, Boleslaw Wierzbianski of Nowy Dziennik, New York, John Tichenor, Wilbur E. Garrett and *National Geographic Magazine*, Mark Bryant and *Outside Magazine*, and the South American Explorers Club. A special thanks also to Marc

Reisner, Jim Keller, Randall Hayes and the Rainforest Action Network, and Manuel Lizarralde.

We were provided with excellent equipment and supplies by Bill Masters of Perception and Aquaterra kayaks, whose vessels we came to know perhaps too intimately; by Sally McCoy and The North Face, whose tents we called home for six months; by Jeanette Smith of Yurika, our main food supplier; and by Jim Stohlquist of Colorado Kayak Supply, who outfitted us with white-water gear.

Of the hundreds of people in South America who helped us along the way, I wish in particular to thank: Luis E. Muga in Lima; Antonio Vellutino and family, the Arana family, Jose Domingo Paz and family, Mauricio de Romana and family, the Hotel Turistas, and the Pizza Nostra restaurant in Arequipa; Edwin Goycochea and Rio Bravo, and Chando Gonzalez and Mayuc Expeditions in Cuzco; Enrique "Kike" Toledo in Iquitos; Foptur, the Peruvian department of tourism; and Aero Peru.

In Brazil, Ivano F. Cardeiro of Emamtur shielded us from the bewilderment of Manaus, and Maria Severa of Paratur and the staff of the Equatorial Palace Hotel buffered our return to the modern world in Belém. As, in Rio de Janeiro, did Mateusz Feldhuzen, of Nowy Dziennik. Thanks also to ABC-TV's *Good Morning America* and Pan American Airlines for bringing us home.

During my journey I saw much that I did not at first understand and could not explore as fully as I would have preferred. Many written works later helped to clarify my impressions. In particular, regarding the complex and wholly fascinating culture of the Quechua, I owe a debt to Ronald Wright's *Cut Stones and Crossroads*, Billie Jean Isbell's *To Defend Ourselves,* and John Hemming's *The Conquest of the Incas.* On the lower Amazon, the classic studies by Alfred Russel Wallace, Henry Bates, Richard Spruce, and William Lewis Herndon, all recorded in the nineteenth century, remain surprisingly and fully relevant.

Finally, on the long river that is the writing of a first book I have been loved, nurtured, advised, ably critiqued, and rescued from some mighty dark spiritual holes by Elyse Axell, who along the way also consented to become my wife. This book is for her.

Introduction

The Amazon, with its more than eleven hundred tributaries, seventeen of which are more than a thousand miles long, has provided river-running adventure for centuries.

On December 26, 1541, the Spanish conquistador Francisco de Orellana and about fifty of his countrymen, who had come down into the jungle in search of El Dorado and the Land of Cinnamon, set out in a jerry-built brigantine down the Napo, one of the Amazon's Ecuadorian tributaries, having no idea where they were going or what awaited them. They became the first Europeans to penetrate the Amazon basin. They passed riverine settlements that went on for miles, a civilization that recent research by archaeologist Anna Roosevelt suggests was as advanced as that of the Incas. Here they were attacked by apparently female warriors, the Amazons for whom Orellana named the river.

In 1913 an expedition including Theodore Roosevelt, who had just lost his presidential reelection bid, descended a sub-sub-tributary of the Amazon called the Rio Dubido, the River of Doubt. The Rio Dubido flows into the Aripuana, which feeds the Madeira, one of the Amazon's major right-bank tributaries, and is labeled on modern maps as the Rio Roosevelt or the Rio Tedoro. It has some major white water, and the expedition encountered tragedy. One of Roosevelt's paddlers went mad and killed another paddler, and Roosevelt's own health never recovered from the harrowing adventure. He died a few years later.

In 1960 the young explorer and writer Peter Matthiessen shot the Pongo de Manique on the Urubamba River, one of the Amazon's Peruvian headwaters, on a *balsa*, or log raft. His account of the adventure in *The Cloud Forest* remains terrifyingly vivid. The Pongo is the final sluice, at the bottom of which the river—having dropped ten thousand feet in fifty miles from the Andes to the jungle—slams into a wall of water, followed by furious whirlpools. Matthiessen told me years later that it was the most foolish thing he ever did.

The literature inspired by Amazonian river adventure also includes books which are, to put it politely, greatly embellished. For example, Leonard Clark's *The Rivers Ran East* was published in 1953, and in those days the Green Hell school predominated in books on the Amazon. Clark made it seem as if poisonous snakes dripped from every tree, and savages lurked in the foliage, waiting for an opportunity to shrink his head, but his route was basically the same one taken by Margaret Booth in 1910. Ms. Booth wore full Victorian skirts, and for much of the way she was carried in a litter and experienced nothing even vaguely unsettling.

There is, however, no embellishment in Joe Kane's *Running the Amazon*, and no need for it. *Running the Amazon* recounts the ultimate feat of Amazonian river-exploration—traveling the entire length of the drainage, some four thousand two hundred miles, from the source to the sea. In 1985, when Kane joined a kayaking expedition with this ambitious itinerary, it was one of the few remaining "firsts" in global exploration. No one had even survived the initial and most difficult leg—the terrifying rapids of the Apurimac River. As Kane tells us, the Apurimac "drops almost thirteen thousand vertical feet, a gradient five times that of the Colorado River through the Grand Canyon. Before the Apurimac collapses, spent, into the Amazon basin, she carves a gorge that for miles at a time is more than 10,000 feet deep. It is one of the deepest river gorges on the planet." The Grand Canyon is a mere 5,000 feet deep.

In 1976 the leader of a German expedition had been killed within three minutes of putting into the Apurimac. Another team, led by J. Calvin Giddings of the University of Utah, had bailed out of one section, Black Canyon, a few years earlier. Going further, Giddings believed, "would be suicide." He returned the following year, putting into the river below Black Canyon, and he and his four-man team narrowly managed to get through the Acobamba Abyss.

It was against this intimidating background that Joe Kane's expedition, including nine men and one woman, set out in 1985. What possessed Kane, who had no experience with white-water kayaking, to accept a stranger's invitation to chronicle such a perilous, perhaps even suicidal adventure? He suggests that he had found something missing from his life in the American mainstream: "I felt that the life I lived was a step removed: filtered, rehearsed, relayed." He had traveled to Guatemala and Mexico, and he spoke Spanish. Perhaps, as I did at the same age, he had "a burning desire to do something notable," in the words of Sir Walter Raleigh, the Elizabethan buccaneer who explored South America's other great jungle river, the Orinoco.

My first experience with the Amazon was at age thirty. I had contracted to write a book for the Sierra Club, and arriving in the fall of 1976, I spent nine months exploring the basin. For a month I lived in the Cayapo Indian village of Mekranoti, cataloging their medicinal plants. Later, near the Venezuela border, I canoed for ten days up a jungle river and trekked to a Yanomami village that had never been entered by white so-called *civilizados*. The region has since been overrun by prospectors, and the isolated stone-age existence of the Yanomami has been devasted. Since that trip I have returned to the Amazon half a dozen times to trace the historical basis of the Amazon-women legend, to write about the murder of Chico Mendes, the Brazilian labor union martyr, and on other projects. I have covered some of the same ground Kane writes about and can attest to the accuracy of his descriptions.

Toward the end of my first trip I remember descending into the stupendous gorge cut by the roiling Apurimac and crossing the river at Pillpinto. I was shuddering and hallucinating from blackwater fever, the most virulent type of malaria, which I had picked up in the jungle a few weeks earlier. I barely made it to Cuzco, barely escaped from that abyss with my life. I had done a little white-water canoeing, and I remember looking at the torrent smashing around boulders and thinking that you would have to be completely nuts to even think of running this river. And was it even a sane idea to shoot the Pongo de Manique, which I still planned to do?

Joe Kane's riveting narrative belongs with the classics of Amazonian exploration literature, but unlike its predecessors it brings a modern sensibility to the genre. He has an unusual gift for characterization. He deftly and compassionately brings to life his fellow-expeditionaries, their ego clashes and character flaws and heroic qualities. The people he meets along the river emerge as fully drawn human beings; they do not remain primitive stick figures as they do in most of the early exploration literature.

Even the river itself becomes a character—the central character, in fact—an awesome, almost godlike presence, which is how the native Amazonians themselves see it. "She would barrel along straight and fast for a quarter mile," Kane writes of the stretch known as the Tambo, "lulling us with a bouncy joyride, her rolling boil drumming lightly on the raft's underside and only hinting at the force at work below. Then she would slam into a curve and snap us awake with powerful turbulence and huge whirlpools that surfaced and sucked and disappeared like some kind of carnivorous aquatic giants."

After the confluence of the Tambo and the Urubamba just below Atalaya, the white water and most of the attendant hydrological danger were over, but there were thirty-five hundred miles remaining, and they were to prove a severe ordeal. Only two members of the expedition—Kane himself and Piotr Chmielinski —would make it to the Amazon's mouth after three more grueling months on the river. That no one was killed in the white water or by guerrillas of the Shining Path or by *narcotraficantes* is a miracle, and Kane and Chmielinski's feat is an extraordinary one. The river had selected those who had the right stuff.

Soon after Kane and Chmielinski got home, the Shining Path overran the province of Chumpivilca, which includes the Apurimac Valley. Although the guerrilla's leader, "Presidente Gonzalo" Guzman, was subsequently caught and is now behind bars in Lima, the status of the Shining Path and the safety of the Apurimac region for foreigners is unclear. So it may be a while before

Kane and Chmielinski's feat is repeated—if ever.

Kane's experiences in the Amazon changed his life, as my own experiences there changed mine. The trip awakened in him a love of white water. In 1991, on assignment from the *National Geographic*, he ran the Colca River in Peru, which has the world's deepest canyon. It also awakened him to the environmental threats to the world's largest, most mysterious and biologically diverse wilderness, and to the Amazon's native people. He went on to write an article about the Huaorani, a nomadic group in Ecuadorian Amazonia, known as the Oriente, who are sitting on rich oil fields that have been leased to American oil companies. The article, published in *The New Yorker* in the fall of 1993, chronicled the appalling physical and cultural destruction that is taking place in the Oriente. It won Kane an Overseas Press Club Award for "best environmental reporting in any medium" and forms part of a book he has recently completed on the subject.

Running the Amazon was Joe Kane's first book, and it will endure for many years as a classic in the literature of Amazonian adventure.

Alex Shoumatoff
Keene, New York, 1994

ONE

HIGH COUNTRY

1 *The Pacific*

Southern Peru, late August 1985. Beneath a rust-colored winter sky an old GMC flatbed bounced slowly through the high Andean badlands known as the *puna*. It is a lunar landscape, flat, treeless, ringed with bald dun hills and sharp gray peaks, bone-dry nine months of the year, beaten by frigid, dust-coated winds. At fifteen thousand feet, where the oxygen content of the air is about half that at sea level, the head throbs, and in those rare moments when the sky brightens, cold sunlight races down uncut and stings the eyeballs. I beheld the *puna* through an involuntary squint. And I thought, uneasily, that I did not at all understand what I was getting into.

There were five of us hunkered down on the truck bed. We proposed to make the first source-to-sea navigation of the planet's longest river, the Amazon, to see with our own eyes every foot of the four-thousand-mile chain of water that rises in southern Peru and spills north through the Andes and east to the Atlantic. To do that we had to find the river's source, hidden somewhere in those bleak highlands. But in searching for the birthplace of the Amazon, we had found only dust. Though we hacked and spit and squeezed our eyelids shut, the howling puna wind drove dust into every throat, ear, eye and pore. Dust penetrated food crates, water bottles, the soul itself.

Sitting to my right was a thirty-year-old Pole, Zbigniew Bzdak, a squat, bearish man with soft blue eyes, a flowing red beard, and a balding dome fringed with blond hair. Despite the conditions, he could no more go without talking than without air.

"Six years ago I was living in Krakow," he shouted to me. "I was studying photography and nuclear physics. Not a great life, but not bad. You have coffee in the morning and beer in the afternoon. One day my neighbor, this is Piotr, comes to visit. He tells me that he is going to Latin America to kayak every big river he can find." Piotr was Piotr Chmielinski, who had recently earned a master's degree in mechanical engineering. He and his nine-man expedition had finagled a seven-ton truck from the Polish military, stocked it with twenty kayaks and a year's supply of kielbasa, and loaded it on a freighter. "The boat is ready to leave but the photographer has disappeared," Bzdak said. "Piotr wants to know am I interested."

They left Poland together two weeks later, thinking they would be gone for six months. Neither man had yet returned.

"First river we run is the Pescados, in Mexico. We put seven kayaks in the river. In fifteen minutes we lose six of them. River just takes them away. Big Polish joke."

But they persisted, ultimately running twenty-three rivers, thirteen of them first descents, in eleven countries. The Mexican government hired them to study six previously uncharted rivers. The National Geographic Society commissioned them to report on the deepest canyon in the world, Peru's Colca. Jacques Cousteau invited them to join the white-water team for his Amazon film project (an invitation they declined in the face of other commitments).

"Big difference between Cousteau's Amazon expedition and this one," Bzdak said.

"What is that?" I asked.

"Four million dollars. Even in the Amazon Cousteau is drinking good wine. We are flat broke."

In 1981 the Poles made the first recorded descent of the Colca canyon. When they returned to the Colca in 1983 for *National Geographic*, they recruited a South African, Tim Biggs, to be their lead kayaker. Biggs was now sitting across from me with his knees pulled up beneath an Abe Lincoln beard. Thirty-three, short, muscular, dark-eyed, his curly brown hair going gray, Biggs had a reputation as a bold riverman with extraordinary energy (once, solo, he had beaten an eight-man rowing team in a twelve-hour race) and strong, sometimes perplexing convictions. He was, for example, a third-generation vegetarian from a family that raised beef cattle. For the past two hours he'd been blowing a harmonica nonstop into the teeth of the wind, playing the only tune he knew, "Waltzing Matilda," again and again, faster and faster.

Biggs, of British ancestry, had been a world-class distance kayaker for nearly a decade, but eventually, banned from one country after another as a South African athlete, he had retired from competitive racing. He had met the Poles in Peru in 1981, when he captained a South African expedition on the deadly Urubamba River, which flows beneath the walls of Machu Picchu. Afterward, Biggs had joined Chmielinski on a first descent of the most difficult section of the nearby Apurimac River, considered the furthest tributary of the Amazon. Later, in the city of Arequipa, he'd led the Polish team through long evenings of drinking and dancing. Bzdak had nicknamed him "Zulu."

Since then, however, Biggs had married, adopting his wife's evangelical Christianity, and he now spent long evenings reading his Bible. He was ready to settle down, work the family farm, and raise kids. Still, he figured he had time for one more expedition.

Next to Biggs sat Dr. Kate Durrant, her teeth chattering despite the sleeping bag in which she'd wrapped herself. Thirty, sharp-eyed, lean and British, she had a long, aristocratic face and auburn hair cut in a short punk style laced with orange. She stuck her head up and, as best she could, surveyed the barren *puna*. "At times like this," she shouted, "I wonder why I ever came here."

"You come because it is better than your boring life in London," Bzdak shouted back.

"I suppose so."

She was the only woman on the expedition, which included five other men in addition to the four of us on the truck bed. Prior to her arrival in Peru she had met only two of her teammates face-to-face. She had been working in London as a general practitioner for the National Health Service when friends in the television industry mentioned a project to film the first descent of the Amazon. Thinking a female doctor would lend romance to their story, the film's producers selected Durrant from some sixty applicants. Ultimately the producers withdrew from the project, but Durrant pushed ahead. She had spent the last year researching high-altitude and tropical medicine and assembling a medical kit designed to prevent, or nurse the team through, malaria, yellow fever, hepatitis, rabies, gangrene, intestinal parasites, toothaches, poisonous snakebites, dysentery, broken bones, and a list of other horrors up to and including the wretched *candiru,* a tiny, parasitic catfish that pins itself inside the human urethra with nonretractable spines. Once in place it must be cut out.

Leaning against me for warmth, suffering in silence, was Sergio Leon. A devout Christian Scientist (only with reluctance had he agreed to ingest the twice-weekly malaria prophylaxis upon which Durrant insisted), he was short and dark, the strong cheekbones of his Indian ancestry mixing handsomely with a leafy black mustache bequeathed him by Spanish forebears. He had taken leave from his post as director of Costa Rica's Corcovado National Park to participate in the expedition. He was the team's only native Spanish speaker and its expert on tropical biology. Though as cold and uncomfortable as he ever had been, he displayed a bright-eyed tropical sang-froid. He looked twenty-five; he was forty-seven.

I was the expedition's only American, and, as I was to see with the painful clarity of hindsight, by far its most naive member. It was, or should have been, a telling sign that I carried in my duffel bag a copy of *The Portable Conrad* and wore a new great-white-hunter felt safari hat and a khaki shirt with epaulets—the sort of vogue paramilitary garb that can get one shot on sight in a violent country such as Peru.

I was miserable, freezing, and nauseous from the altitude. I was also bewildered, what self-knowledge I possessed arising from panic rather than insight. When I'd left the United States for Peru

I'd seen myself in a romantic light—as a man on the run from something, though from exactly what I hadn't determined. On that bone-jarring truck ride, however, I vaguely, and with some horror, understood that I was also running *toward* something: the black hole of the Amazon. With nine complete strangers.

For me it did not start with a wild love of the Amazon, though later I did learn to love it. It began in a more ordinary way, with a telephone call from a stranger.

The call came on one of those bright June San Francisco days when, as they say, the weather is so perfect there does not seem to be any weather at all. The bay's sweet-salt air drifted in through the open window of my office as I sat at my desk trying to finish a newspaper column, a sort of consumers' service I wrote for the San Francisco *Chronicle*.

The voice on the line was guttural, Germanic in tone; later I would learn it was Afrikaans. The caller identified himself as Dr. François Odendaal and said he studied butterflies for an American university. But he wanted to discuss an independent project, one that he had been developing for the last six years. He intended to become the first man to navigate the length of "the greatest of all rivers," the Amazon.

I was skeptical. Man had golfed on the moon but had yet to travel his planet's most famous river from source to sea? Still, I listened.

Odendaal's expedition would begin with a climb to the source of the Amazon, a snowfield high in the Andes. There his team would mount white-water kayaks, which they would paddle some four hundred miles down the Apurimac, one of the most dangerous white-water rivers on Earth. Once on the jungle floor, they would switch to sea kayaks for the three-thousand-eight-hundred-mile haul through the Amazon basin to the Atlantic Ocean. Odendaal estimated his journey would take four months.

He had a problem, however. At the last minute, the British film company that was to have sponsored him had withdrawn its backing. The expedition, scheduled to depart for South America in six weeks, was about to collapse. He said mutual acquaintances had suggested I might write press releases to help him raise money.

I said I didn't do that kind of work; he should try a public relations firm instead. I gave him a name and wished him luck. We hung up.

I finished the newspaper column in mid-afternoon, bought a six-pack of beer, and walked to the beach. I swam in the cold Pacific. Then I lay down in the sand, opened a beer, and settled into that glazed state that precedes an afternoon nap. Tropical images bubbled up from my subconscious: parrots, palm trees, monkeys swinging on vines.

I bolted awake, anxious, and found myself ticking off the reasons a man like me could not go to the Amazon. I had just begun living with a woman who had recently graduated from law school. We might soon marry. Though my job was nothing spectacular, I was competent at it, and it was secure.

The relationship scared me and I was bored with the job. That was the source of my anxiety. When I got home, I called the night line at Odendaal's university.

"Don't look at the dog!"

I looked at the dog, looked right into the beast's beady eyes. It sprang at my face but got instead the car window between its fangs and my neck—and a swift fist from François Odendaal.

"My apologies," he said. "I should have warned you sooner." He leaned into the car and cooed to the whimpering animal. "The dog is a dingo. I found him when I was studying in Australia. He wandered in from the outback, starving and nearly dead, and I saved him. He has been with me ever since. He hates people. He would tear your eyes out."

The small dog frightened me. It was shorthaired, wiry, and ugly, and even after the punch it glowered at me, muttering from low in its throat. When I looked at it again it exploded in wild barking and threw itself at the window a second time. I didn't look at it after that.

I looked at Odendaal. We were about the same age (he had said he was thirty), but he was not what I had expected. He was tall and had thinning red hair and the beginning of a pot belly and a funny kind of bouncing limp when he walked, as if he had sprained an ankle. He did not look like an athlete. He said, "You do not look like the man I expected," and I thought: Well.

I stared at his feet, rudely. I couldn't help it. They were oddly small for his height. "Polio," he said, without reproach, as if my reaction were one he often experienced. Offering no further explanation, he asked, "May I buy you a beer?"

We were in a resort town high in the Colorado Rockies, near where Odendaal was spending a part of the summer supervising a butterfly research station. We found a bar and sat down at a table. Odendaal spread out a map rendered in garish colors, as if it had been lifted from the bulletin board of an elementary-school classroom. Here, on what turned out to be a map prepared by the Peruvian military, were the mountains, in lurid orange; the cloud forest, in bubbly pink and screaming gold; the jungle, in—of course—funky, primordial green.

I watched Odendaal trace the blue vein that would define his journey. It was an intoxicating exercise; maps are such seductive fictions. The river names bewitched me. *Apacheta, Lloqueta, Hornillos, Apurimac, Ene, Tambo, Ucayali, Marañón, Solimões, Amazon.* Pronounced, they twisted the tongue in sensual ways. They sang, they enticed.

So did the campaign Odendaal laid out. He would climb big mountains, kayak wild rivers, at least one of which had never been run, and travel areas that were virtually unmapped. In one of those unmapped places, called the Red Zone, the Peruvian government was engaged in an exceptionally grisly war with the Sendero Luminoso, or Shining Path. "These are guerrillas," Odendaal said. "You may have heard of them. Every once in a while they kill people, including journalists." He looked at me and laughed. The Red Zone was under martial law and closed to outsiders. Odendaal would have to sneak through it. Later, he would spend weeks in the heart of Peru's cocaine-producing country. He would meet exotic tribes. Britain's prestigious Royal Geographical Society had already invited him to speak upon completion of his journey.

Odendaal lit a cigarette and sat back. "What do you think?" he asked.

The deal was this: If I could raise money from a publisher and contribute it to the expedition, Odendaal would let me write about his adventure. I would shadow the team as best I could. For the first month I would ride in a support truck, but after that, when we ran out of road, it would be raft, banana boat, whatever.

I wasn't particularly qualified for the trip. I spoke Spanish, and I was in decent physical shape—I ran five miles a day and did two hundred push-ups—but I had never been on a white-water raft, and I was not a good swimmer. By no means was I an "explorer." Still, I felt that the life I lived was a step removed: filtered, rehearsed, relayed.

Six weeks after that first phone call, I quit my job and kissed my girlfriend good-bye. Feverish and sweating from a battery of injections received the night before, I met François Odendaal at the San Francisco airport, where we boarded a plane for Lima, Peru.

Over Mexico we spoke about the expedition. Odendaal was worried about the river, about his health, about money. But the thing that worried him most, the thing that had his guts in an uproar, was Piotr Chmielinski.

Chmielinski was the expedition's co-organizer. Odendaal had met him only once, but he said that he had found the Pole brilliant, tireless, and ambitious. Chmielinski's first descent of the Colca had made him a celebrity in Peru, and he had an easy way with the Byzantine workings of the Peruvian bureaucracy. He knew how to get equipment into the country without its being confiscated, was adept at wheedling favors from government officials, understood the peasants who lived along the rivers.

But Odendaal feared that Chmielinski would try to seize control of the expedition at the first opportunity. In fact, he said,

Chmielinski had already attempted one such coup. When Odendaal's film backing had collapsed, Chmielinski had found new money, from a Wyoming millionaire who'd cornered the U.S. market for highway-stripe paint. Odendaal said that Chmielinski had then tried to force him to surrender his role as leader, but Odendaal had contacted the sponsor himself and won his support. Odendaal said he would have thrown the Pole off the expedition had he not sorely needed his expertise. But he was worried. Peru was Chmielinski's turf.

The plane bounced twice: Lima.

2 *The Colca*

Lima, Melville wrote in *Moby Dick*, is "the strangest saddest city thou canst see . . . there is a higher horror in the whiteness of her woe." There was woe aplenty in the city the night we arrived, but we couldn't see it, for its color was not white but black. Guerrillas had bombed the city's main power plants, plunging her into a darkness punctuated only by an occasional oil-drum fire.

Sergio Leon, with whom Odendaal had worked in Costa Rica, arrived on the flight after ours. We spent three days together in Lima, but I never got a good look at the city. My perspective was jaundiced. I fell sick the second day, erupting in a fit of spasms brought on, I suspected, by nerves, travel fatigue, and the medicine I was taking to prevent altitude sickness, one of whose side effects, apparently, was altitude sickness.

That third morning I awoke drained and beaten, my clothes soaked with sweat, my head hot with fever. Nevertheless, while Odendaal remained in Lima to await other expedition members, Leon and I set off on an eighteen-hour bus ride down Peru's desolate Pacific coast. We were bound for Arequipa, from where we would commence our climb to the source of the Amazon, and where we hoped to meet the notorious Chmielinski and his partner, Zbigniew Bzdak.

At some time during the night we veered east and began climbing into the Andes. At dawn we pulled into Arequipa, Peru's forgotten metropolis, a high, sunny, desert city set against a spectacular trio of snow-covered volcanoes. Arequipa is home to six hundred thousand short, calm people, no flies, and no joggers. The city takes its name from a Quechua expression that means "You are welcome to stay."

We went to our lodgings. That night I received a phone call.

"*Hola*," I said when I picked up the phone.

"Hello," the voice came back in English. "How going is everything?"

Piotr Chmielinski proved to be a crisp, auburn-haired man of medium height, lean but muscular, with a dapper mustache and the cool blue eyes of a wolf. Polite but reserved, he did not smile as we ate ice cream in Arequipa's Plaza de Armas and watched a shuffling parade of Quechua Indians play "Jesus Christ Superstar" on *quena* flutes, their round tones soothing after the jarring bus ride.

I was surprised when Chmielinski said he had rented a house to serve as expedition headquarters. It seemed extravagant. Odendaal, I said, had told us he would be in Arequipa in a few days and that we would leave the day after he arrived.

"Two weeks," Chmielinski said. "At the least." His tone implied that the discussion was closed.

When Leon and I reported for duty the next morning Chmielinski assigned us to help Bzdak provision the expedition.

"Call me Zbyszek," the photographer said, offering a Polish diminutive that rhymed roughly with *fish shack*. "It is easier." He was wrong about that, but he didn't seem to mind my fumbling his name. He was Chmielinski's opposite, loose and easygoing, and he quickly formulated what would be our only guideline in securing food: "No mess." If it couldn't be boiled, dissolved, or eaten cold, we didn't want it.

We had a few supplies on hand already. Chmielinski had persuaded a Canadian company, Yurika, to provide us with a stock of their product, which was designed for the survivalist market. It was whole food vacuum-packed into aluminum envelopes. You dropped an envelope in boiling water for five minutes, then dumped the stuff over instant rice or potatoes. Our diet in some of the planet's most desolate locales would include beef burgundy, chicken cacciatore, and, for those nights of complete abandon, sweet-and-sour shrimp.

But that alone wouldn't be enough. We spent the next week scrambling about Arequipa's labyrinthine marketplace. One old woman sold us cinnamon and oatmeal, another canned sardines, a third tins of black-market chocolate. We found local cheese in waxed two-kilo wheels, which would keep well. We bought all we could afford, as well as bagged tea, instant coffee, powdered milk, sacks of sugar.

Once, urchins jumped me and tried to steal the bundles of paper money (*soles*) strapped to my body in bulging lumps. Bzdak slapped them away and, unbowed under twenty kilos of chocolate, continued his charge down Arequipa's narrow cobbled streets, stopping to chat every block or so in Spanish, English, or Polish with some old friend or recent acquaintance. Leon and I staggered along behind, gasping in the thin mountain air and wondering if the expedition would ever begin.

Tim Biggs arrived in Arequipa next, accompanied by a tall, blond, twenty-nine-year-old South African named Jerome Truran. Biggs, appointed river captain by Odendaal, would have final say over how each section of the river would be run. Truran would assist him, sharing the lead through the most difficult rapids. The two men had been teammates on the South African kayaking circuit for almost a decade, a relationship that had ended in the face of international sanctions against South African athletes. Biggs had retired, but Truran had emigrated to England, where he eventually gained citizenship (his great-grandfather had been British). Truran had quickly won a berth on the British national team and established himself as one of the world's premier kayakers, winning a gold medal at the 1980 European Wild Water Championship, a silver medal at the 1981 World WWC, and a gold medal at the 1982 National WWC.

Biggs had turned to exploring. During three river trips with Odendaal (to Africa's Limpopo River, Alaska's Colville, and the Urubamba) he had developed a deep affection for the Afrikaner. Biggs had seen the hell of polio firsthand—his older brother had been crippled by it—and he respected the effort Odendaal had made to rise above his handicap. For Biggs, Odendaal had the soul of a poet. He was a visionary, a mystic.

But Biggs worried about him. Odendaal's handicap stoked a great ambition, but he was not much of a kayaker, and his expeditions were not always smoothly run. And so Biggs had urged Odendaal to invite Chmielinski and Truran. Biggs admired the Pole's organizational skills and his knowledge of Peru, and Truran he trusted with his life. Biggs knew he would spend most of his time on the river protecting Odendaal; he wanted someone looking out for Tim Biggs.

Kate Durrant rode the bus into Arequipa alone, a day behind Biggs and Truran, and immediately set to work assembling individual medical kits for each of us to carry, going over our medical records, bringing us up to date on injections, and double-checking the hundreds of items in the big aluminum medical crate that would accompany us down the Amazon.

Meanwhile, Chmielinski managed to borrow a Land Rover—no small feat in Peru—and he, Truran, and Biggs took on the imposing task of retrofitting it. *El Condorito* ("The Little Condor") would be our mother ship for the first four to six weeks of our journey, rendezvousing with the kayakers (Odendaal, Biggs, Truran, and Chmielinski) every week or so and hauling the support-team members, food, the medical crate, spare kayaks and paddles, camping gear, and film.

Or so we had hoped, until we made a test loading. When Chmielinski drove poor Condorito down one of Arequipa's pitted streets the truck rocked violently and listed hard to port. We would have to reduce our load. More important, we saw for a fact what most of us had suspected: Condorito could not possibly carry the entire support crew.

That night I studied the topographic maps I had bought in

Lima. The headwaters and the upper Apurimac flowed through high, desolate plateaus and steep, sparsely inhabited canyons, but there did appear to be trails. I told Chmielinski that if I were able to handle the climb to the source, I would then be willing to try to walk the first leg of the trip.

I couldn't determine exactly how long that walk would be. It would cover about a hundred and fifty river miles, but given all the climbing and descending of canyon walls, it might be three hundred miles by foot. (A British man, John Ridgway, had hiked the lower country in 1970. It would take weeks just to get down to the point at which he had begun his walk.)

Despite the trek's length, my plan was selfish and pragmatic. I was bound to be the first man booted off the overcrowded truck, in which case I would have to fly ahead to the city of Cuzco and hole up there for a month or more while I waited for the rest of the expedition to work its way down out of the high mountains.

I was relieved when Chmielinski endorsed my proposal.

When the British filmmakers pulled out of the Amazon project (Odendaal said they had demanded more control of the project than he was willing to relinquish), Odendaal decided to make his own documentary. He recruited a two-man camera crew from South Africa. Two weeks after Leon and I arrived in Arequipa, Odendaal flew in from Lima with Fanie Van der Merwe, who taught at a film school in Pretoria, and Pierre Van Heerden, one of Van der Merwe's former students. Both had experience as cameramen for mountaineering expeditions, and both were tall, dark, hard-drinking, chain-smoking Afrikaners.

A few nights later we gathered by candlelight around the broad wooden table in the kitchen of our Arequipa headquarters. Odendaal sat at one end of the table, Chmielinski at the other, while the rest of us sat between, passing a bottle of the Peruvian grape brandy called *pisco*. Odendaal delivered a long speech, emphasizing that he had included Chmielinski as co-organizer of the expedition out of respect for his skill and his knowledge of Peru, but that he, Odendaal, was the leader, alone and uncontested, and anyone unwilling to accept that was invited to leave.

When he had finished, he looked to each of us, and then to the end of the table. He asked Chmielinski for comment.

"What is the problem?" the Pole asked in a low voice. "You are the leader. We all know that."

Through a Peruvian friend, Mauricio De Romaña, the resourceful Chmielinski borrowed a second truck, an old but sturdy GMC flatbed. This and Condorito would haul the entire team up to the Colca valley, some fifty miles inland from, and five thousand feet above, Arequipa. From the Colca, Odendaal, Chmielinski, Bzdak, Biggs, Van der Merwe, Van Heerden, and I would attempt to climb by foot to the source of the Amazon, a snowfield atop 18,000-foot Mount Mismi. Durrant, Truran, and Leon would drive Condorito around the mountain and meet us fifteen miles beyond the source, on the Atlantic side of the continental divide. From there, on foot, we would trace the runoff from the divide until it grew deep enough to support the four-man kayak team.

This, at any rate, was the plan, and the next morning, beneath a blood-colored dawn, we loaded the trucks and set course for the high Andes. We made our jarring ascent via a dirt track that contoured the flank of Mount Chachani, one of the trio of volcanoes hovering over Arequipa like brooding monks. Arequipa was quickly swallowed by the dust-swept *puna,* and within a matter of hours, as we climbed to fifteen thousand feet (higher than any point in the continental United States), my every effort became concentrated on choking back the nausea of *soroche,* or altitude sickness.

Given my pain and the lunar bleakness of the landscape, it was easy to see why the indigenous Andeans, who refer to themselves as Runa, or "the people," but who are more widely known as Quechua (the name describes a linguistic group; Quechua was the language the Incas imposed on their subjects), call the *puna* "savage" and consider it forbidding not only physically but spiritually. It is, for example, where one must go to perform sexual acts, such as incest, that are prohibited within the villages, and it is home to the most powerful deities in the Andes, the *apus* and *wamanis,* often described as bearded white men who wear European clothing and live inside mountains and lakes. If not placated through ritual offerings, a *wamani* may eat a man's heart, cause his wife to miscarry, or kill his infant child.

Shrouded in dust, rumbling through the lonely Aguada Blanca Reserve, the truck offered the only wrinkle of motion on the *puna's* dun canvas until, flushed by our intrusion, five long-necked, goggle-eyed vicuña galloped suddenly along a ridgetop. They were a sight at once otherworldly and heartbreaking. They and their fellow ruminants, the guanaco (both, though humpless, are related to the camel), are the largest wild creatures in the *puna,* but they are not big at all, about the size of small North American deer. By the late 1960s the vicuña had been hunted almost to extinction for their fine wool. Though they have come back strong in the reserve, and though they are swift, graceful beasts, moving easily at thirty miles an hour, their speed seemed annulled by the sprawling brown plateau. They ran and they ran, but they appeared not to get anywhere at all.

Such immensity of scale overwhelms the first-time visitor to the Andes. They are the planet's tallest mountains outside the Himalayas and the Pamirs, running north and south like a spine along the west side of the continent in a series of ridges, or *cordilleras,* separated by impossibly deep canyons and high, endless *puna* plateaus. However, although the Andes are never more than a hundred miles from the Pacific coast, their quixotic and frequently violent weather is greatly influenced by the mass of hot, moist air that rises from the Amazon basin and drops its moisture as it moves west. Consequently, the Atlantic slope is lush, the Pacific parched and nearly lifeless. It is said that in the Atacama Desert, southwest of Arequipa, one can travel a hundred and fifty miles at a stretch without finding life large enough to be seen with the naked eye.

I witnessed the *puna* from the bouncing bed of the GMC. The bodies around me changed constantly, shifting from bed to cab and back, but the ride was miserable, and I quickly abandoned any effort to communicate. Instead, silently and without success, I tried to divine some order, some binding pattern, in the babble of strange tongues that percolated above the wind: Polish, Spanish, Afrikaans, English spoken in dialects I had never heard before coming to Peru. Altogether, nine men and one woman; a born-again Christian, an Old World Catholic, a Christian Scientist, agnostics and pagans of various stripes; two Poles, one Brit, three Afrikaners, two South Africans of British heritage, a Costa Rican, an American; four husbands, two fathers; political convictions from far left to far right.

Only four would reach the sea.

Late in the day we dropped down below twelve thousand feet into an immense patchwork of delicate agricultural terraces rising sharply from the Colca River, which runs northwest through the Andes, hairpins south, and drains into the Pacific. The hand-worked terraces (tractors would fall off the steep walls) give the lower reaches of the otherwise arid Colca valley the look of a verdant amphitheater.

High overhead, two Andean condors, the world's largest birds of prey, floated easily on the valley's strong thermals, their ten-foot wingspans casting shadows hundreds of feet below. Viewed through binoculars, the condors, showing a white neck ring on an otherwise black body, looked like hooded executioners. Behind them, white-tipped volcanoes guarded the valley rim, and a few miles downriver, a black slit identified the point where the Colca River has carved the world's deepest gorge, more than twice as deep as the Grand Canyon of the Colorado. At one point the canyon rim is two and a half miles above the river.

When emissaries of the Inca first penetrated the Colca valley, about 1450, they found the Collaguas, a people who worshiped volcanoes and shaped their heads like cones. (Their bizarre cranial effect was achieved by strapping boards to the soft skulls of their infants.) A century later, when the Spanish arrived, the Colca was the second-most-productive unit in the Inca agricultural system, generally recognized as the most sophisticated in the New World.

Assisted by Franciscan missionaries, Gonzalo Pizarro wound up with control of the Colca. Within thirty years half the native population was dead, the rest herded into towns and their farms and irrigation systems all but destroyed.

It was a tragedy repeated throughout sixteenth-century Peru, where the Quechua death rate was two and a half times that of Europe during the Black Plague. Though there are some ten million Quechua-speaking people in Peru today (there were an estimated six million when the *conquistadores* arrived), they have never really recovered from the Spanish conquest. They occupy the lowest position in Peru's variegated social stratum. The country is controlled by an oligarchy of *criollos,* people of predominately Spanish, or white, descent. Between *criollo* and Indian are several vaguely defined *mestizo,* or mixed, classes. Through cultural assimilation and the shedding of their traditional ways, some urban Quechua have managed to assume *mestizo* status. But the rural Quechua most definitely have not, and often the face they choose to display to those who bother to look back down the social ladder at them is hard as stone.

In the four centuries since Pizarro's butchery the Colca valley has regained a delicate equilibrium, though it is not nearly as productive as it once was. Now there is also a new joker in the deck, the $900 million Majes project, which, if ever completed, will pump Andean water westward over the mountains into Peru's coastal desert.

The Majes dam on the upper Colca was inaugurated two months before we arrived. What long-term effect it will have on the valley is unclear, but so far, according to Sister Antonia, a Brooklyn-born Maryknoll nun who has lived in the Colca for fourteen years, it has been devastating. The delicate indigenous economy, based on barter, subsistence agriculture, and cooperative labor, was blasted out of balance by the project's sudden infusion of high technology, hard cash, and steely pragmatism. Precious farmland was bought up and destroyed, farm animals were killed on the fast new roads, and the local cosmology, which held the river and many of the surrounding mountains sacred, was callously assaulted. The few people wise enough to save money during this period left the valley quickly. Most of those who remained rejected the old life for sunglasses, Polaroid cameras, cheap cane alcohol, and, when the project closed down, unemployment.

Chmielinski had hustled free accommodations for us in Achoma, a chunk of contemporary suburbia plopped down square in the middle of the valley and protected from the rest of Peru by chain-link fence, barbed wire, guards, and an electronic gate. At one time Achoma had housed more than one hundred and forty Majes engineers and their families, from Canada, the United Kingdom, Spain, Sweden, and South Africa. Beyond the fence one smelled dung fires and the musky, freshly turned earth of fields that had been tended by the same families for generations. Inside the fence were rows of identical ranch-style houses, graded streets, yards, electric stoves. I felt I could walk into one of the houses, turn on a television set, and watch baseball.

Left with the compound, the Peruvian government had been promoting it as a tourist hotel. We had the place completely to ourselves. We spent two days there, sleeping fitfully and nursing headaches and queasy stomachs as we tried to adjust to the eleven-thousand-foot elevation. Then, on an ice-cold clear-blue Andean morning, we reloaded the trucks and followed the dirt track back along the Colca River. An old Quechua man chased us in silence, until he could run no more. We rounded a turn with two crosses erected on the outside curve. The smaller one, made of twigs, marked a road death. The larger one, aluminum, supported the power line that ran to the Achoma compound.

We crossed the Colca and drove west along the river for six miles, into the village of Lari. From there, Odendaal, Chmielinski, Bzdak, Biggs, Van der Merwe, Van Heerden, and I would begin our climb to the source. The GMC and its Peruvian driver would return to Arequipa. For the moment, Condorito waited with us in Lari. After we climbers hired burros and set off, Leon, Durrant, and Truran would drive the Land Rover back along the Colca and around the mountain to what our map said was a small weather station in the high *puna* some fifteen miles north of the source. We would try to meet there in three to five days.

The Lari sun stood alone under a brutal silver-blue sky. Its glare singed the eyes, and the air, dry as cotton balls, seemed to suck the moisture right out of them. Two dozen crumbling earth shacks and one sturdy Catholic church, the largest in the valley, lined an empty, baked-earth plaza. The whole hung on the lip of the sheer canyon like a snail climbing a wall. Quechua—stocky pink-faced women in bowler hats and enormous skirts, pinched leathery men in blue jeans and holey sweaters—slouched in doorways or nodded in the sun. No one moved.

Odendaal and Chmielinski were not having an easy time hiring burros. "It's like walking into East Selsby, Texas," an exasperated Odendaal said, "and trying to borrow someone's Cadillac."

I stood at the edge of the village and peered down. The Colca's deep drop begins just downstream from Lari. Staring into the canyon, I was overcome with a numbing, jelly-kneed vertigo, and I felt as if a little man with a hammer were beating against the backs of my eyeballs. If I had altitude sickness here, at eleven thousand feet, how would I handle the further six-thousand-foot climb to the source?

Inside my skull, the man with the hammer shouted: "MGFLARHA!"

But it was Bzdak, standing next to me and shouting above the wind that now swirled up out of the canyon. He opened his mouth to reveal a green quid. He spit it out.

"Coca leaf," he said. "You want?"

"I don't know."

"You feel like shit?"

"Yes."

"You want."

In the Andes it is legal both to grow and to chew the leaves, and according to what Durrant had told us, they are an effective antidote to the ravages of high altitude. But that endorsement didn't really matter to me. I hurt. I was willing to try anything.

Bzdak extracted half a dozen finger-sized leaves from a clump wrapped in newspaper and folded them in half. I tucked the wad into my right cheek. It tasted like tea leaves. Then he gave me a half-fingernail sliver of charcoal, or *llipta,* which I worked into the leaves. The ash, from the quinoa bush, is extremely bitter, but it catalyzes the leaves' cocamides. Without it the leaves would have no effect.

Nor with it, at first. When my soggy wad started to disintegrate I replaced it with another, and a bigger chunk of *llipta.* My gums burned horribly. Minutes later the right side of my mouth went numb, then the back of my throat. I felt none of the mule-in-a-stall kick of cocaine, but the hammering man put his instrument away, and Lari no longer seemed so grim, or our expedition so improbable.

Bzdak and I walked to the plaza and joined the rest of the team around Condorito. Odendaal and Chmielinski were negotiating with two Quechua men, Pastor and José, who owned four burros between them, but there was some sort of snag.

A crowd had gathered. An old woman drooling coca-green saliva yelled "Filthy gringos!" then walked from one to another of us screaming obscenities. She was toothless and barefoot, her rumpled cotton dress torn and covered with mud. She stuck her hand on my chest and pushed me backward over one of the kayaks. Dignity shot, I left the plaza.

I found a cold, dark, windowless shop, and from amid its bags of white rice and cans of fish and evaporated milk dug out a warm bottle of soda. Shivering, I paid a dour Quechua woman and stepped toward the sunlight that filled the shop's door.

Suddenly, through the glare, I saw a dust ball of pounding hooves and Vibram soles and plastic boats stampeding down the dirt street. Urgent cries of "Chorro! Chorro!" filled the air. Beneath the dust, sticks in hand, Chmielinski and Biggs were beating four bewildered, nostril-flaring burros.

"Get one and go!" Biggs yelled. I did as commanded, falling in behind the last wild-eyed beast and screaming "Chorro!" in a manner that convinced neither of us.

Van Heerden and Van der Merwe were trotting alongside Biggs.

"They tried to burn the truck!" Van der Merwe shouted. "Chased it out of town! We hijacked the animals!"

Back at the roadhead, Odendaal and Bzdak were holding off the Indians. "We find the end of town," Chmielinski yelled, "then we make a deal."

I ran down the street screaming at the clod-flinging hooves before me and thinking: It was not supposed to be like this. Three weeks in South America and already I had degenerated into burro thievery. I pictured myself strung up in sullen Lari like some raunchy outlaw in a spaghetti western.

But Chmielinski had it figured correctly. We passed the last hut on the trail and stopped. Odendaal and Bzdak caught up with us, and behind them came not an angry mob but only the burros' owners, Pastor and José.

"It was the women," Pastor said. "They did not trust you."

"Yes," José agreed. "The women. My wife does not want me to go with you."

"What do women know?" Pastor said, and gave a dismissive wave.

The trail turned sharply north, and up. One by one, the two Quechua men in the lead, we began to climb.

3   *Headwaters*

Marching at the rear of our ragged parade, free at last of engines and wheels, I soon found myself rejoicing in the solid thump of foot on earth. "One felt the happy sense of being free," Graham Greene wrote in *Journey Without Maps*. "One had only to follow a path far enough and one could cross a continent." *We're off!* I thought, chasing the tips of my boots with heady anticipation. *Into the wilderness.*

Wilderness? A tittupping procession of men, women, children, cattle, sheep, mules, burros, llamas, alpacas, goats, and dogs came slip-sliding toward me down the steep trail, an endless clattering farrago bound for Lari and below. Here a stony Quechua face, here a primordial goat eye cowering behind a quinoa bush, here—*phoot!*—a warm wad of llama goober shot squarely at the chest.

"Don't get close to llama!" Bzdak yelled from up the trail, too late.

I stopped at a spring to clean myself and met a Quechua man.

"What is above?" I asked.

"Nothing."

"Where are you coming from?"

"Nowhere."

He hoisted a load of gnarly wood and set off downhill, the calluses on his bare feet thick and creased like old boots. One cracked heel had been sewn shut with red yarn.

Two hours later I found Biggs and Chmielinski resting on a broad sandstone outcropping. Chmielinski pointed to a spot five miles southwest, where the Colca plunges most deeply into her canyon. Glinting ochre in the afternoon sun, her sheer ramparts soared out of the earth like giant organ pipes.

Chmielinski said that a month earlier he and Bzdak had rafted through the area searching for the body of their close Peruvian friend Alvaro Ibañez, whom Biggs had also known—the four men had run the Colca together in 1983, Ibañez becoming the first Peruvian to make the descent. The spring before I arrived in Peru, Ibañez and four fellow Peruvians had returned to the Colca. The river was at high water when they put their raft in, and it flipped in less than a minute. One of the men disappeared, never to be found. Another crawled out on the far side of the river. A third washed up on a boulder only to see his girlfriend flushed by a foot beyond his reach. Ibañez had also made the rock but dove into the Colca to try to save the drowning woman.

"Last time anyone saw Alvaro," Chmielinski said. "The helicopter found the girl's body a few days later, on big rocks. Somebody tied a yellow life jacket there to mark the spot."

"Alvaro?" Biggs asked.

"Must have been."

"And Alvaro's body?"

"We found his raft. It was the one we had given him. No body. One life jacket. It was a bad day when we found the raft. We could not talk or eat. We turned over our own raft. Zbyszek took the worst swim of his life. Our trip was very dark after that."

"Alvaro had a wife, didn't he?" Biggs asked. "I think I met her once. She was very pretty."

"She was seven months pregnant when Alvaro drowned," Chmielinski said. "Now she has his baby."

We continued up the dry, dusty trail in silence, hiking steadily through the hot afternoon. The altimeter loaned us by the Royal Geographical Society ticked off our altitude in meters, which I converted roughly to feet: twelve thousand five hundred, thirteen thousand, thirteen-five.

The trail climbed steeply into the young, soft, harshly eroded Andes, and my heavy pack hurt. But there was pride in hauling one's weight, and, in a sense, identity. Bzdak lugged his cameras and film; Biggs, his Bible and sketchbook; Chmielinski, the maps he would pore over each night. Van Heerden and Van der Merwe had cameras and cigarettes. I carried my notebook, photos from home, the thick socks I wore to bed in cold weather.

Only Odendaal did not bear a pack. Instead, he loaded his gear on a burro, saying that if one of us were to be injured, his back would be available. After the first few hours on the trail, however, he seemed naked without a pack, and strangely alone. He went from man to man offering to carry his load, but no one would give it up.

The burros plodded along before us. The kayaks that were fastened awkwardly to their backs banged their heads, pinched their ears, and blocked their vision. We would meet Condorito before the kayakers entered the river, but Odendaal wanted to carry two boats to the source as props for his film. Suddenly, as if they understood the impurity of this exercise, the burros knelt down in the middle of the trail, jiggled their ropes loose, and pitched the kayaks.

Odendaal and Chmielinski shouldered one boat, Pastor and José the other.

Late in the afternoon thick clouds filed along the canyon rim. A cold wind picked up, and within minutes the temperature dropped below freezing. We made camp on a narrow ledge where the trail widened slightly. To one side rose a sheer mountain wall. On the other, a thirty-foot cliff dropped into a creek.

By then my euphoria had evaporated. The wind had whipped my face raw, my sweaty socks had chilled, my fingers refused to uncurl. I was cold and tired, and I didn't know anyone else well enough to share my misery without embarrassment. My head was too thick for small talk. It would have looked bad if I had simply gone to sleep ("The lazy sod!"), so I helped Biggs cook our communal dinner. We fired up our little gas stoves, and by the light of candles that flickered and died in the wind we boiled a pot of powdered-something soup followed by what its aluminum jacket alleged was Swiss steak. This sounds like a simple task, but at fourteen thousand feet it was an awkward, woozy chore. By the time we finished, the idea of actually eating the slop made me want to vomit.

I stumbled off to my tent, which I had pitched near the cliff, facing into the Colca canyon. Though tempted to dive fully clothed into my sleeping bag, I forced myself to shed my filthy trail gear and stand naked to the night wind for one frigid instant. Then, like a knight donning battle armor, I scrambled into clean long underwear, turtleneck, down booties.

The moon, waxing and nearly full, loomed over my left shoulder, and fifteen miles in front of me reflected off the iced face of 19,600-foot Mount Hualca Hualca so brightly that the mountain seemed close enough to touch. The Southern Cross hung over the glistening peak, beaming through the thin, dry air as brilliantly as a movie marquee. I had never seen the cross, but instead of awe and exhilaration I felt only an immense loneliness.

By mid-morning the next day, beneath a high, hot sun, we had gained a ridge at fourteen thousand five hundred feet. The thin air made me so giddy I took delight in the increasingly arduous task of planting one foot in front of the other.

"What a marvelous world!" I thought, but that was only the last rattle of a mind about to go jelly soft. My red corpuscles were begging for oxygen. Altitude sickness is, in its own perverse way, wonderfully egalitarian. An old, fat, chain-smoking drunk is no more likely to suffer its headaches, vomiting, confusion, diarrhea, dehydration, nausea, and short-term memory loss than is a champion athlete. It's mostly in the luck of the genetic draw. The best way to prepare for altitude is to drink plenty of water, until, as the maxim goes, one's urine runs "clear and copious." And to climb slowly, giving the body time to adjust. The rule of thumb is one day of ascent for each thousand-foot gain above six thousand feet, and one day for each five-hundred-foot gain above twelve thousand feet. At about fifteen thousand feet, if not properly acclimated, one risks pulmonary and cerebral edema, which can strike quickly, do permanent, painful damage to lungs and brain, and even kill. Above eighteen thousand feet—what mountain climbers often call the "death zone"—the body can no longer acclimatize fully.

We needed two weeks to adjust correctly, but we were so far behind schedule that we had decided to try to reach the top of the continental divide in a matter of days. We weaved and staggered up the mountain in a long, scraggly line. Though walking slowly—planting one foot deliberately, then stopping as if to make sure it was in place before lifting the other—the first man, Van der Merwe, was more than a mile ahead of the last, Odendaal. The rest of us were spread along the narrow trail, mountain wall to the right, cliff to the left.

I was second in line. By fifteen thousand feet my euphoria had crashed. By fifteen-five I felt as if I were carrying a balloon in my bladder, but try as I might I couldn't pass water. Slightly above sixteen thousand feet, I vomited. Pastor, hiking behind me with the burros, offered coca leaves. I accepted them with no small gratitude.

The sky grew gray, then black, and a hard wind roared up, followed by snow. I pulled my wind suit tight around me, head to toe, tied my ridiculous safari hat to my head with a bandana, and leaned into the wind. One step, two steps. Blinded by the snow, I could no longer see anyone in front of me, and I was too tired to turn around and look back.

I crossed a ridge, dropped down, climbed another, each step lung-draining and leaden. The trail bent into a canyon, then wound out to a glacial moraine. Tiny creeks and spongy *ichu* grass spilled like a brown skirt beneath Mount Quehuisha, a glistening pinnacle of snow and ice standing bold against the storm clouds clinging to the divide.

Van der Merwe waited at the turn. When our teammates joined us, each greeted the sight of the splendid mountain with a look that was part reverence, part stupor. The usually ebullient Biggs was quiet and withdrawn. Bzdak's face had gone puffy and gray.

Van Heerden, the chain-smoker, hacked deeply and continuously. Chmielinski slogged along with the burros; the frustration of paying attention to the headstrong animals, and also to their owners, had rendered him short-tempered and agitated. Odendaal, still taking up the rear, looked weary and confused, his eyes bloodshot and foggy. Searching for the source of the Urubamba in 1981, he had suffered two edemalike attacks at sixteen thousand feet and collapsed in spasms and convulsions that had nearly killed him.

Pastor and José, their big mountain-adapted hearts pumping some 20 percent more blood than ours, cruised right past us. Chmielinski yelled to Pastor, and after a brief consultation told us, "He says *media hora*. Half hour to source."

We pushed on. The storm intensified, at times cutting visibility to ten feet, and two hours later we seemed to be no closer to the divide. Our pace slowed. It took thirty minutes to walk a quarter of a mile. The trail steepened into switchbacks up a near-vertical slope.

It was too much, but Pastor and José refused to make camp. There was no forage for the burros, and besides, they insisted, the pass was only *media hora*. They kept going. As he had all day, Chmielinski urged the rest of us on, then chased after the burros. No one had the strength to argue with him.

The wind blew harder still, at what I estimated was thirty knots, and gusted so severely that no matter how far forward I leaned, it stood me straight up. I could no longer feel my face.

I drew my wind suit tighter, popped a golf-ball-sized wad of the local chew into my left cheek, and settled into a high-altitude walking meditation: left foot, right foot, count each step, *one, two, three, four* . . .

At seven hundred thirty-one the snow cloud rolled down into the canyon below, the sun burst through, and Quehuisha glistened white and gold. The trail flattened. In front of me Chmielinski drew a line in the snow. I looked back down the trail, but I could not see the others. I staggered up to the Pole.

"Ten *soles*, please," he wheezed. "Now crossing continental divide."

As best I could I studied Chmielinski's line. It took a moment to register. On one side he had written "Pacific," on the other, "Atlantic."

I stepped across, dropped my pack, and breathed deeply in the thin air, failing to draw the lungful I so desperately wanted. Behind and below, to the southwest, black clouds hung in the canyon we had climbed, sealing it off as if there were no retreat. Quehuisha's insouciant flanks rose immediately to the right, or east, her coned peak now less than six hundred feet above us. Half a mile beyond her stood Mount Mismi, and between them a ridge flecked with the pale-blue icefall that we would call the source of the Amazon. A rock cairn about six feet high sat in the middle of the divide, and at its peak two sticks were tied in a cross. Travelers had built this *apachita* stone by stone as an offering to the *wamani* who dwelled within the mountain. As custom dictated, I contributed a stone and my coca quid, an offering to the guardian spirit and a recognition of my pain. Then I turned to Chmielinski.

"All downhill from here." I said. Ho-*ho!*

"Yes," he said, "for next forty-two hundred miles."

One by one the others struggled up after us, their faces so many flaring turquoise medallions. One by one they dropped their packs in silent exhaustion, and when, one by one, they erupted in hooting celebration, one by one they were punched short by wracking coughs. Cameras came slowly from packs, and slowly we reenacted the crossing of the divide.

The black clouds swelled and rose out of the valley below, blowing hard across white snow. We had found the top of the Amazon, but there was nothing tropical about it. Minutes later we stumbled quickly down the Atlantic slope, anxious to make camp before the bitter Andean night fell upon us.

Below the divide meltwater had built a webwork of brooks and tundralike islands, one of which had room for all but two of us. Bzdak and I hopped the rivulets and established our own little kingdom.

Never, not even on my very first attempt, had the simple act of

erecting my tent required more than fifteen minutes of my attention, but at seventeen thousand feet it was like trying to tie a
shoelace in the middle of a roaring drunk. I couldn't decide which
end was top, which bottom. I unfurled the ground cloth and
circled it again and again, trying to gain perspective. Finally, the
authoritative *crack* when I snapped the shock-corded poles into
rigid order gave me a fool's courage, and I proceeded to poke, pull,
and zip for a good forty-five minutes.

When I finished I had a surprise: The tent had grown an extra
pole. An extra pole! That was rich. The tent seemed fine without
it. Chuckling to myself, I stuffed the pole into my sleeping bag,
anticipating another good laugh after dinner.

"Joe," Bzdak said, "how you feeling?"

"Like a million *soles!*" I replied. What a knee-slapper!

"That fifty bucks. Not so good, eh?"

I followed Bzdak as he meandered herky-jerky to the big island.
Biggs shared a big two-man tent with Odendaal, and he had
volunteered it as a galley. We wormed in, pitched ourselves onto
bags and packs, and removed our shoes.

Biggs, tucked in his sleeping bag, was not feeling well at all.
Somewhere in his travels he had contracted chronic brucellosis, an
incurable infection whose symptoms include depression, extreme
lethargy, and fever. Usually Biggs could control the condition with
antibiotics, but a few months before leaving home for the Amazon
he'd developed glandular fever (akin to mononucleosis), which in
turn had triggered an attack of brucellosis. He'd been bedridden
three months, and had yet to fully recover.

"Evening, mates," he said. He smiled, but he was wheezing.

"How you feeling, Zulu?" Bzdak asked.

"Zbyszek," he said slowly, "you're getting so big they'd make you
King Zulu."

"What for dinner?" Bzdak asked.

Without getting out of his bag Biggs pawed through the supplies. "Chili. Sweet and sour pork. Beef burgundy. I think . . .
Zbyszek, I think I'm going to puke."

"What make you feel that?"

"Your feet stink."

This was no small declaration. At high altitude the sense of smell is greatly diminished. The molecules that build scent are too heavy to travel well in thin air. And so the dominant smell of high mountains, really, is no smell at all. Unless you're trapped in a tent with . . .

"Sorry, Zulu. What I can do?"

"It's okay, Zbyszek."

"Don't want to make you sick, Zulu Man. I will leave."

"No. No! Just kidding. Nowhere I'd rather be than right here with my buddy Zbyszek. Really."

"How about with wife?"

"Let's not talk about it."

Soon the tent was a jumble of arms and legs and pots and spoons, one man lifting stoves, another reaching for food bags, a third lining up bowls. Now a hand held the big pot while another pumped the stove. Here were tea bags and coffee cups, and later a steaming pot of soup.

A head in the tent door, vapor billowing from mouth and nostrils.

"Food ready?" Odendaal asked.

"Soon, soon."

We cooked and poured, and Odendaal, recovered from the hike, carried soup through the snow to the men in the tents, returned with reports—"Pierre's coughing badly, Piotr can't hold food, Pastor and José like the tents we gave them"—and departed with bowls of chili and rice.

Biggs couldn't eat. I managed a bowl of chili. Bzdak gobbled seconds.

When my head felt as if it were being punched from inside, Bzdak led me back to our tents. I shook with cold the night through.

When I awoke I forced my head out the tent door into a wet gray cloud that seemed to have smothered all sound and shredded the day's light into a shadowless pall. It could have been dawn, or noon. Below the gray spread a white plain of fresh snow, from which I retrieved my frozen boots.

"Zbyszek."

A thick voice gurgled up through the white mound next to my tent. "What you want?"

"Breakfast. "

"I take your order. Breakfast to bed for Señor Amazon. Then you puke."

He was right. I could no more hold food than stand on my head. Or, for that matter, my feet. I stood, wobbled, sat down, pulled on my heavy clothes. The day's plan was for Pastor, José, and me to leave camp ahead of the others with the burros, hauling all the expedition kit we could carry to the weather station where we hoped to meet Condorito. Our map said the station was on a plateau some fifteen miles north of the source. The rest of the team would stay behind to film the icefall, then, with lightened packs, hurry down the trail to join us that night.

Before we set out, however, I wanted to see the source for myself.

Compass in hand, I slogged back up to the divide, gave the *apachita* a nod for luck, and turned left, east, groping uphill through snow and scree. An hour later, the fog spread below me like a gray sea, I was locked alone on top of Peru with the solemn, treeless peaks that guard the birthplace of the Amazon like court eunuchs: Quehuisha, Chayco, Mismi, Huillcayo.

And there, suddenly, not fifty yards away, hung the blue veil of the icefall. I started toward it but stopped. I have never been sure exactly why. I had to get back to camp and on the trail, and I was drained by the effort of climbing, but that was not all. It seemed irreverent to say, this is it, I'm—what? *Touching* the source of the Amazon?

It seemed vaguely silly, too. Defining the source of the Amazon is like unwinding a ball of string and trying to decide which of the tiny frayed threads at its core is, in fact, the end. By generally accepted definition, the source of a river is that tributary farthest from the river's mouth (as distinct, say, from the tributary carrying the greatest volume of water). For years—centuries—the Marañón was considered the Amazon's source, but aerial photos taken of the Andes in 1955, and later translated into excellent topographic maps for Peru's Instituto Geographico Militar, revealed that the Apurimac, one of the Ucayali River's feeder streams, made the Ucayali system some sixty to a hundred miles longer.

Which left only thread measuring: Which of the brooks and creeks feeding the Apurimac is the longest?

In 1971, after studying the Peruvian maps, an American, Loren McIntyre, traced three Apurimac tributaries (the Hornillos, the Challamayo, and the Lloqueta) to a spongy cirque, and from there to the continental divide. He reported on his exploration in *National Geographic* magazine:

On October 15, 1971, we reached an ice-edged ridge above Carhuasanta, longest of the five headwater brooks. The Indians call that 18,200-foot summit Choquecorao. . . .

A thousand feet below the ridge we sighted a lake, its crust of ice thawed by the midday sun. We clambered down to quench our thirst with its transparent meltwaters. Here at 17,220 feet was the farthest source of the Amazon—more a pond than a lake, just a hundred feet across.

[My partners] named the lake after me, more or less in fun, knowing it may not always be the most distant water of the River Sea. It could disappear in a single season. The Andes are new mountains; they still buckle and break. . . .

McIntyre was right about the shifting terrain, but I think he was wrong about Carhuasanta being the longest of the feeder brooks. Our maps clearly showed that the Apacheta, two streams west, is longer, that a third stream, Ccaccansa, is longer still, and that another system altogether, draining nearby Mount Minaspata, is at least as long if it runs year-round. Nicholas Asheshov, an expatriate British journalist living in Peru, climbed Minaspata in 1970 and claimed it as the source; to the writer Alex Shoumatoff (in his book *The Rivers Amazon*), Asheshov dismissed McIntyre's pond as "a marshy lake one kilometer above the mine where everybody goes and has a pee."

Do these differences matter?

No. What we are talking about, after all, is a distance of perhaps a mile, which in the context of a 4,200-mile river hardly merits debate. Man must name, even if his definitions drain the natural poetry of a thing, but the source of the Amazon is not one particular pond or a single nugget of ice. It is the whole place, all of that cold gray web. The icefall, yes, and Lake McIntyre, but also the fog, the wind, the peaks, the fragile lace of mud and grass that spills below the mountain wall.

Snow fell. Weren't these flakes the first drops of the Amazon? Can you separate snow from creek, ice from air, wind from sun?

The wind howled, the snow fell faster, the fog obliterated the icefall. Wheezing and confused in the thin air, I stumbled back down the mountain.

Our camp was nearly whited out by the storm. After loading the burros and conferring quickly with the others, Pastor, José, and I set out, slipping north through the tundralike sponge along a defile some three hundred yards wide. The storm descended, lifted, descended. In the spaces between the enveloping whiteness the dark peaks loomed menacingly, softened only slightly by their mantles of fresh snow.

No sign of people, no trees, no boulders, nothing but the odd patch of golden *ichu* jutting up through the white blanket. A splendid isolation. Creeks burbled down out of the mountains every hundred yards or so and buried themselves in the valley floor. Then, half a mile below our camp, they formed the Apacheta, the first coherent body of flowing water on the eastern side of the divide. A mile later we passed a *quebrada,* a deep, narrow slice in the valley's west wall. *Quebrada* is Spanish for "broken," and no one word better describes what is the most common geological feature in the high Andes, cracks deep and eroded out of all proportion to the often minuscule flows that carve them. The *quebradas* look as if they have been struck by some *wamani*'s giant axe.

That was Quebrada Calomoroco, and there—the true source?—the Ccaccansa, flanked by two steep, bouldery walls that looked exceedingly difficult to climb or descend. I was glad that we had chosen to follow the easier Apacheta.

Behind me, a Quechua family had worked its way into our line, but I could not spot any place from which they might have come. Their dark, hunched figures kept quiet pace with us. Half an hour later, when I looked back again, they were gone.

Suddenly the sun came on so strong that within minutes my eyes stung and I was stripped to my undershirt. Pastor and José overtook me as I removed my clothing. For the next hour we hiked together.

"Where are you from?" Pastor asked in Spanish.

"The United States."

"Miami?"

"California. San Francisco."

"That is near Chicago."

"No." I was surprised. The Peruvian peasants I'd met knew Miami, New York, Los Angeles, and Las Vegas; that was the United States. But Chicago? "Not exactly," I said. "I suppose it is if you are from Peru."

"That is where I am from," Pastor said. José nodded his head in vigorous agreement. "But Alkapohnay is from Chicago."

"Alkapohnay?"

"With the pistol." He made a shooting motion.

I said, "He has been dead a long time."

"He was a great man."

Our conversation lagged until we stumbled across what appeared to be a llama shank, picked clean to the bone, the hoof intact. During our hike we had spooked one herd of the domestic beasts, which are related to the vicuña. That and the mysterious Quechua family (it dimly occurred to me that they and the llamas were connected) were the only living creatures we had seen. Pastor suggested that a fox had eaten the llama, but I could not fathom any wild animal surviving in a land so barren.

Pastor said we should cross the little valley. Leading the burros, he and José waded into what the map said was now the Lloqueta River. It came to mid-calf. I threw my pack across and leapt to the far bank, a feat that winded me but drew applause from my fellow travelers. For a moment I reveled in the ridiculous notion that I had leapt the breadth of "the greatest of all rivers."

Pastor said, "*Media hora.*"

"Fine," I said, and figured on at least four.

Both men stuck close with me through the afternoon, chattering away in Quechua and switching to Spanish whenever I indicated a desire to converse. Unfortunately, that wasn't often. We were still above fifteen thousand feet, and the hiking exhausted me. Black clouds built up behind and above us, overwhelming the hoodlum peaks. If the men back at the source weren't moving quickly, they were in trouble. The sun broke through briefly, the temperature jumped twenty degrees, the sun departed. I erupted in fits of hacking that split my head.

"Look!" Pastor hissed.

He pointed to our left, to a slate-gray lake about half a mile long. On its far shore stood a low wall of blazing pink. Pastor shouted, and the wall flapped up from the earth: Andean flamingos, their unanticipated beauty hypnotic against the stark gray landscape.

Blue-white lightning flashed behind the hirds, followed by a peal of thunder and a sudden dizzy squealing. An army of frantic rodents scurried in and out of the rock pile along the right side of the trail. They looked like a cross between a rabbit and a squirrel, with long fluffy tails. Pastor identified them as *vizcacha* (a relative of the chinchilla), and added, rubbing his stomach, that they were good eating.

Beyond the lake the valley opened to waves of rolling, snow-dusted hills. I asked Pastor how much farther we had to go. He hesitated, and we spoke at the same time:

"*Media hora.*"

He was lost. *We* were lost.

The day still held about an hour of light. We huffed up and down hill after hill. At the top of one I stopped to catch my breath. The effort was, as always, useless, but a mile distant I saw a tree, leafless and completely out of place. I hadn't seen a tree in two days.

It was a weather vane, and beneath it the station, a dreary two-room affair manned by a single soldier, Roberto. His fortress held a small wooden table and a stone bench. Landscapes from a three year-old calendar decorated one wall, along with a photo of Peru's national soccer team. Hanging like a shrine on the biggest wall was a poster of Miss Inca Cola. Her blond hair and thin bikini made the hut seem even colder.

Roberto said no truck had arrived. I hustled outside to reconnoiter in the dying light. The hut stood on a hill directly above the point where the Challamayo River becomes the Hornillos. Below, a dirt track ran along the river, and a mile downstream I saw a dusky beige bulb that stood out only because it had launched itself into the one ribbon of contrasting color—the green Hornillos—that ran through the endlessly gray landscape, now fading to white with snow.

Condorito.

I waved and shouted, but the wind threw my pleas back in my face. Condorito turned downstream and drove away. My heart sank —though I had known Leon, Durrant, and Truran less than three weeks, I missed them.

I sat with Pastor and José and even the obliging Roberto, who brewed me a cup of tea and said I was welcome to stay for as long as I needed to. My loneliness paled by comparison to Roberto's— he had been on duty at the shack for almost three months. His village was a six-day walk.

An hour later, like cavalry to the rescue, Condorito burst over the top of the hill, a wild-eyed Durrant at the wheel, Leon and Truran beside her. "Bloody useless maps!" she yelled out the window. We piled into the hut, lit our stoves, boiled water.

Minutes later a white mass blasted through the door: Chmielinski and Odendaal, covered with snow.

"Bottom of the hill," Chmielinski sputtered. "The others."

Durrant grabbed her medical kit and flashlight and followed him back out. Odendaal stayed in the hut.

"Got lost," he said, warming his hands over a stove. His teeth chattered and his face was blue. "Zbyszek and Pierre split off from the rest of us. Defied my orders. We were to stick together at all costs." Beneath his fatigue burned an intense anger. As night had fallen Bzdak and Van Heerden had spotted the fires of a small settlement off the trail. Realizing the team was lost, they had left the other hikers and gone to the lights, where they had found a man willing to guide the team to the weather station.

Freezing, hungry, and dehydrated, the rest of the crew now stumbled into the hut. We melted snow and boiled soup and searched in vain for camaraderie, each of us too tired to think beyond himself.

We pitched camp outside, in the snow. That night I couldn't sleep. My breath came in gasps, and my tent and bag seemed to surround and squeeze me. I tore free of them and launched myself into the gelid night.

The moon, mother to the Inca nation, sister-wife to the sun-god Inti, had come full and scaled the blue-black sky. To the Quechua, in the months of late winter and early spring it is the moon, not the sun, that dominates life. I didn't find it hard to understand why. The snow that lay on the rolling *puna* like a glossy skin reflected the moonlight so brightly that I felt I could see farther there, in the dead of night, than I had during the day.

Apu, in Quechua, means "lord"; the Apu Rimac was the Lord Oracle, or the Great Speaker. Considered the most powerful of the Inca oracles, he spoke through the river's tremendous rapids. It is said that approaching the Apurimac on foot during the rainy season, one can hear the rapids from miles away.

It was the Apu Rimac who foretold the coming of the bearded white gods, the *viracochas,* who would take command of the Inca nation. So it seemed faintly ironic that on the day we were to set off in search of the oracle's river, Tim Biggs gathered us—nine bearded men and one woman—and asked our permission to say a group prayer, that day and each Sunday thereafter. The Afrikaners and Leon agreed, and though the rest of us were noncommittal,

Biggs bowed his head and, speaking loudly and with a slightly nervous stutter, delivered an invocation on all our behalfs.

Then, in the clear, cold morning, we said thanks and good-bye to Pastor and José, who would return home with their burros. They seemed happy to have traveled with us, and displayed no residue of the venom that had accompanied our departure from Lari. I regretted not having gotten to know them better. Bzdak and the cameramen left, too. They would drive Condorito around the mountains and meet us downriver.

We waded the Hornillos, which was little more than a canal, and climbed to a ridge above it. A mild argument erupted. Odendaal and Biggs maintained that to claim to have "run" the entire river, they must follow its every inch, never losing sight of it. They wanted to walk low, right next to the water. Their argument contained an admirable purity, but also a disheartening literalness: It defined a river as separate from its watershed, from the land it drained, from its people and wildlife.

We split up. Odendaal, Biggs, and Truran hiked low, Chmielinski, Durrant, Leon, and I high. The absurdity of our disagreement struck home within an hour, when the trails converged. But we were ahead of the others by then. We would not meet again until late that night.

In fact, we saw almost no one. Once, we heard shrieks from behind a boulder, and rushed over to find two Quechua matrons sitting as serene and implacable as the rock itself. Only much later would we learn that their unsettling ululations had been Quechua song.

As we worked our way down the Hornillos, caught one moment in a blast of snow and the next in a burst of sun, the *puna's* washed-out dun tones took on a green patina. Tiny cactus flowers dotted the minimalist landscape, their reds and yellows screaming against the treeless brown hills. Verdant Spanish moss vibrated along the banks. A squadron of Andean geese glided upriver, low to the water. We saw a trio of cormorants, a klatch of squeaking terns, some coots, and two tall, stalking waterfowl, black and white . . .

"Brings babies," Chmielinski said.

A horse and rider charged across the *puna* and reared up before us, blocking our path. The horse was huge—my head barely reached the bottom of its shoulder—and its bridle, inlaid with gold and silver, stood out regally against the scoured landscape. The rider wore a florid llama-wool poncho, a wide-brimmed sombrero, and a wool skull cap pulled down low over a Quechua face red as the volcanic soil. His cheeks bulged, and the wind had blown a green line of saliva and coca juice across his face.

But it was the man's eyes that startled: Spanish eyes, as pale and distant a blue as the icefall at the source.

The ghost rider stared at us but said nothing. Finally he let fly with a shrill, manic laugh, as if we were the most absurd thing he had ever seen. Then he wheeled his heaving beast and barreled across the blank *puna* as urgently as the wind.

Two days below the weather station we met Condorito at La Angostura ("The Narrow Place"), where the Hornillos joins the Apurimac, and where the river first becomes deep enough to support kayaks. The last five miles of our trek traversed a broad alluvial plain flanked, like almost every part of the high plateaus, by menacing volcanic peaks. In my notes I had come to refer to these peaks as "The Enforcers."

At the slim confluence Bzdak and I climbed a lava spire and saw, on the rock wall opposite us, chalk markings and hardware for a dam and reservoir that will be part of the far-flung Majes project. If the dam is built as scheduled, much of the country we had hiked over the preceding two days will be flooded behind the first, and only, dam on the entire 4,200 miles of river we hoped to follow to the sea.

"How long have you been coughing up blood?" Kate Durrant asked Pierre Van Heerden that night at La Angostura. We were in my tent.

"Two days," he said. He took a long drag off his cigarette. "It's spasms. Once I start I can't stop."

Tap-tap, tap-tap, tap-tap. Probing knuckles led a stethoscope across his back.

"It's the altitude," she said. "And the dry air. Smoking doesn't help."

"I know." Inhale, exhale, smoke ring, *hack.* Van Heerden tilted his head back on my lap while Durrant worked the scope along his chest.

"Crackling on one side. We'll try antibiotics."

Van Heerden exploded in a fit of deep coughing that quickly built to spasmodic retching. Though he seemed to be suffering the most, we all had similar problems. A deep draft of the thin, cold, dry air, a puff of dust, and an invisible hand doubled one over, lungs burning, throat trying to rip itself out. Each night ferocious hacking erupted from the camp like death cries.

Loud voices and laughter drifted to us from the big South African tent nearby, into which the rest of the team had crowded to share the *pisco* the cameramen had found in the tiny mining town of Cailloma, a few miles up the Apurimac from the Hornillos confluence. Durrant packed up her gear and she and Van Heerden left to join the party. I stayed behind to work on my notes.

Or so I tried to tell myself. In truth, after nearly a month with this crew I still felt like an outsider. In a way, it was my role. They were the expedition, I the observer. But that role had been designed in a different world, a world from which I now felt completely removed, and in the lonely *puna* those lines seemed cruelly artificial.

Wind blasted the tent. My thermometer read five degrees Fahrenheit. I blew on my fingers and scratched a few more lines.

I heard scraping at my tent door, then, "We come to visit Château Joe," and Bzdak and Durrant tumbled in. I lit a second candle and fluffed up the foot of my sleeping bag to make a seat. Bzdak offered a bottle of anisette.

The tent flap opened again, and Chmielinski ushered himself in. Bodies mushed together. Amid them flew stories of Poland and the Andes and London. The flap opened yet again ("Hey, mates!") and Tim Biggs crawled in over the bodies. Then, "*Hay fiesta?*" Leon shoved in from behind, and the stories took on a tropical hue.

We talked and drank and talked. Hours later, when the party finally broke up, my thermometer read a comfortable forty-five degrees. And I did not feel bad at all.

4 *The Upper Apurimac*

Running roughly northwest through the heart of the Andes, the Apurimac is a river left to herself, the wild young issue of a wild young mountain range. She is not a civilized river. There are few villages on her banks, fewer bridges. Roads cross her four-hundred-mile course only eight times, and they are terrible crossings. At the top, during her first fifty miles, she wriggles gently through the high *puna* in a shallow red volcanic trench fringed with golden *ichu*. Over her next three hundred miles, however, she drops almost thirteen thousand vertical feet, a gradient five times that of the Colorado River through the Grand Canyon. Before the Apurimac collapses, spent, into the Amazon basin, she carves a gorge that for miles at a time is more than ten thousand feet deep. It is one of the deepest river gorges on the planet; many believe that it is second only to her neighbor, the Colca. Down on her boulder-strewn floor, the Apurimac's whole untethered act of simply running, of sheer velocity, overwhelms all other life. Since the 1950s a half dozen attempts have been made to kayak her. At least two people drowned, and no one succeeded in navigating her length.

It is understandable, then, that the Apurimac canyon has always been shrouded in mystery (parts of it remain among the least-known areas on the South American continent), and yet it holds profound historical and religious significance for the Quechua. According to a widely accepted version of the Inca creation myth, it was near the village of Paccaritambo, high on the canyon wall, that four brothers and their sister-wives crawled out of their caves and at the bidding of their father, the sun-god Inti, founded an empire in the neighboring valley of Cuzco.

The deep Apurimac protected this fledgling Inca state from the mighty Chanca nation to the west until the mid-fifteenth century, when the two nations clashed at Cuzco, and the Incas emerged victorious. The spanning of the Apurimac with four bridges woven entirely of hammered grass played a critical role in their subsequent, frenetic westward expansion. (When the Spanish *conquistadores* arrived a century later, they regarded these bridges—their cables, two hundred feet long and as thick as a man's body, were capable of supporting entire armies of animals and men—as among the New World's most awe-inspiring sights.)

In 1533 the Inca ordered the grass bridges burned to block the *viracocha* invasion from Lima, but the river was uncharacteristically low that year, and the white gods managed to ford it. They sacked Cuzco but failed to settle the inaccessible Apurimac, and in 1536 the canyon became a strategic flank for what would be the last Inca state, Vilcabamba.

Two centuries after the fall of Vilcabamba, the Apurimac village of Surimana spawned José Gabriel Tupac Amaru II, who in 1780 led the second rising of the Incas. Though his revolt failed, in terms of territory, participants, and bloodshed it dwarfed one taking place at roughly the same time in a tiny, recently declared nation far to the north.

And it was the Apurimac canyon that gave birth, exactly two hundred years later, to the Shining Path movement—the Sendero Luminoso—which would grow into one of the most ruthless and clandestine guerrilla organizations in modern South America.

I awoke to the river's easy rush. Outside my tent the frozen droppings of burro and llama glistened in the dawn's half-light. The night before, having found no other level ground, Bzdak, Leon, and I had pitched camp right on the trail, on a thin rock ledge etched into the gorge wall a few yards above the river. The three of us had become a team. The previous day, at La Angostura, Chmielinski, Truran, Biggs, and Odendaal had put their kayaks in the Apurimac, and the cameramen, Van der Merwe and Van Heerden, had conscripted Durrant as driver for Condorito and left the river. Bzdak and Leon had volunteered to walk with me, and in that desolate country we had trekked under the giddy intoxication of being alone, unobserved, in a place no one cared about.

But of course we were not really alone. That we saw no one that first day out of La Angostura was probably a consequence of our garish appearance—bulging aluminum-and-nylon packs, Goretex jackets, sunglasses, big leather boots. I imagined Quechua hiding in the mountains, giggling as we passed.

Or perhaps we had simply been too fatigued to notice anyone. At dinner, after struggling through fifteen miles of steep switchbacks and descents, Bzdak had wobbled away down the trail. Leon and I heard vomiting and found him crumpled in a clump of *ichu*. We helped him to his tent, and Leon brewed him a stomach-soothing tea from foraged mint.

In the morning, however, Bzdak was in good cheer ("I get sick from no beer"), and the trail ran smooth and level, a foot wide and centuries old. It cleaved to the ledge, then retreated behind soft, loamy slopes. Ducks and geese cruised by, fish surfaced in the river, the weather turned temperate and welcoming. We passed the charred remains of a llama-herder's fire, a stone hut, and small fields plowed right down to the trail but never violating it. I began to think of us as honorary members of the Quechua Department of Highways. With each step we did our part to preserve the trail, to maintain order. Here an encroaching clump of ichu stomped down, there a revolt of loose dirt tamped into place.

A red-faced Quechua woman studied us from her mud-brick hut, perched like a storybook home on a boulder wedged between trail and river.

"I like your house!" Bzdak yelled in Spanish. The woman blushed redder and ran inside.

In late afternoon we reached the ruins of an Inca fortress. Tucked into craggy folds of rock at the point where the Totorani

River joins the Apurimac, it reflected the Incas' ability to blend into that cleavaged landscape, to hide. The buildings, unlike the famous jigsaw puzzles of the Inca religious and cultural centers, were simple, utilitarian, and long since looted, but their stone lintels continued to define doors and entranceways, and young corn sprouted between the walls. Corn and stone, agriculture and architecture—the material achievements of the Inca state. Their presence in such austere highlands hinted at the dogged endurance of the mountain culture.

We met the kayakers and the camera crew that night, four miles down the trail, at another set of ruins, Mauccallacta. There is an old and complex tradition of reciprocity in the highlands, one form of which, *mita*, the Incas elevated to a kind of social-security system. In compensation for rotating terms of state labor, the Incas built large public projects for the workers' communities—roads and irrigation systems—and guaranteed those communities against harvest short-ages and famine. Mauccallacta's round, crumbling stone towers, looming like frozen druids beneath the half-moon, might well have been storehouses for various commodities provided under the *mita*.

That night I worked in my tent with Durrant, helping her to prepare the packets of antimalarials that we would begin taking six weeks before we reached the jungle.

"Come here, Doctor!" Fanie Van der Merwe shouted through the cold night air. "I have something that needs a little attention." Cackles rose from the Afrikaner camp.

"Bloody hell," Durrant said under her breath. She had not enjoyed driving the truck for the two "cowboys," as she called the Afrikaner cameramen. They had spent one night with a South African engineer connected to the Majes project. While Durrant had cooked and washed dishes, the men had pored over the engineer's collection of Peruvian erotic art.

"That was all right," she said. "It diverted their attention. But in the truck, my Christ. They kept winding me up."

"Come quick, Doctor!" Van der Merwe yelled. "Now it needs a *lot* of attention." Howls erupted from the camp, followed by the sound of Van Heerden hacking deeply.

"They're trying to get me to lose my temper," she said. "My only defense is to bloody well ignore them."

I asked if she would prefer to walk with Leon, Bzdak, and me. "How far?" she asked.

"Ten to twenty miles a day," I said, and added that it would be harder work than our two-day trek on the Hornillos. As we moved farther down the canyon the country would become much steeper, and we would probably meet Condorito only once a week for resupply. We would have to carry full packs.

"I'm keen to try," she said. "But do me a favor. Talk to François. Our relationship seems a bit strained. I don't know what the problem is, but I'm not up to finding out just now."

I went to the Afrikaner camp, where a pot of coffee bubbled on the fire. Odendaal poured two cups. Then we walked into the dark and the wind, and took shelter in one of the ruined towers.

Odendaal said he welcomed the idea of Durrant joining us on the trail, and agreed that if she handled the walk to Yauri, she could continue to hike with us. We didn't go into her reasons for wanting out of Condorito. Odendaal had other things on his mind. He was worried about his film, worried mainly that his cameraman, Van der Merwe, would try to usurp his role as director, if not now then when Odendaal went to South Africa to edit the film. This was an understandable concern. Van der Merwe, several years Odendaal's senior and a professional filmmaker, had clearly established himself as the de facto leader of the Afrikaner triumvirate.

I asked Odendaal about the river itself. He said the first two days of kayaking, the first thirty miles, had been easy, mostly flat, soft runs. Overall, he was disappointed. The expedition was lacking in adventure.

"I would think there was adventure in the whole effort," I said. "In the perseverance."

"We're too organized," he said. "Watch Piotr. He keeps notes on everything. *Everything.* He knows precisely how much coffee we drink. He wants to bring tourists in here."

"Doesn't his organizing make it easier for you?"

"Maybe. I don't know. We have too damn many people. If it was just me and two others I'd be halfway down the river by now." He said the Apurimac would rise quickly once the rainy season began, which could be as soon as a month. We had to get moving.

On that note we said good night. I went back to my tent, and Odendaal returned to the fire, where, judging by the intensity of the whoops and hollers, the ribaldry seemed to have increased.

Parched, dust-ridden Yauri is the capital and only substantial town in the mining province of Espinar. It hovers over the brown *puna* like a withered mirage, its two hundred or so sun-baked mud-and-tin buildings perched on a low rise that amid the numbing flatness of the surrounding plain is as imposing as a mountain peak. Long before we arrived we could see the imperious spire of the church. As in most poor Latin American villages, it was ostentatious well beyond the meager resources of its flock. Brittle shacks huddled around it like orphans clutching at the skirts of a wealthy matron. In front of the church a man labored shoulder deep in a sandy trench, digging up old graves. Stacked behind him, in a neat row, were a dozen human skulls.

The Spanish conquered Peru primarily for the mineral wealth buried in the Andes, and to extract that wealth, they corrupted the *mita* into a brutal system of forced labor. There is no accurate count of how many Quechua died as a consequence of the Spanish *mita*, which lasted more than two hundred years, but the most conservative estimates run to about a million. (It is also estimated that during the first fifty years of the Spanish conquest the native population declined from about six million to less than two million.) Many more fled their homes, and to this day some of the highland valleys remain depopulated.

That bitter legacy continues to haunt mining towns like Yauri. We made camp near the center of town, at a fortresslike weaving cooperative that had been organized by an order of Canadian nuns, with assistance from an Irish priest. That the Irishman had also begun to organize the local Quechua politically and to teach them to read and write had not sat well with the town's ruling powers, and he had been replaced by a *criollo* priest from Lima. The Roman Catholic Church in Peru is notoriously conservative (it is the only Peruvian institution that continues to employ the *mita*), and as a Quechua man working in the cooperative storefront said of Yauri's new priest, "The poor are not his business." The nuns had carried on, however, and in the cooperative's cavernous weaving room we rolled out our sleeping bags beneath handpainted posters urging support for the Sandinistas, voting rights for the poor, and breast-feeding.

Bzdak and Durrant went in search of food and returned with news of beer and *pollo dorado* ("golden chicken"). After eight days on the trail I could hear nothing sweeter. They disappeared immediately. Truran and I charged out right behind them, only to emerge into darkened streets lit solely by the refracted light of dung cook-fires spilling through open doorways. As we walked in the dark we talked to keep from spooking ourselves.

Although the expedition had been in Peru almost a month, that was the first time I had found myself alone with Truran. This was a function of the expedition's crowded nature, not any reserve on Truran's part. Indeed, among the ten of us he seemed the most carefree, the most contented with his life. He was six feet tall, blond, with classic, square-jawed good looks and the natural physical grace of a champion athlete. In Arequipa, girls and women had pointed to him as he passed on the street, giggled shyly behind their hands, and called him "Geronimo," after a Peruvian soccer star. Thus far, his chief concern on the expedition, other than rigging his kayak with a device that would enable him to breathe underwater in an emergency, had been to keep his waterproof Walkman alive to play the black African pop music he relished.

Once the kayakers left Yauri, Truran said, the Apurimac would drop steeply, and his real work would begin. In 1983 Biggs and Chmielinski had made the only known descent of a twenty-mile stretch of the river, a week below Yauri, that Biggs had named the "Black Canyon." It had taken the men ten days to kayak those twenty miles. They had run out of food, become quite sick, and endured several serious accidents. Truran described the canyon as the upper river's "crux move," its hardest section, but one that had to be run if the team was to claim a complete kayak descent of the river.

Truran was concerned about the team's ability to execute that crux move. He said that Chmielinski was physically strong and mentally disciplined ("He will do the right thing under pressure") but weaker technically than Truran had expected. Something was bothering Biggs—he seemed timid on the water—and Odendaal was not prepared at all. "He hasn't done his homework," Truran said. "He should have spent every weekend of the past year working on his paddling, but he hasn't. It shows. I think Tim will end up carrying him down the river."

"Are you worried about that?" I asked.

"Not really. That's Tim's problem, isn't it?"

His cold tone caught me short, but before I could ask him anything more we heard Bzdak's high laughter cutting through the night. We tracked the sound to a dirt-floored cantina lit by one bare bulb. The rest of our team arrived right behind us, in Condorito, and parked in front of the cantina. The vehicle quickly attracted a crowd of sullen young men.

Meanwhile, when our *pollo dorado* was served a beggar boy and a phlegmy drunk took up posts inside the cantina door. We heaped food on a plate and passed it along to the boy. He sat in the dirt and bent himself to the task of eating, the unshaded light throwing into relief the scabs on his shaved head. The drunk cajoled a cigarette from Van der Merwe. One of the young toughs entered the cantina, reached behind me, and tried to slip my plate off the table.

"Fuck off!" Van Heerden yelled, and swung at the thief, who retreated beyond striking distance without saying a word.

"Many beggars here," Chmielinski said. "If you are not watching, they will take your head. Better they should go find work."

"A man can make of himself what he wants to, can't he?" Van Heerden said. "If he'll work at it."

"Do I hear the voice of the Nationalist Party?" Odendaal said.

"You hear the voice of a white male," Durrant said.

There was a commotion outside, and, being nearest the door, I bolted for the truck. The strong young faces retreated into the shadows, but no farther.

Two women approached me. They wore tight denim jeans, silky blouses despite the cold night air, high heels, thick makeup, and cascades of cheap jewelry. One introduced herself as "Nancy," the other as "Mary."

"Would you like to go to the disco?" Mary asked in Spanish.

I tried to imagine what would constitute a disco in the dark folds of that poor town, and declined their invitation. Van der Merwe and Van Heerden appeared in the doorway.

"Who are these lovelies?" Van der Merwe asked.

"Mary and Nancy. They want to go to a disco."

"I think we could manage that," Van der Merwe said. Neither of the Afrikaners spoke Spanish, but that didn't seem to matter. Grinning, they strolled off arm in arm into the shadows.

Biggs felt weak, and soon the four kayakers left, too, together with Leon, driving Condorito back to the cooperative.

Two men and a boy entered the cantina carrying a guitar and flutes. Bzdak, Durrant, and I ordered three more bottles of Cuzqueña. The beer was warm, flies buzzed our table, the drunk leered at Durrant. Bzdak told us about the time in Lima that he had almost died from malaria. He had slept in a bathtub filled with ice.

"Why do you stay over here?" Durrant asked. "Why don't you go home?"

"Cannot. Same with Piotr." He said they had come to Peru in 1979 with permission from the Polish government to stay six months. Half the team returned on time, but two years later five still remained in the West. They scheduled a flight to Krakow for December 23, 1981. On December 13 the Polish government outlawed the Solidarity movement. When the news reached Lima, the Poles organized a five-thousand-person march led by the novelist Mario Vargas Llosa. They went first to the Polish embassy, where Llosa delivered a letter of protest to "the only person with enough nerve to stick his damn head out the gate," and then moved on to a nearby park, where they were met with water cannon.

Peru maintains strong ties with the Eastern bloc, and for the next six weeks the Poles were kept under surveillance by the secret police. Harassed, and with Chmielinski suffering a severe case of hepatitis, they fled to Casper, Wyoming, which they had visited briefly in 1979. They settled in Casper, gained U.S. residency, and eventually returned to Peru, where, after running the Colca, they were embraced as heroes by then-President Fernando Belaúnde Terry.

"Does it bother you, Zbyszek?" Durrant asked. She had the pronunciation of his name down cold. "You know, that you can't go back to Poland?"

"If I go to Poland I have an interview, they take my passport away, and I go to prison. For sure I am never let out of Poland again. So it is not so bad. No home, but no prison."

"What about your family?"

"No trouble for my parents, I think, or my little sister. It is five years now. They write me a few letters. They were . . . interviewed a few times, but there was no trouble." He hesitated, then finished his beer. "At least no one ever tells me there is trouble." The man with the guitar began to play a soft, soulful *huayno*, a kind of Andean folk song. The boy accompanied him on flute, its tone at once melancholy and comforting.

"I don't see how you do it," Durrant said. "I've only been in Peru a month and I'm wondering why I came at all." Her feet were swollen and blistered from the hike, but she did not want to return to driving Condorito. "And I have this feeling I'll forget everything I see here as soon as I go home. I feel like, I don't know, like this won't *affect* me."

"You will learn more on this expedition than in five years at home," Bzdak said. "It will always affect you."

"Do you really think so?" she asked.

"Yes."

Four beers to the good, Durrant disappeared behind a greasy

curtain in one corner of the cantina. Lurching, the drunk was about to follow her in when Bzdak shouted a Spanish oath across the room. The man met Bzdak's glare with a dull look and slumped against the wall. When Durrant returned, she and Bzdak danced to the guitar and flute, her feet miraculously, if temporarily, cured.

I returned to the cooperative. Van der Merwe and Van Heerden tumbled in behind me, sweating despite the cold and breathing heavily. Their dates, they explained, had walked them past an alley. They had heard low whistles, upon which the girls had apparently experienced a change of heart. *Run,* they had gestured frantically, *or your throats will be cut.*

The next morning the expedition once again divided into three teams. The kayakers manned their boats and we hikers set off on a trail along the river's left wall. Condorito would drive east out of Yauri, pick up a road that ran northwest through a valley that paralleled the Apurimac, then cut back into the Apurimac some thirty miles later, at the site of the only grass hanging bridge left in Peru. We agreed to meet there in four days.

As Truran had anticipated, below Yauri the river began to demand from the kayakers increased technical expertise and physical stamina. As the Apurimac cut deeper into the earth, huge rocks formed sieves that could suck a body underwater in seconds and keep it there forever. For hundreds of yards at a stretch two-story boulders buried the river completely. The kayakers hauled their heavily laden boats over the boulders and committed several flying "seal-launch" reentries, but weary of portaging, they took greater risks, at times running open pools without first scouting below them.

All four kayakers suffered, but Odendaal suffered most. Though with his weak feet and legs he was the man least capable of portaging his boat, he did so twice as often as the other men, slowing the team severely. Frequently, Chmielinski, the strongest portager, would race ahead with his own boat, then return to carry Odendaal's. Despite this help, Odendaal grew increasingly shaken and temperamental, and sometimes seemed overwhelmed even by the

simple demands of making camp. Biggs worried about his friend.
The river would only get tougher.

The second night below Yauri, Biggs sat quietly before the campfire, playing his harmonica, wishing the orange flames could burn
away the conflicts he felt brewing within and without. Beyond the
fire's warmth the canyon air was frigid and foreboding. Above him,
in the narrow slit between the high black canyon walls, he could
barely make out a thin ribbon of gleaming pinpricks. He thought
about his new wife, Margie. They had been married only a few
months, and he felt uneasy about being away from her for such a
long expedition. The least he could do was come home alive.

He promised himself that he would not paddle the way he
always had before, back when he had shot any rapid he thought
he could run and many he didn't. It was time to change his
attitude. He would run only those rapids about which he felt
absolutely sure, and portage the rest. It was the first time in his
kayaking life that he had conceded there were limits to his ability.

Biggs pocketed his harmonica and left the fire. As the cold air
stung his face he recognized faint symptoms of his illness, especially the drained lethargy, and hurried to his tent. He lit a candle,
crawled into his bag, and finished reading the Book of John. Then
he blew out the candle and settled in for a long sleep. He knew
the river would demand all his physical and emotional strength.
He had to get himself down it safely. And somehow he had to get
his good friend François down it as well.

When I woke up that third morning out of Yauri, fog hung in the
canyon, and in the chilly predawn air my body felt stiff and sore.
And it stank. I found a quiet sandstone pool amid the bucking
rapids, took two steps into it, and sank unsuspecting up to my
neck in the freezing water. I emerged shivering, betrayed, and
coughing from deep in my lungs.

"Please turn off cough alarm." That was Leon, curled up tightly
in his snug bag. Farther down the tiny beach Durrant and Bzdak
had zipped their bags together.

As penance for my rudeness I made coffee and oatmeal and

served it in bed, or bag. Then we packed and were off, climbing, as the game but exasperated Durrant described it, "fucking up and fucking down," a thousand feet up the canyon wall and down and up again, seeing nothing but rock and grass and the deep gray pit of the Apurimac. I fantasized about mules. Mules and bicycles. Mules and bicycles and cars, big cars, mountain-flattening monsters with horrible power plants and stereo tape decks and coolers of cold beer.

From the ridgetop, at about thirteen thousand feet, sharp *quebradas* fell away to either side like the widespread fingers of a bony hand. The scale of the terrain was immense. We hiked for hours between each small sign of man, the few we did see popping up like unrelated snapshots: a stray llama, strings of bright yarn hanging from its ears; a plume of smoke curling from behind a ridge; a shocked, bowler-hatted Quechua woman standing in the trail, her woven blouse dyed with a blue so vibrant it seemed to dance against the dun landscape.

We tramped along in a pattern that would last the duration of our three-week trek. Leon and I walked in front, Leon first, moving with the steady rolling gait he'd developed in Costa Rica's volcanic mountains. He called out the names of plants and flowers, sang songs, and coached my Spanish—this last routine instituted after I'd asked a man we met on the trail to sell us not the eggs he was carrying but his testicles.

Durrant and Bzdak tripped along at the rear, slowly. Bzdak felt it his duty to explain each nuance of the countryside, its history and culture and geology. He was an enthusiastic man, and once he got going on a subject he was hard to stop. Unfortunately, as his lips picked up speed his feet slowed down. Several times each day Leon or I backtracked to prod the chirping lovebirds into forward motion.

As we climbed that morning I considered the budding romance between doctor and photographer, which I knew was exactly the sort of thing Durrant had vowed to avoid. They seemed an unlikely match, Bzdak the anarchic artist, Durrant the urbane professional, even here in the wild. In part, perhaps, a matter of balance.

And for Durrant, after the hard time in Condorito, of refuge.

Late in the afternoon we reached our first settlement since Yauri. Hueco (colloquial Spanish for "hole") consisted of a dozen mud huts squatting amid a ring of the humpy bald peaks called *cerros*, which aside from the canyon's walls and *quebradas* are the dominant feature in the Apurimac moonscape. Each *cerro* is believed to harbor a benevolent spirit, a spirit that may be made godfather to a newborn child. I liked that idea—how spiritually fulfilling to tramp about one's personal godfather hill, talking things over with the dirt.

Next to the first hut a young man pressed mud into forms and laid the bricks in the sun to dry. He was soon to be married. The home he was building, beside his parents', would be the size of a small shed, with barely enough room for two people to sleep. However, like so much else in that lean country (where a third of the crops fail, and the economy is for the most part a cashless one), marriage is a cooperative venture designed to further the community as a whole. The newlyweds would enter a trial period of perhaps a year to see how well they meshed with their new relatives. If things did not work out, the union would be honorably dissolved. Neither church nor state would be party to it.

Fangs bared, a barking little shepherd dog harangued us through Hueco, until a squat beardless man ran down from one of the *cerros* and gave the cur a solid boot.

"I am the mayor of Hueco," the man said. Despite the run, he was not breathing hard at all. "Where are you going?"

"To Cuzco."

"By foot?"

"Yes."

He hefted Bzdak's pack. "You are crazy," he said, then ran back up the hill.

We pushed on, and late that evening made our rendezvous at the Hanging Bridge.

As the Incas had directed, the one hanging bridge that still spans the Apurimac is rebuilt every year in a spirit of cooperation between the citizens of Chumbivilcas province, on the west side of the canyon, and Canas province on the east. It is woven entirely of grass, and though its purpose is ceremonial—a modern wooden bridge stands two hundred yards upriver—it is an impressive structure. Once, according to the villagers of nearby Huinchiri, it attracted a film crew from *Disneylandia*. (Perhaps a convenient identification. After the Pope and Fidel Castro, no icon is more ubiquitous in Peru than *El Ratón Mickey*.) The villagers demanded payment before they would allow the crew to film. Refused, they burned the bridge.

Years later, when Condorito chugged into view laden with the arcane matériel of the cinematographer, Huinchirins attacked it. The kayakers arrived at the bridge shortly thereafter, and the entire crew quickly found itself on trial, sat down, like prisoners of war, on a stone bench in the middle of the village and surrounded by a hundred or so angry locals. For nearly an hour Chmielinski argued with the mayor, argued, as Biggs later described it, like a Prussian statesman. Finally, desperate, he offered the villagers a group medical plan—free examination by the expedition doctor. With that, the men were released.

We hikers limped into camp that night to find the expedition's mood raw and shaken, and when Odendaal announced that we would carry film equipment upriver the next day so that his crew could stage a shot of the kayakers running a rapid, I made the mistake of protesting. (Odendaal had appointed me "Leader of the Hiking Team.") I said that we had been hiking twelve hours a day with full packs for the last four days. Bzdak's heart was bothering him, Durrant's feet were painfully swollen, Leon was exhausted, my knees were shot. We needed a rest.

"I am responsible for every person on this expedition!" Odendaal yelled at me. "I know exactly how they feel!"

His vehemence caught me off guard; our relationship had been cordial until then. I believed he hadn't spoken to the other hikers—Bzdak, in fact, was asleep, and Odendaal hadn't said a word to me before announcing his plan—and when I pressed him for some proof that he had, he would not answer me. Stalemated, we walked away from the campfire to hash things out.

Odendaal leapt to the offensive. He threatened to throw me off the expedition. "And Piotr wants you off, too," he said.

"Look," I said, "I'm sorry—"

"He wants Kate out as well. What good is a doctor who can't kayak? And he says Sergio is a needless luxury."

Numbed by this drastic escalation in what I had thought a contretemps, I said nothing, though I wondered idly how far I would have to walk to find a ride to Lima.

"I don't understand it," Odendaal said after a while, when we had both calmed down. "You and I got along very well in the United States."

"We're all pretty tired right now."

"I have been on many, many expeditions. This is nothing. Nothing at all. You will see."

"I'm sorry."

"Yes. Well, I hope it will work out."

Perhaps, I suggested, traveling alone in a group of strangers had affected my judgment.

"Alone?" he said. "You?"

"Yes, I—"

"What about *me?*"

That was a surprise. I said that it had been my impression that most of the men he had brought with him were his friends.

"Oh, no," he said. He shook his head sadly. "Oh, no. You don't see it, do you? You don't see it at all."

I admitted that I didn't.

"I'm the one who is most alone here," he said. "I have Fanie pushing me from one side, Tim from another. I have to figure out how Pierre will support his family while he's gone, because we certainly won't finish on time. Piotr is just waiting for me to make a mistake. And the river . . ." He shook his head again. "No, you don't see it at all. *I* am the one who stands alone here. *So* alone."

We shook hands, and he left me sitting there by the river, chewing on what he had said. I believed that it was my duty to speak up on behalf of my fellow hikers. Nevertheless, I regretted having further burdened a man so troubled already. And I began to suspect that I had no real understanding of how terrifying a river could be.

The next morning, while the rest of the expedition marched upstream (Leon pressed into service as a film-crew mule, Bzdak carrying only his own cameras), I, the squeaky wheel, was assigned to be interpreter and factotum for the offices of Dr. Durrant. Patients began to assemble at dawn, and by the time she had her clinic erected in the big tent, two dozen Quechua were huddled silently near Condorito, with more arriving hourly.

Most were women who appeared to be suffering from rather vague ailments. None spoke Spanish, nor I Quechua, either of which might have rendered their pains more specific. Though several had brought husbands or sons to translate for them, I found myself fumbling for unfamiliar Spanish words. I had no idea how to say, for example, "Is she still menstruating?" and so bumbled forth with "Does she continue to have a river of blood falling from time to time from between her legs?" Hesitant consultation between man and woman, then, "No. No river."

One young woman had back and stomach trouble. In the preceding seven years she had borne four children and suffered three miscarriages. Another had given birth to ten children, five of them still alive. Another had eight, three alive. And so on. Few of these women were over thirty.

We saw about three dozen patients. Several had walked as far as five miles. None had ever visited a doctor. A few had the deteriorating gums and missing teeth that are the marks of coca-chewing and dietary deficiency, but other than that, Durrant said, most seemed healthy. All had remarkably low blood pressure: "No fat in the land, no fat in the people."

What these peasants seemed to want most was an ear, and sorcery. To the more insistent Durrant dispensed aspirin, which cannot be found short of the daylong trip to Cuzco and is quite expensive by local standards. But she did this reluctantly. "It's too much like a laying on of hands," she said. "The magic white doctor dispensing magic white pills."

Our final patient, the fish-eyed young wife of a very old man, had been hit in the head with a rock three years before. Her head still hurt, and her eyes focused on two entirely different places, like the headlights of a funky car. After a quick examination Durrant determined that she probably needed glasses, considerably more difficult to obtain than aspirin, and not at all what the old man wanted to hear. At first they refused to leave. After a few tense minutes, however, they hit the trail.

"There didn't seem to be many serious problems," I said.

"These people are like anyone else," she told me. "Medical problems are not always the point of a visit to the doctor. When they're sitting around with the neighbors they want to be able to say, 'I went to the best specialist in town.'"

Two hours later the old man shuffled back into camp, alone, carrying a pot filled with small, sweet potatoes and pieces of marinated lamb. He watched silently as we ate. The food was delicious. We cleaned the pot. When he left he said only, "Thank you."

At the Hanging Bridge we once again split up into three teams. We agreed to rendezvous in five days, at the village of Surimana, in the notorious Black Canyon.

Two days after the kayakers departed the Hanging Bridge camp Biggs made a decision he found distasteful: Odendaal would have to leave the Apurimac and portage around the entire Black Canyon. Biggs believed—wanted to believe—that his friend had the physical ability to run the river. Emotionally, however, Odendaal was faltering. He took forever to decide whether to portage or paddle a rapid. Mostly he elected to portage, which meant he spent twice as long at each rapid as the rest of the team. Too often on those occasions when he chose to run a rapid, he froze up and endangered himself on the water. Meanwhile, the other kayakers carried most of his gear in their boats, which made their own portages that much harder.

Biggs tried to persuade Odendaal to shoot more of the smaller rapids, so as to build up his confidence, but Odendaal refused. Biggs thought about forcing him to run them, but he was afraid this might backfire, that Odendaal might break completely. Yet something had to be done. Odendaal's fear was rubbing off on the rest of them, especially Biggs, who was second-guessing himself, running the river through Odendaal's terrified eyes.

At lunch that day, Biggs told Odendaal of his decision. At first Odendaal was shattered. Though he would be allowed to rejoin the team later, his journey would be broken. He would not be able to say, in the strictest terms, that he had kayaked the entire Amazon. However, he agreed that the plan was for the best. The team would push on that day and make camp near the Chaca bridge, where they would hire porters to carry Odendaal's gear into Surimana, six miles downstream.

Then a difficult thing happened.

The canyon broadened and the river flattened out. The rapids became easy, open, gentle. In the unconstricted river, Odendaal began to paddle well, and over the next couple of hours his confidence soared. Then, above an unexpectedly tight turn, he froze up once again. Chmielinski was bearing down behind him. Trying to avoid Odendaal, the Pole flipped his boat. Biggs and Truran, scouting along the bank ahead, scrambled for their rescue lines. As they did, Biggs looked up, and saw that Odendaal had successfully negotiated the rapid and was whooping with joy in the calm water below. Biggs knew what Odendaal was thinking: If Chmielinski could not handle this stretch of water, he too should be made to leave the river.

Truran and Biggs rescued the battered Chmielinski, but Biggs stuck to his decision. That night they made camp at the Chaca bridge, and the next morning Odendaal was sent off, his kayak borne on the shoulders of two Quechua men.

5 *The Black Canyon*

Below the Chaca bridge the Apurimac began to show her darkest side. Now she began her great plunge, boring through a turquoise-and-steel-blue canyon clotted with mile after mile of bouldery blockages and frothing water. "We came to a place where enormous rocks covered the valley floor. The water charged in frenzy at these giants, boiling between and beneath them in search of a distant sea." That is how a University of Utah chemistry professor, J. Calvin Giddings, described the entrance to the Black Canyon of the Apurimac. In 1974, he and a partner made the first recorded attempt to kayak the canyon, but abandoned the effort almost immediately. "Navigation," Giddings concluded, "would be suicide."

When Biggs, Chmielinski, and Truran entered the Black Canyon, they were already feeling lonely, isolated, and run-down from the hard work and insufficient rations of the preceding leg. Almost at once Biggs met the hole that in 1983 had given him one of the worst scares of his life.

It was a siphon, really, a powerful sucking maw that lurked behind an overhanging boulder. Truran and Chmielinski scouted it and waved Biggs through. It did not look like a difficult run. Biggs had only to skirt the boulder. But when he hit the first drop above the boulder a little too slowly, the river snagged the tail of his boat and threw its nose high in the air. By the time Biggs corrected, he found himself heading for the heart of the siphon.

For one horrifying moment he realized that he was in exactly the same predicament as two years before. Here it was again, like a recurring nightmare, this agent of the *apu* Rimac tugging him slowly to his death. How could this be? Paralyzed for a moment, shocked, he could only stare at the rock he would be sucked under. It was a "tea strainer." The river went under the rock in one big flood, but it went out the other side through holes too small to pass a body.

He snapped out of his trance and tried to pull away from the siphon, bracing his paddle against the overhanging rock. No luck. His boat flipped. He stole his last breath. The river tore the paddle from his hands. When he bailed out of his boat he felt himself going down, felt the siphon sucking him under, deep under, to a place without light or sound.

His lungs ready to burst, he fought in vain against the unseen power pulling his feet and torso farther under the rock.

This was it. The end.

Dear God, Biggs prayed, *don't let me go like this.*

He thrust his hands up into the swirling green above him. His last hope was his boat, rocking overhead. He slapped one hand on the kayak and one on the granite roof and pulled.

Air!

The siphon sucked him back down. It slammed him along the rock, into a different boulder. Here was hope: tiny fingerholds in the moss-covered granite. Then from behind, a shove—his boat again!—and he was pinned to the boulder.

The river poured over him, tore at him, but his right foot found purchase on a rocky nub. His head struggled out of the siphon, his shoulders, his back.

Biggs heard shouts: Truran and Chmielinski. A yellow rescue bag bobbed in the water scant feet away, its white line—life!—leading to Truran.

But the bag bobbed just behind his head.

Give up his hold to lunge for the line? He couldn't do it, couldn't abandon the rock.

Water, tons of it, crashed over and around him. The river raged and ripped at him, tried to pull him back from the light. She yanked his feet from the rock. He was going down again.

He prayed strength into his fingertips. They found tiny cracks and nubs, arrested his slide, pulled him back, inch by inch, from eternity. Now he was out to his waist. Now he hauled himself free of the siphon. Now he gained the top of the boulder.

Then he lay facedown in the sun for a long time.

So much river left to run.

We hikers left the Hanging Bridge camp relieved to be on our own again. After two weeks on the trail, our ragged quartet had developed a mobile domesticity, an idiosyncratic routine, that didn't mesh with the rest of the expedition. It was hardest, perhaps, on Kate Durrant. For one thing, she and Bzdak were not ready to reveal their relationship to the rest of the expedition, and did not sleep together when we were with the film crew and kayakers.

Further, as she noted in her diary, with nine men in camp, much more attention was paid to "what I look like than most of the men. Most of them are not exactly Paul Newmans, to put it mildly . . . [but I sense] a certain disappointment that I don't live up to the [image of] glamorous expeditioneer—perhaps the price one has to pay for being taken on because of being female."

On the trail, dusk was the best time of day. No one would have spoken in the last two hours, except to consult and denigrate our torn, tyrannical map. ("It says we have to do *what*? It's *got* to be kidding!") Beaten silly, we would trudge through our last jarring descent and collapse on a sandy beach. Slowly at first, then quickly as the temperature plummeted below freezing, we would open packs, discard sweaty clothes to dry, build a fire, boil water, erect tents.

I was on kitchen detail that first night, and I discharged my duties in sullen silence. After my tiff with Odendaal at the Hanging Bridge, I had decided unilaterally that if we were to be removed from the expedition, it would not be because we were too slow. That day I had set a hard pace on the trail, pushing the others to keep up, and they had glared at me with angry eyes.

But something melted over the campfire, its dancing flames a warm center in the cold mountain night. Bzdak initiated a preprandial ritual that we would repeat whenever possible—"Quechua Moonshots" (cane alcohol, or *cañazo*, he had carried from Huinchiri, mixed with a powdered fruit drink favored, the package alleged, by *los astronautas*). Leon helped me fix chili, spicing it with wild garlic and onions he had foraged along the trail. Durrant teased me gently into dropping my arrogance, and with it my pants.

I was due for a shot, a rabies prophylaxis against the jungle bats we would encounter if we ever reached the jungle.

"Off with the trousers, Kane. Doctor's orders."

"It's cold."

"Off."

"I will make a big fire," Bzdak said.

He heaped driftwood on the blaze, and I capitulated, whatever dignity I still retained evaporating with an involuntary yowl when the doctor found her mark. There was a round of applause. After dinner, as the three who could still do so sat and watched the river by starlight, I rummaged in my pack and fished out three chocolate bars. I offered them, wishing I could offer more.

We awoke at dawn and climbed hard all the next morning, to thirteen thousand five hundred feet, gaining the canyon rim at about noon. It was like climbing out of a cave. Ten yards away, a solitary gray eagle held at eye level in the thermals swirling up out of the canyon. Forty miles to the northeast, 21,000-foot Auzangate floated like an iceberg above the lesser brown peaks of the Cordillera Vilcanota. In fact, turning in a full circle, all one saw was peaks. Wind tore across the exposed ridge and lightning flashed in the gray-black sky above.

Two thousand feet below us, we could see the point where the Apurimac's black-and-red walls shifted abruptly from their forty-five-degree slope to nearly vertical. Even from that height the Black Canyon revealed itself as a boulder-strewn mess, its feathered rapids whipping the once-green river into a boiling white.

We were looking for the village of Chocayhua. From there the trail would drop back down to the river and eventually cross the bridge, near Surimana, where we hoped to meet the kayakers.

Our trail forked. Here was a Quechua man. Could he direct us to Chocayhua? "That place does not exist," he said, and took the left fork. We went right. Fifteen minutes later we were in Chocayhua, watching a Quechua crew hew eucalyptus trunks into logs for a schoolhouse. Under yet another form of reciprocal labor, *faena*, community members would build the school. The government would provide the workers with coca, *cañazo*, and cigarettes. And, perhaps, when the project was completed, a teacher.

We pushed on down the trail. As we reached the end of the tiny village a voice shouted to us from behind a courtyard wall: "*Chicha!*"

Beer or the dusty trail? Not a difficult choice.

We entered the courtyard. Six barefoot Quechua men in clean white alpaca suits sat before three ancient manual Singer sewing machines, drinking freely from bottles of *cañazo* and sewing banners for a fiesta scheduled to begin the next day. There would be a bullfight, and this being planting season, any human bloodshed would be considered a fertility offering to the earth.

Two stout gap-toothed women moved among the men, refilling their bottles and the ornate ceremonial coca pouches that hung from each man's neck. They poured us cups of home-brewed *chicha*, a thick, slightly sweet corn beer. We sat in the sun and drank and watched the men sew. Every few minutes they asked how we were doing, which seemed, increasingly, to be just fine.

An old, drunken man with a big belly entered the courtyard. This was "Papa," who said he was the father of several of the men, although he could not remember who their mothers were. One of the women began to wail in a high, eerie voice. The men ignored her. Papa attempted a shot of *cañazo* but missed, a rich stream pouring down his lower face and across his chest. The young men stood and anointed their banners with *cañazo* and toasted themselves. After a while one fell down and did not get up.

When we inched toward the courtyard gate hands clamped my arms in a way that was not entirely friendly. I tried to pry the leathery fingers loose, but they were firm and unyielding. Two men grabbed Bzdak. They hauled us to another home, another courtyard. The two families sponsoring the fiesta that year were honorbound to outdo each other. If the moonmen had fun at one home, they had better have fun at the second.

They said Bzdak must take photos, which he did energetically, though without film in his camera. They said we must drink *chicha.* This I did as fast as I could, until my stomach started to cramp and felt as if it would burst. Leon and Durrant did likewise.

When a commotion at the courtyard gate distracted our hosts' attention, we ran for it. We were cut off at the gate. A horse reared up on the trail, its rider swinging a kind of lariat looped around a golfball-sized stone. A skilled man can fling the stone some fifty yards with considerable accuracy. But not this *mal hombre:* After demanding in a gurgling voice to be photographed, he slumped forward in a stupor and fell to the ground like a sack of rice, headfirst, his skull landing with the squashed sound of a dropped melon.

Someone else jumped on the horse, and the mob—the whole of Chocayhua seemed to have spilled onto the trail—trampled poor melon-head. A fight erupted. In the confusion and encroaching darkness we made our escape down the trail and back to the safety of the deep, dark canyon.

Two nights later we found the kayakers camped at the Surimana bridge. Odendaal had gone ahead to Surimana. From there, a road led out of the canyon and into the city of Cuzco. He was to meet Condorito in the village, then drive into Cuzco with the cameramen. Fanie Van der Merwe had decided to fly out of Cuzco and return to South Africa to teach. Pierre Van Heerden, who would stay with the expedition to continue filming, and Odendaal would drive back to Surimana, where Odendaal would again hire burros and try to meet the other kayakers below the Black Canyon.

Truran appeared tired but, as always, cheerful. He was dressed only in long gray polypropylene underwear with horizontal black stripes, and looked something like an escaped convict. "Do you have any bread?" he asked. "We're out of food. Would you like tea?"

Chmielinski wore a bold red gash across his nose, and his knee was swollen big as a grapefruit. "Everybody had a tough time," he said. "One time I was in a hole and it was kind of nice, I was feeling weightless. Then I was dying." He had bailed out of his boat and been washed a hundred crunching yards through three bad rapids.

"Pinball," Truran said.

"Tim had the worst," Chmielinski said. "He was half a meter from no way."

Bad as the water was, however, they were equally worried about news gleaned from a gold panner. Two European kayakers had also set out from La Angostura. They were two weeks farther down the river, and bound for the Atlantic. It was a race.

Truran brewed tea and we pitched camp in a downpour. Thirty feet up the bank, in a small cave lit by two candles, Tim Biggs drew river scenes in his sketchbook, as if with black ink and white paper he could conjure order from the chaos of the Great Speaker.

It rained the night through. In the morning, shivering in the damp air, we climbed the two miles into Surimana.

An army of morose children followed us through the village. Their leader, a tall, skinny girl, hissed at us in Andean Spanish, but the idiomatic expressions for *shit, whore,* and *fucker* tumbled from her lips uneasily, without much venom, as if she were experimenting with them.

A bust of José Gabriel Tupac Amaru II stood in the plaza, near the locked doors of a church that is opened but once a year. The neglected memorial, its base cracked and in need of paint, marks the end of the dirt road chiseled into Surimana from Cuzco in the 1970s by the government, which had hoped the birthplace of one of the Western Hemisphere's great revolutionaries would attract tourists. But the tourists did not come. There is nothing to eat in

Surimana and nowhere to sleep.

The road, the only one into the Black Canyon, does not seem to have helped the village much—the local store offered only a basket of white flour, three candles, and a tin of *cañazo*. The only vehicle we saw was a jeep bearing the acronym of a government relief agency. Judging by the appearance of the townspeople, the road was used mainly when in need of Cuzco's polyester shirts and aviator sunglasses.

In a way it is the road, not the neglected bust, that embodies the spirit of Tupac Amaru II, whose story seems to capture all the desperation and wild hope the Apurimac canyon provokes. He was born José Gabriel Condorcanqui, a great-great-great-grandson of Felipe Tupac Amaru Inca, whose sadistic beheading in 1572 signaled the end of the Inca dynasty and the final subjugation of indigenous Peru by Spain. The Spanish forced Felipe's two daughters to watch the beheading. Magdalena died within a year, but the penniless Juana married Felipe Condorcanqui of Surimana and settled in this forgotten canyon.

Under an Inca system bent by the Spanish to their own ends, the Condorcanquis, like other Quechua of Inca caste, were *curacas*. They governed the Apurimac canyon and the surrounding high lands for their absentee Spanish overlords, overseeing conscription for the terrible *mita* and enforcing the feudal *encomienda*, by which the Quechua were forced to pay the Spanish vast tributes of produce and precious metals. By the time José Gabriel Condorcanqui was born, about 1743, the family had become one of the most prosperous in Peru. Raised as a nobleman, he was well educated and wealthy, with a serene disposition and the elegant manners of a European aristocrat.

When José Gabriel became *curaca* of the Surimana area, Spain was in decline and its exploitation of the Quechua had increased. Millions died in the mines during the first half century alone. Unable to ignore the suffering of his people, José Gabriel adopted his ancestral title, then journeyed to the Lima courts. He believed that the laws of Spain were just, but that greedy tax collectors, a corrupt clergy, and a sadistic military had grossly perverted them.

His entreaties were ignored. In 1780, declaring himself a loyal servant of the King of Spain, Tupac Amaru II revolted against the colonial administration.

His revolution was short-lived—it ended in 1783—but at its height, reaching from Colombia in the north through Ecuador, Peru, Bolivia, and northwestern Argentina, it was grander in scope than the American Civil War and almost every European war preceding World War I. Tupac Amaru, however, was captured in 1781 and marched to Cuzco. The Spanish handcuffed him, his wife, his son, his uncle, and five compatriots, stuffed them in sacks, and dragged them through the streets with horses. They forced the Inca and his wife to watch while his eighty-year-old uncle and twenty-year-old son had their tongues cut out and were garroted, then made the Inca witness his wife's garroting. When the iron collar failed to crush her tiny neck, the hangman wrapped a lasso around her throat and yanked on it until she died, beating her all the while. Then he cut out the Inca's tongue, tied his limbs one each to four horses, and drove the beasts in the four directions. When they failed to tear him apart, the exasperated hangman first disemboweled the Inca, then hacked off his head.

News of the barbarous execution reached Spain, drawing attention to the other atrocities in Peru, and a new administration was installed. A half century later, however, Quechua and *criollo* joined forces to drive Spain out of Peru. Whether this freed the Quechua from the barbarities visited on them by men of lighter skin is, of course, another matter altogether, one that is at least partially addressed by the fact that, two centuries later, much of the Apurimac canyon was under martial law, Peru's *criollo* leaders locked i a brutal war with an army of guerrillas whose veins ran thick w Quechua blood.

Everything about the Andes is abrupt: the geology, the p weather, the people. You walk but a few miles and feel have traveled into an entirely new region, or an entirel season. Two days below Surimana our dusty trail sudder a mossy carpet. The omnipresent *ichu* drowned in a flo daisies, pink-flowered bromeliads, cactus blooming in purple and white, wild roses as big as fists, blood-red geraniums, yellow broom, bright tiny flowers that ran among the rest like golden ants. The air smelled of mint, peppermint, chamomile, and, as we drew near the village of San Juan, eucalyptus, freshly turned earth, and the first buds of pear, apple, and *maracuya*. Small birds strafed the fruit trees and the honeyed tones of Andean panpipes drifted down the hillside.

A hedge ran along the uphill side of the path. A battered straw hat rose above it, followed by a well-used earth-brown face, a gnarly hand, a plastic jug . . .

"*Chicha?*"

Our narrow escape from Chocayhua notwithstanding, could we refuse? We had marched out of winter into spring: Here were Quechua families preparing their fields, the men working the ancient foot plows, the women laying out bowls of boiled corn and pitchers of *chicha*. It is custom in that roadless, wheel-less country to treat the traveler as kin. We sprawled in the dirt and sampled the local brew.

The fields in San Juan, like the families who work them, have a lineage at least a dozen generations old. (Parts of the Peruvian highlands have a native agriculture that can be traced back four millennia.) That those fields continue to produce, and produce well, is, as the American writer and farmer Wendell Berry put it, evidence of "an agriculture of extraordinary craftsmanship and ecological intelligence."

Consider the potato. Nobody knows how many varieties of potato grow in the Andes, though estimates run from four hundred to two thousand. In addition to wild potatoes, an extraordinary array of native varieties is grown for table—as many as forty-six have been found in a single half-acre field. (My conceptual favorite is an exceptionally tough table potato called *lumchipamundana*, "potato that makes the young bride cry.") There are also potatoes called *chuño*, which are freeze-dried. Each day for about a month the Quechua hand-squeeze the water out of them and let them freeze by night. The end product has a shelf life of years and tastes about like any other freeze-dried product, which is to say, awful.

A seven-year fallow cycle controls a predator nematode with a six-year life. Rows carefully contoured to the land minimize the overwhelming threat of erosion. If these peasants must sing to their fields to get them to produce; if they offer *chicha* to spirits they believe live in the rocks and trees and caves; if they choose to measure their plots of land not in square meters but according to their fertility; if they name each plot after the plants that grow best in it—well, it works. Here, where the land is so steep it seems to spill right off the sides of the mountain (stand up and your head is closer to corn sprouts than it is to your feet), the Quechua have evolved a system of sustainable agriculture in sharp contrast to our topsoil-devouring corporate farming. Farmers in tabletop-flat Iowa lose a foot and a half of topsoil every year. A Quechua farmer can't afford to lose an inch.

A crowd of barefoot schoolchildren, wearing white shirts and black pants, led us to the sea-of-mud plaza. Behind us, between teetering mud houses, mud streets twisted up the canyonside. Before us they accelerated toward the canyon, ending there abruptly, as if one could walk to the edge of town and step directly into the abyss of the Apurimac. Staring down into that chasm, one respected the Quechua's decision not to invent the wheel—what chaos it would cause in such precipitous country.

Fifty dark, Asiatic faces stared at us. The smallest boy singled me out. His hair was close-cropped and, like so many children we had seen, his scalp was covered with scabs.

"What is your name?" I asked. No answer, then a mumbled response, "*Solitario*," in a voice too deep for that diminutive frame. Solitary. Lonely.

Suddenly, from among the sea of children there appeared at our feet a bottle of beer, a bottle of rum, an onion, a head of cabbage, three eggs, a sheaf of chamomile, and one of mint. Then a man pushed through the crowd, a giant compared with everyone else we had seen, six feet tall, his white hair and blue eyes loud as neon in that world of brown-eyed, black-haired elves. He breached the wall and stopped, as shy and dumbstruck as the children. His name was Adán. "For your health," he said, and quietly poured yet another round of *chicha.*

He took us to his house, a simple two-room affair with a garden and a big earthen oven in which he baked loaves of whole-grain bread. ("For the children," he said. "When their nutrition is poor they cannot pay attention.") He gave us five fresh loaves. His own children had gone to Lima, where two attended a university. "I hope they come home soon," he said. "That city is a terrible place."

The urchin army escorted us out of town, along a trail that followed the canyon wall, wound into a *quebrada* and back out to a breathtaking view of the Black Canyon. Now bathed in the golden-red light of dusk, it looked something like the Grand Canyon of the Colorado, but steeper, narrower, deeper, lonelier.

A last glance at isolated San Juan, clinging to the side of the canyon without roads, phones, or power lines to cinch it into place. *Solitario.*

Down below us the kayakers plowed slowly through the boulder-strewn Apurimac. Relieved of the burden of Odendaal's gear, they traveled for the first time with full rations. Freed of Odendaal himself, they now moved twice as fast as they would have if Odendaal had been with them. But at times they found no more than fifty runnable yards between each portage, and even then the river, with its sieves and undercuts and siphons, was tougher than ever. Some days they were lucky to advance a mile.

Despite the river's demands, Biggs felt his confidence returning. Jerome Truran had a lot to do with that. His kayaking style was smooth and unflinching. He scouted each rapid carefully, but when he had decided how to run it, he did so directly, without hesitation. He alone among the kayakers had yet to be torn out of his boat.

Off the water Truran was funny, charming, not easily perturbed. Like Biggs, he loved the river life. Competing in the United States in 1978, Truran had discovered the big white water of the Rocky Mountains and the Sierra Nevada. South Africa and Europe had nothing quite like it. Now, after making camp in the fading light of day, Truran and Biggs would often don their paddling gear and play in the Apurímac's murderous rapids, exulting in the river's sheer power.

Biggs was happy, indeed proud, to see the younger Truran developing an appreciation for the rhythms of expedition kayaking, perhaps the one thing Biggs could teach his world-champion friend. No car waited downstream to haul you away if you were injured. You didn't have a week to rest up after a weekend of hard paddling. You carried as much food as you could in your boat, and when you ran out you went hungry. You settled in for the long haul, adapted to the river's pace, moved as the river allowed you to move. It wasn't all exhilarating runs and beach parties. Truran, Biggs thought, was learning a river.

The days grew warmer, and cactus and small fir trees splashed the canyon walls with a refreshing green. But the river became no easier. Day after day the three kayakers fought to gain a hundred yards here, a quarter mile there. To lighten their boats they ate big meals, gambling that they would gain speed on the river. Frustrated by the long hours spent scouting the river, climbing boulder after boulder, they ran some rapids blind, and paid for it. Biggs suffered another bad swim, Chmielinski broke his nose.

Six days after entering the Black Canyon the kayakers reached its terminus, the Apurímac's confluence with the Livitaca River. As they approached it they heard shouts coming from the right. They looked up to see porters lowering a scratched, muddy, but quite happy François Odendaal and his equipment down the canyon wall at the end of a rope. When the rope came up short, the kayakers beached their boats and eased Odendaal down to the river. Then he packed his boat and they set off, a quartet once again.

Below the Livitaca confluence the Apurímac changed. Its high, pinching walls receded slightly, their sculpted granite broken by long formations of soft rock that the river had ground down to create stretches of wide, flat water. Where the granite reappeared, however, the river narrowed into funnels, creating spectacular, cascading rapids. One of these shook Odendaal out of his boat and nearly pinned him to the face of a boulder.

That night around the campfire Odendaal mounted an anguished monologue, arguing that the ethics of portaging was a gray area, that his trip with burro and porters did not differ fundamentally from the portages the other kayakers had made, and that, therefore, his claim to having run the entire river remained intact. The other men listened quietly. Clearly, Odendaal was obsessed. Biggs alone tried to assuage his friend's anxiety. Odendaal, he said, had run the river to the best of his ability. That was all any man could hope to do.

The next day was hard. All four kayakers had close calls, Odendaal took another mean swim, and in one spot the river was completely blocked, requiring a long, slow, bone-jarring portage. The following morning Piotr Chmielinski called a summit meeting.

It was time, he said, to address the subject of the competition, and to adjust plans accordingly. They had to move faster. He had not come to South America to be the second crew down the Amazon. If they did not intend to be first, he would go home.

This was the moment Biggs had been dreading. He did not want a race to the sea. This was a river trip, a journey of exploration, an adventure to be shared with friends. He had had his fill of racing.

On the other hand, if the expedition's goal was to be the first to travel the Amazon from source to sea, then so be it. As river captain, it was his duty to realize that goal.

Then things really went crazy.

Jerome Truran had an idea or two about this whole so-called race. If Odendaal regarded his long portage around not only the Black Canyon but much of the water above it as tantamount to paddling it, if he believed it was legitimate to complete the river's crux move by burro, then why were the other kayakers risking their lives on the water? Why paddle at all? Why not hire burros and porters and catch the competition by land? Hell, why not *fly* to the sea?

No, Truran said, if it really was going to be a race, then Odendaal was out. He simply did not have the ability to kayak the river. He was like a beginning client on one of the commercial trips Truran led in South Africa. Truran, Biggs, and Chmielinski were "buttering" the river for him, carrying his gear and coaching him through the few rapids he actually ran. That the three of them would battle the Apurimac while Odendaal took credit for the descent was an outrage.

In fact, the way Truran saw it, Odendaal didn't belong on the river at all. He hated kayaking. On the water his face was tortured with worry and fear.

Truran said he hoped, for all their sakes, that there was another François Odendaal beneath the one he knew. But he hadn't seen such a man, not yet. If Odendaal wanted Truran to help baby-sit him down the river, fine. Truran could never afford such a trip on his own. But Odendaal's money bought only Truran's skill, not his complicity in a lie.

Shattered, Odendaal turned to Biggs, but Biggs, though upset with Truran for lashing out, was also upset with Odendaal. For six years he'd been after Odendaal to master at least the basic skills of kayaking. Odendaal had known how dangerous the Apurimac would be, but had not adequately prepared himself. Now his lack imperiled them all.

Biggs let Odendaal stew for the rest of the day, but that night the two of them had a heart-to-heart talk to straighten out their differences. Meanwhile, Odendaal spoke to Chmielinski about removing Truran from the expedition.

In other circumstances Chmielinski might have agreed with Odendaal's suggestion. On an expedition of which he was the sole leader Chmielinski would not have tolerated Truran's insubordination. But now he was not sure what to do.

For one thing, Chmielinski had never seen a kayaker with Truran's skills, or his courage. As the river grew, it produced the most thrilling runs the team had yet encountered. This was Truran's country now. A white-water river was so *alive*. If one were good enough—confident and skilled and strong—one became part of its spirit, absorbed its rhythms. Truran was that good, and more. It was not simply luck that only he among the four of them had yet to come out of his boat and swim at the mercy of the Great Speaker.

Chmielinski's technical skills had improved rapidly under Truran's influence. He knew that with Truran leading the descents, the team would continue to move quickly. Speed was now foremost in the Pole's mind. To him, the news of the second kayaking team made this situation similar to Amundsen's and Scott's race to the South Pole.

But speed concerned Chmielinski for another reason as well. A year before, in Wyoming, he had received a telephone call he had been expecting for months. When he had left Poland in 1979, he was in love with a woman named Joanna. They had spoken of marriage but had agreed to postpone their wedding until Chmielinski's return. A year later they managed to meet briefly in New York, but shortly thereafter martial law was declared in Poland and Joanna could no longer leave the country. In 1984 Joanna learned about the possibility of going abroad with a tourist group. She wrote Chmielinski, who contacted an old friend from Krakow, a monsignor who had become right-hand man to the Pope. The friend began the arrangements for a Vatican marriage.

Two months later Joanna called Wyoming: She was in Italy. Chmielinski landed in Rome twenty-four hours later, and within days they were wed. (The Pope himself gave the couple his blessing.) Then they began the sticky process of getting Joanna out of Poland legally and into the United States. They filed papers with the Vatican, with the U.S. Embassy, with the Polish Embassy. Joanna returned to Poland, Chmielinski to Wyoming.

There were delays, and more delays. He had not seen her since, and it had been months since he had been able to speak with her by phone.

She was due to arrive in the United States, alone, shortly after Chmielinski finished running the Amazon. He had to be there to receive her, but now that schedule was in jeopardy. Odendaal's slowing the team on the river was concern enough, but if he became separated from the other kayakers and had a bad accident, the expedition would grind to a halt.

The best thing for all of them, Chmielinski thought, would be for Odendaal to leave the river for good. On the other hand, he needed Odendaal. If Chmielinski could learn something about filmmaking on this trip, he might someday be able to translate his own adventures into profit.

Chmielinski had a business agreement with Odendaal. He would stick to it. But he decided that removing the skilled and courageous Truran would seriously jeopardize the expedition.

Intact, the team pushed on. That afternoon they reached Pillpinto, and their rendezvous with the hiking team.

6 *Trail's End*

According to our map, we faced a long, steep hike out of the Black Canyon. From San Juan we would climb the canyon wall, gaining two thousand feet of altitude, then cross a pass at fourteen thousand feet that would probably be covered in snow. Coca-leaf time. We were getting used to the altitude, but such severe climbs still left us gasping and achey headed, and as the Quechua discovered centuries ago, the leaf is an excellent tonic. I had read many accounts condemning the locals for their coca use, but I now suspected most had been written by people who owned cars.

A woman on the trail offered a fistful of leaves and a chunk of *llipta*. When Leon asked directions to Toccorani, she pointed straight up in the air and laughed in the shrieking way the Quechua sometimes did, a laugh all the more unsettling for the rarity of its appearance.

The Andes display staggering contrasts—weather that changes forty degrees in minutes, monolithic geological formations that erupt from flat, eroded tracts, waterways that burst and explode rather than flow—but the most surprising are found in those few places in which man has wedged his tinkering fingers: his villages. Each village in the Black Canyon had an air, a tone, that was distinct and identifiable. Hueco had been primeval and isolated; Surimana sullen and unsure of itself, corrupted by the road; San

Juan fertile and welcoming.

As we circled Toccorani, on the trail to the pass, we saw a manicured soccer field and near almost every hut a horse of impressive size and coat—something like finding a Mercedes-Benz in every driveway in an American suburb. The field suggested a surfeit of what in the States we call leisure time, but leisure time in the Andes also means time to quiz the gringo. We avoided Toccorani, hiked through the pass, spit our wads on the *apachita*, slouched through the snow and down into deserted, forlorn Santa Lucia, fifty huts clustered wall to wall and perched like a muddy pulpit two thousand sheer feet above the Apurimac. Where was everybody? (In the fields, planting.)

Across the canyon Omacha's tin roofs glinted in the sun. Omacha was a couple of miles away as the condor flies, but the immensity of that country was deceptive. It didn't encourage things to expand and connect; it compressed them into tiny, isolated universes. To visit Omacha we would have had to climb back to Surimana, cross the bridge, and walk down the far side of the canyon. The trip would take a week.

Black clouds coagulated along the canyon rim, amplifying Santa Lucia's barren, marooned feeling. We hustled up the trail. Rain fell and stopped. Below us a sea of cotton-topped clouds obliterated the river. A black wall rose from that white sea, rose and whitened, and snow fell on the mountain peaks across the canyon. Beyond the peaks the sky swirled with a thousand shades of purple. The colors mixed with such slow subtlety that, unable to bring the sky into focus, I felt as if I were about to lose my balance and fall down.

The sun slid out of that purple pocket and lodged between two of the peaks. We sat on a rock and ate chocolate. The storm ascended the canyon once again, rained on us, and receded. The sun, which appeared to have set, burned through the clouds. Chimneys of cold fog levitated up from the canyon floor.

This meteorological wizardry, dizzying and eerie, lent the mountains an air of mystery. Like most travelers stumbling into a mysterious place, we felt as if we were discovering it. But there, clinging to the mountain ledge three-quarters of a mile below us, was a tiny hut. On our map was a corresponding dot. The hut had been there at least thirty years, perhaps hundreds.

We wouldn't reach Huayque that afternoon. Instead, we pitched camp on the only flat place we could find, the trail itself. As a friend once wrote, traveling narrows one's horizons. Moving from place to place, securing food and shelter, become full-time work. In the three weeks since I had stepped out of the truck at Lari and first set foot on the trail, the Andes had stripped me of excess. I slept on the trail, scrounged food, and traveled by the oldest and simplest means known to man.

To reduce our weight, we now carried a two-man rain fly instead of tents. This we hurried to erect before the storm hit, and squeezed into it hoping that four bodies would generate heat sufficient to keep us from freezing. We needn't have worried. Though it snowed all night, our body heat stoked the humidity beneath the plastic to unbearable levels. In the dead of night Leon bolted headlong into the storm, dragging his sleeping bag with him. He returned five minutes later, stark naked, soaked, shivering, and asleep on his feet. Bzdak dried him off and dressed him in long underwear. Then Durrant and I laid him down between us and wrapped our arms around him until, half an hour later, he stopped shaking, and we heard the sound of deep, rhythmic breathing. In the morning he said he had dreamed he was Superman.

It was late September, but in the Andes the seasons have as much to do with altitude as with time. The next day we once again hiked down out of winter into spring, walking through a chorus of yellow daisies, hot-pink bromeliads, the blue medallions of flowering wild potato, and aromatic eucalyptus groves, which are planted near settled areas for reforestation.

Huayque, too, was a surprise. Cobbled streets and a stone canal ran through the village carrying water and, from the looks of it, anything else that would float. But the biggest revelation was the houses. They had two stories, a design we had not seen before, but were built on Quechua scale. It was like walking through a children's amusement park, or a Hollywood set, where everything is slightly smaller than real life. I stopped in front of one mud-and-thatch home, reached up, and touched the top of the second-story shutters.

A woman more ancient than old waddled up to us. She was hunched over and dressed in filthy rags and her gray hair hung to below her waist in a sloppy braid. She had one tooth, in the center of her upper gum. She yelled and shoved a pitcher of brown *chicha* in our faces. It looked as vile as the effluent running through the clay canal.

Bzdak, Durrant, and I refused it, but Leon, ever polite, drained the horn.

"You must stay here tonight," the woman said.

Leon pointed to me. "He will stay if he can sleep with any woman he wants."

Bzdak said, "Are there any girls in the village who would like gringo babies?"

"Yes," she said, nodding seriously. "Some young ones."

This frightened me. The young Quechua women had a tranquil beauty that broke one's heart with a glance. But the idea of a sexual liaison on the dirt floor of a flea-ridden hut, while Mom boiled corn over the open fire and Dad sharpened his machete—that was not my idea of romance, especially given the mercurial and at times violent moods we had seen among the locals.

I left quickly, and let the others catch up.

On the trail out of town we met men and women returning from their fields, carrying wooden foot plows and drinking from bottles of *aguardiente* and *cañazo*. Two hours from town they were still coming, spilling down out of the mountainside like rainwater. For a mile above and below us sweeping rows of terraced fields cut the mountains like lines on a topographic map. I could not see a single patch of uncultivated land.

The men grunted, a few said hello. The women hurried silently behind them. They had a long hike home, and they would be back on the trail before dawn.

We camped in a cow pasture next to a stream. I heard a loud report and looked up the slope to see a man holding a rifle, which when he again slapped it against a tree I saw was actually a foot plow. I turned back to the camp. Six Quechua men stood in a row a few feet in front of me, passing a bottle of *cañazo*. More than one found the ground beneath his feet a little shifty.

A man stepped forward and pointed to another, who appeared to be the oldest of them, though with the Quechua it was hard for me to judge age.

"This is the lieutenant of Huayque," the younger man said. "It would please him to see your license."

"License?"

"Your permission."

"Permission?"

Fortunately, Bzdak knew this ritual, its steps as prescribed as those of a formal dance. He explained that we were visiting Huayque as representatives of the Peruvian government, that we were exploring sites for a great film project, that we hoped to tell the world of the glory of Peru. And so on. Meanwhile I rummaged through my pack and found a photocopy of a letter from the Peruevian tourist board. The *teniente* studied it carefully, impeded not at all, apparently, by the fact that he was reading it upside down.

"We will be here only one night," Bzdak said.

The man grunted and returned the paper.

"Please be our guests," he said. "We did not mean to offend you. We were afraid that you would steal our cattle."

He wished us well, bowed deeply, and led the men back to the trail in single file. A few stumbled slightly as they went, but overall, I thought, they carried themselves with an earthy dignity.

From Huayque we dropped down, way down, breaking toenails against the insides of our boots. Late the next afternoon we arrived on the canyon floor at the point where the mud-red Chacco River empties into the turquoise-green Apurimac. At the town of Acos, a mile from the confluence, we picked up a dirt road used for bus traffic to Cuzco. But we followed it the other way, into Pillpinto, where we were to meet the kayakers.

Where it flowed through Pillpinto the Apurimac was wide and

shallow, lacking the power and urgency it had displayed farther up the canyon, and the town itself had a surliness similar to that of Yauri, the Hanging Bridge, and Surimana. The staring crowd that wouldn't leave us in peace went with the territory, but these people had none of the brightness we had seen in, say, San Juan, or even Huayque. It was impossible to carry on a conversation. We sat in the dirt, surrounded, until long after dark, went to sleep with the townsfolk staring into our tents, and in the morning pulled back tent flaps to find them still there.

In the end, lacking a better explanation, I decided that it was the road that triggered this impotent hostility. It promised so much—trade, culture, escape—but judging by the beaten-down look of the town and its people, it delivered very little.

The kayakers had arrived in Pillpinto the same afternoon. All looked battered except Truran. Odendaal's face was bloody and swollen, Chmielinski's nose reinjured. Biggs's appearance was drawn, his ebullience forced. There was evident tension between Chmielinski and Odendaal (at one point I heard the Pole mutter, "On the river he is a baby"), and Chmielinski, if not directing the expedition, certainly was not following Odendaal's lead. Given my fragile perch on the journey, this did not augur well for me. I was sure that Chmielinski saw me as Odendaal's soldier, and I suspected the only reason I (or, for that matter, Durrant or Leon) remained on the expedition was that Bzdak had put in a good word.

I decided I had better establish some kind of communication with Chmielinski. Try as I might, however, I could not find a way to do this. In conversation he was polite but formal. He was also one of the most intense men I had ever met. On the nights we had camped with the kayakers, I had watched him labor by candlelight until long after dark, his ledgers and maps and notebooks (which he carried in a waterproof plastic box tucked deep in the nose of his kayak) spread out on some cleverly built driftwood desk or on the floor of his tent.

From what Truran said, this intensity carried over to the river. It was Chmielinski who harangued the South Africans to wake before dawn, Chmielinski who pushed them onto the river and kept them on it until late in the day. Truran said that Chmielinski attacked the river like a military man. He was brave, and though his kayaking skills were self-taught, he had a superb feel for white water—he refused to let the river's power intimidate him. He felt the river in his bones and respected it the way a general does a worthy enemy: It was something to conquer.

Each day Chmielinski prepared himself as if for combat. He was the first man awake, the first man packed, the first man with his boat in the water. His daily uniform—long polypropylene underwear and crisp paddling shorts—was so unvarying, and so fresh compared with the rags the others were now wearing, that Truran half suspected the Pole kept spares hidden in his boat.

The final steps in Chmielinski's matutinal ritual were the most telling: Using a pocket mirror, he carefully combed his hair and applied a combination of lotions and sunscreens that looked, to Truran, exactly like war paint. Then Chmielinski hauled his boat down to the Apurimac and paddled off to do battle.

The morning after we arrived at Pillpinto Chmielinski and Odendaal outlined what would be the next, and thus far the longest, leg of the campaign. Once again we would divide into groups, and reunite ten days later, at the military bridge near the town of Chinchaypujio. The expedition would meet Van Heerden and Condorito in Cuzco, which was connected to Chinchaypujio by a dirt road, take a short break, then return to the Apurimac and continue the journey by kayak and white-water raft only. From there down, the canyon would be too steep to hike. Bzdak and I would remain in Cuzco, buy supplies for the next two months of the trip, and drive Condorito back to the Apurimac to rejoin the expedition at a second bridge, Cunyac, some twenty-five miles below the military bridge. Condorito's owner would meet us in Cuzco, ride with us to Cunyac, then take the vehicle home to Arequipa. The road to Cunyac would be the last to reach the river until we were well into the jungle.

The plan disappointed me for reasons that were completely

selfish. Although our long trek had been unanticipated, I had become attached to the idea of traveling along the entire river. In the jungle, that might mean banana boats. But the white-water raft would be the only way to see the lower Apurimac canyon. It was therefore conceivable that of the Amazon's four thousand two hundred miles, I would miss only those twenty-five between the military bridge and the resupply point at Cunyac. I found the distance both insignificant and monumental.

The plan was fair, however. No one had promised I would be on the entire river in the first place. At least I would remain a member of the expedition. Nor was it hard to reconcile myself to a week of fresh food, cold beer, and hot showers in Cuzco.

But first our ragged "B" team had to reach Chinchaypujio.

We marched out of Pillpinto with packs stocked for seven days, but we did not expect a difficult hike. According to our map, the trail ran right next to the river, and would be fast and level. Domestic tobacco growing just outside Pillpinto signaled fertile country. We would be able to flesh out our rations, stretch them to a ten-day kit, as we went.

We hadn't counted on the new road from Pillpinto to the provincial capital of Paruro. It went through the next valley beyond the southwest wall of the Apurimac canyon, and the Apurimac trail had been abandoned in favor of the road. A few miles below Pillpinto the trail vanished.

We laughed that first day when the lone Quechua man we met in the canyon insisted we hire him as a guide. By the end of the second day, after climbing twenty-five hundred vertical feet up the canyon wall, some of it hand-over-hand technical climbing, we weren't laughing. Each of us but Durrant had taken nasty falls (after her two weeks on the trail, the doctor had blossomed into a strong, nimble hiker), and we stumbled into the village of Colcha sporting open wounds. But Colcha proved friendly in the Quechua way—implacable, calm, unimpressed—and a helpful family herded us into their courtyard and assisted as Durrant cleaned us up. They plied us with *chicha*, boiled corn, eggs, and cabbage, and said we were idiots for following the river. If we thought that last stretch was bad, wait until we saw the next.

With that warning we chose to cleave to the canyon's upper rim. The canyon floor, meanwhile, plunged deeper and deeper in the earth. A few days later, we hiked along the rim a half mile from the river horizontally but some six thousand two hundred feet above it. (By comparison, the Grand Canyon of the Colorado reaches a maximum depth of five thousand three hundred feet, but at its narrowest point is four miles wide.)

We found this new country both wilder and tamer than any we had already seen. The towns reached by road—Paruro, Paccaritambo, Huanoquite—seemed, after the time we had spent in the primitive upper canyon, almost modern. Paruro had a streetlight, and Bzdak bought a banana, our first fresh fruit in a month. In Paccaritambo no one knew the location of the sacred caves from which had sprung the mythical founders of the Inca empire. In Aravito we met a colony of Quechua Jews. It was Saturday morning and we heard wailing more than a mile away. Señor Apasas, a gentle, prosperous-looking Quechua man (full set of teeth, leather shoes), explained that a rabbi had lived there for eight years, and that many of the village's people had adopted Judaism. Bzdak said he found such a wholesale conversion mind-boggling. Señor Apasas replied, without a hint of cynicism, "We will do anything for entertainment."

In the gaping spaces between these villages, however, the country was as wild as anything in the Peruvian Andes. Hawks and eagles calmly stood their ground as we hiked by them in the high passes. Often the trails marked on our map no longer existed. The few people who lived there, according to the village dwellers, were *bravos,* which literally means "bold ones" but in idiomatic use connotes something more. The *bravos,* we were to believe, were bogeymen. They were crazy, they had guns, they would eat us.

Quite the opposite was true, of course. The outlanders were for the most part humble, quiet Quechua folk who apparently wanted nothing more than simply to be left alone. Few spoke Spanish, but because we were so often lost (there were no roads or signposts, and the trails were obscure), they felt bound to guide us. Unable to communicate, they would increase the velocity of their replies, hoping to overcome mutual incomprehension with sheer exuberance. More than once we left an exasperated Quechua standing alone on a mountainside, pointing in all directions and chattering away in frustration.

But it is this scene that sticks: Two squat Quechua women watch us descend a barren hillside. For at least an hour they stare without moving as we approach the tiny, dry basin that holds their two mud huts. Trembling, they study us until they can see our eyes, then turn their backs and stand stiff and silent as stone. We pass within a few yards and begin to climb the opposite hillside. Only then does one of them yell, "*Hola, viracochas*"—"Viracocha" being an Inca creator god associated with the sea and with white, and emissaries of whom the brutal *conquistadores* were at first thought to be.

Though the word is now used commonly, the equivalent of "gentleman," I shuddered involuntarily.

The river swelled and picked up speed. The three lead kayakers handled it well, but Odendaal all but stopped running it. Even above small rapids he hesitated and, often as not, elected to portage. At times he was able to hire local people and pack animals to help him carry his gear, which enabled him to move quickly, but the day before the team reached the military bridge, Biggs decided the situation had to change. Below the bridge the canyon would grow much steeper and narrower, and the river would increase greatly in volume and force. Portaging would be much more difficult, if not impossible.

While Chmielinski and Truran pushed ahead, Biggs hung back with Odendaal and coached him in the Eskimo roll, a technique for righting an upturned kayak while still in it, and as critical to navigating high-grade white water as catching a fly ball is to a professional baseball player. Biggs made Odendaal roll and roll and roll. He also worked on Odendaal's ferry glide and reverse ferry glide, techniques essential for traversing rapids safely.

Biggs had faith in his friend, and if nothing else, the attention he paid boosted Odendaal's confidence. On the morning of the day they were to reach the military bridge, Odendaal looked sharper and stronger than he had at any other time during the trip. Biggs's work appeared to have paid off.

A few miles above the bridge they stopped to practice ferry gliding one more time. Odendaal missed his eddy, flipped his boat, failed to execute a roll, and was sucked into the heart of a rapid. When he came up, his face was covered with blood.

"Help me!" he yelled. "I'm bad!"

He managed to crawl up on the bank. When Biggs reached him he was holding his head in his hands and had a vicious bloody gash across his chin. Biggs shaved Odendaal's stubbly blond beard away from the wound, then cleaned and bandaged the wound for the truck ride to Cuzco.

Biggs felt bad about his friend's pain, and worried that the accident would wipe out Odendaal's confidence. After resting in Cuzco they would enter the least-known, most inaccessible part of the river. What would happen to Odendaal down there?

Cuzco is said to be the oldest inhabited city in the Western Hemisphere. Set in a fertile green valley, it is interesting in a dollhouse kind of way, with its cobbled streets, jigsaw-puzzle stone walls, and the splendid mountains rising around it. Its history is palpable: You can shudder in the plaza where the Spanish butchered the Tupac Amarus, you can attend Mass in the same churches in which the Spanish communed with their god. But Cuzco is still a city, and more like any other city in the world than it is the countryside beyond its borders. You can easily find cold beer, American bourbon, hotels with hot showers and sheeted beds, photocopiers, telephones, Michael Jackson records, *Time, Newsweek,* the *International Herald Tribune.* At the end of an October day you will know more about the World Series than you will about the Andean potato crop.

For us, I am afraid, Cuzco was simply a place to eat and sleep and worry about the lower Apurímac. Chmielinski consulted Edwin Goycochea, a river-running friend whose rafting company, Rio

Bravo, was based in Cuzco. Goycochea had rafted the twenty-five-mile stretch below the military bridge three times, but had quit running the river after a confrontation with Sendero Luminoso guerrillas. He had not been on the Apurimac in two years. Since then, the guerrilla conflict had intensified and most of the lower river had been put under martial law and closed to outsiders. No one in Cuzco knew what to expect between the second bridge, Cunyac, and a settlement called Luisiana, two hundred miles below it. Apparently a neighboring settlement, Villa Virgen, had been bombed off the map, first by guerrillas, then by the military.

There were also the sketchy records of several previous explorations. In 1953 a Frenchman, Michel Perrin, and his Limeña girlfriend, Teresa Gutierrez, put two folding kayaks on the river at the Cunyac bridge. They had hoped to open a new route into the jungle and thereby promote colonization of the lower Apurimac, but terrible rapids forced them to quit the river two days later. They left the canyon, traveled overland, and reentered the river eighty miles downstream. They capsized in minutes. Gutierrez drowned. Perrin, heartbroken, left the Apurimac and never returned.

Some twenty years later J. Calvin Giddings made his abortive attempt on the Black Canyon. Though defeated there, he returned to the Apurimac the following year. His five-man team put in at Pillpinto and emerged intact at Luisiana with stories of an awesome gorge that he called the Chasm of Acobamba. At night they had slept in their helmets, to protect themselves from falling rock. They saw no one. They portaged tremendous distances, at one point carrying their boats for five days without finding a place where they could paddle them.

In the late 1970s an American rafting guide, John Tichenor, led three expeditions over short sections of the canyon. Like Giddings, he reported a murderous gorge from which there appeared, after a certain point, to be no exit but the river. The only other recorded attempt on the Apurimac was made by a well-financed German team in 1976. The leader drowned three minutes after putting his boat in the water.

(It is worth noting that Giddings's goal in running the Apurimac was the antithesis of Perrin's: "Soon a dam in the highlands will divert the Apurimac water across the continental divide to the dry Pacific plains. Most of the Apurimac, however, is still untainted by civilization, and its canyon remains one of the wildest in the world. One object of my venture was to demonstrate, while it was still possible, that this river does have lasting values beyond those of hydropower and agriculture.")

As for maps, the excellent 1:100,000 Peruvian topographic series we had used from the source to Cuzco ended at about Cunyac bridge. Below that the river team would have only the unreliable, cartoonish map Odendaal had shown me in the United States. Chmielinski estimated the team would reach Luisiana in three to four weeks, but this was a guess at best. He had to assume that once in the gorge they would be on their own. Goycochea, however, thought it might be possible to bring supplies in from Cachora, a village high on the canyon rim, and he offered the services of his company for this effort.

The map showed one other settlement, Triunfo, near the heart of the gorge, but no one in Cuzco knew anything about it.

In Cuzco the river team gained a new face: Jack Jourgensen, the fifty-one-year-old self-made millionaire from Wyoming who was the expedition's chief sponsor. Jourgensen had met Chmielinski and Bzdak in Casper, and had once rafted the Colca canyon with them. Knowing that Jourgensen aspired to documentary filmmaking, Chmielinski had contacted him when Odendaal's British television deal collapsed. Jourgensen and his business partner, Bryce Anderson, had agreed to back Odendaal's Amazon film and, to a degree, the expedition itself. Odendaal, in turn, would include Jourgensen as a member of his film crew for a short stretch of the river. As a final gesture he named the expedition after Jourgensen, Anderson, and himself.

Given the state of the exchequer after two months in Peru, Chmielinski and Odendaal were delighted by the arrival of Jourgensen and his healthy wallet. The expedition was nearly broke. The money I had raised was long gone, as were the funds Jourgensen had given Odendaal back in the States. In fact, the day before we had departed Arequipa, Odendaal had gathered us together and told us that to keep the expedition alive we would have to give him our "personal money." For most of us, including me, that had meant handing over funds earmarked for incidental expenses and emergencies.

Money had become a sore point between Odendaal and Chmielinski. Odendaal was not much for bookkeeping, and shortly after we left Arequipa had assigned that chore to the meticulous Chmielinski. However, as Chmielinski attempted to put the books in order, he lost patience with what he considered Odendaal's cavalier attitude toward finances and accounting. Equipment purchased in the expedition's name had never made it to Peru. Money designated for the expedition itself had been spent on the film. That Odendaal did not contribute "personal funds" to the expedition further alienated Chmielinski, and by Cuzco they would not stay in the same hotel. Chmielinski roomed with Biggs and Truran, Odendaal by himself.

Meanwhile, after consulting with Edwin Goycochea, Chmielinski proposed a new plan: Put two white-water rafts on the river. He had one stored in Cuzco, and Goycochea would lend him a second and a guide to go with it for those first twenty-five miles. Two rafts could carry all the expedition's food, equipment, and personnel except Biggs and Truran, who would kayak. Bzdak and I would escape our sentence in Condorito.

Goycochea also offered a truck and driver to haul us back to the Apurimac. Once we disembarked, we would not use motorized land transport again. And so, after five weeks of faithful duty, Condorito was fitted with a set of spanking new tires and returned with heartfelt thanks to Chmielinski's Peruvian friend, Antonio Vellutino, who had met us in Cuzco. Then we pared our equipment to the minimum (each member was permitted one small bag of personal gear), loaded Goycochea's truck at dawn, and waited for our river guide.

Morning became afternoon, the shops closed, the city rested, at dusk the shops reopened. We received news both heartening and disquieting—the Swiss team had quit the river. One of the men was badly injured, his leg, according to rumor, crushed by a falling boulder. We did not discuss this. Shadows grew into night. Our guide did not show. A second message arrived: The guide had fled Cuzco. He did not want to run the Apurimac, not any part of it.

It was too late to change our plans. In the morning we proceeded without him.

TWO

WHITE WATER

7 *Meeting the Great Speaker*

At dawn we drove west, climbed slowly up and out of Cuzco's fertile green valley, crossed a pass at about thirteen thousand five hundred feet, and descended just as slowly into the brown chaparral of the Apurimac canyon. In Chinchaypujio, the last town before dropping down to the canyon floor, we stocked up on chocolate bars, hand mirrors, bandanas, toilet paper, soap, insect repellent, and *pisco*—the comforts we would regret having forgotten once on the river. Then we pushed on for the Apurimac. Though we arrived in mid-afternoon, the sun had already set.

Had we paused to think about it—and several of us did—we might have appreciated the splendid idiocy of what we were about to do. We proposed to challenge the most treacherous stretch of one of the most treacherous white-water rivers on the planet with what were, when you got right down to it, novice crews. Chmielinski and Bzdak were experienced raftsmen, Truran and Biggs skilled kayakers. But Odendaal and Jourgensen had only beginning white-water experience, and the rest of us—Leon, Durrant, Van Heerden, and I—had none at all.

That we chose not to stare those rude facts in the face for very long may have had something to do with the bottles of *pisco* Bzdak produced after we carved out a chilly camp amid nettles and cactus. We toasted the river. We toasted the stars. We toasted the frigid Andean night. And then we toasted our impending departure, knowing that if all went according to plan, we would not leave the river again until the river left the continent.

There is an inherent, humbling cruelty to learning how to run white water. In most other so-called "adrenaline" sports—skiing, surfing, and rock climbing come to mind—one attains mastery, or the illusion of it, only after long apprenticeship, after enduring falls and tumbles, the fatigue of training previously unused muscles, the discipline of developing a new and initially awkward set of skills.

Running white water is fundamentally different. With a little luck one is immediately able to travel long distances, often at great speeds, with only a rudimentary command of the sport's essential skills and about as much physical stamina as it takes to ride a bicycle downhill. At the beginning, at least, white-water adrenaline comes cheap.

It's the river doing the work, of course, but like a teenager with a hot car, one forgets what the true power source is. Arrogance reigns. The river seems all smoke and mirrors, lots of bark (you hear it chortling away beneath you, crunching boulders), but not much bite. You think: Let's get on with it! Let's run this damn river!

And then maybe the raft hits a drop in the river—say, a short, hidden waterfall. Or maybe a wave reaches up and flicks the boat on its side as easily as a horse swatting flies with its tail. Maybe you're thrown suddenly into the center of the raft, and the floor bounces back and punts you overboard. Maybe you just fall right off the side of the raft so fast you don't realize what's happening.

It doesn't matter. The results are the same.

The world goes dark. The river—the word hardly does justice to the churning mess enveloping you—the river tumbles you like so much laundry. It punches the air from your lungs. You're helpless. Swimming is a joke. You know for a fact that you are drowning. For the first time you understand the strength of the insouciant monster that has swallowed you.

Maybe you travel a hundred feet before you surface (the current is moving that fast). And another hundred feet—just short of a truly fearsome plunge, one that will surely kill you—before you see the rescue lines. You're hauled to shore wearing a sheepish grin and a look in your eye that is equal parts confusion, respect, and raw fear.

That is River Lesson Number One. Everyone suffers it. And every time you get the least bit cocky, every time you think you have finally figured out what the river is all about, you suffer it all over again.

As white-water rivers go, the Apurimac's dangers lie not in her volume, which is middling until she reaches sea level, but in her extreme rockiness and steep descent. She is inclined less to pound you unconscious with big waves than to trap you beneath an undercut rock or suck you into a "strainer"—a submerged, sievelike boulder pile from which there is no exit. She rewards technique over power. That is, she is better run on a small, maneuverable, four-man paddle raft capable of executing a series of tight turns, rather than the kind of boat often used on high-volume rivers like the Colorado—long, wide rafts that can plow roughshod through big water and are usually controlled by a single man working two large oars.

Though both our boats were paddle rafts, we had problems immediately. The raft Goycochea had loaned us, a lumbering, sixteen-foot-long Avon, was stable—it barreled right through waves that tossed Chmielinski's fourteen-foot Riken willy-nilly— but not easily controlled. And as manned by Bzdak, Odendaal, Van Heerden, and Jourgensen, an exercise in floating anarchy. As the Avon plunged into a hard rapid, each man flailed away with his paddle as he chose, watching out mainly for himself.

Life was somewhat more orderly on the narrower, shorter Riken, if only because Durrant, Leon, and I were so completely hopeless that we reacted to Chmielinski's every command as if our lives depended on it. For Chmielinski, the military man, failure was not an option. By the end of our second day on the river he had intimidated us into a passably competent crew which, if not strong, at least managed to pull together as a team, stroking frantically at his urgent direction.

And we had another advantage. In its own way, the state-of-the-art Riken raft was as profound a breakthrough in river technology as the canoe or the outboard motor. The beast's intelligent beauty lay in its self-bailing design. (Chmielinski called it "safe-bailing.") Its foundation was an independent, inflatable floor affixed to inflatable side tubes by a webwork of rope lashings. When water filled the raft, its weight forced the floor down, stretching the lashings and opening a gap between floor and side tubes. The force of the pneumatic floor trying to rise back up from the river drove the water out through the gap. The manufacturer's claim was that when filled, the raft would drain completely in five seconds.

The primary task for Durrant, who paddled at the raft's left front corner, and Leon, who paddled at the right front, was to propel the raft forward. Manning the back corners, Chmielinski and I supplied both power and direction.

As a "driver" I was also charged with scouting the rapids on foot before we ran them in the raft. Chmielinski scouted, I should say. I scrambled along the bank behind him, slipping so often on the slick boulders and sharp rocks that after two days my shins were plum-colored and mushy and my face and hands were covered with scabs.

Nevertheless, Chmielinski committed himself to the unenviable task of teaching me how to pick a safe line of travel through the Apurimac pinball machine. He believed that he could teach us the requisite paddling skills if we had confidence in ourselves—he would provide the head if we hung in there with a little heart. But as a driver I had to understand the consequence of each flick of my paddle, an understanding that involved the ability to decipher the river's complex hydraulic patterns. However, when asked from the safety of dry land to choose a possible route, I invariably described one that would have condemned us to a watery death— for instance, twisted and pinned under a strainer, dying slowly of asphyxiation and head wounds.

Chmielinski would look at me with quiet exasperation, then patiently explain a more prudent route. As we memorized the turns, stops, and starts we would try to execute when we actually ran the rapid, our conversations proceeded something like:

"Okay, Joe. Pointy rock."

"Pointy rock."

"It is a killer for sure, that one. I am *in* with my paddle, you are *out*, we are turning left, then we are *go,* straight, we are *running,* we are pulling for our lives. A killer. But not a problem."

"Pointy rock. Killer. No problem."

Such conferences were always—*always*—followed, on my part, by a vigorous expelling of urine. I learned to judge the true danger of a rapid, a danger that only my subconscious could objectively perceive, by the volume issuing from my bladder.

Almost without exception our painstaking choreography evaporated the moment we entered a rapid. Then it was up to Chmielinski to bring us under control with his precise set of commands, delivered at a pitch never less than savage.

God help the crewman who got out of position on the raft, which, unfortunately, was all too easy to do. The position one must master to paddle a raft correctly runs counter to all survival instincts. For example, as a driver, I was supposed to sit squarely on the left side tube at its junction with the back tube, tuck my left toes under the cross tube in front of me, and, spreading my legs as if sprinting, push the bottom of my right foot hard against the back tube. Then, anchored to the bucking raft only by the tension on my left toes, right heel, and buttocks, I was to hang my body out to the left, over the water, so that I could dig my paddle straight down into the river.

At first this struck me as mortally ludicrous—Chmielinski wanted me to expose half my damn body to that terrible river, daring it to snatch me. Over time, however, and after the Apurimac had once too often treated me as a blender does a banana, I learned that being extended over the water, my paddle dug into it, was safer than bouncing about the raft's interior. Our supplies were stored dead in the center of the raft, under a net. Carrying this weight, the raft floor—one was desperately tempted to dive onto it, hug it shamelessly, and weep—delayed slightly before responding to the river's turbulence, in fact moved in counterpoint to it, while the lighter, independent side walls moved in synch. Riding the floor was like sitting on a trampoline while someone else jumped. One quickly vaulted up and out, into the smothering arms of the Great Speaker.

And so one fought one's instincts, a battle in which Commander Chmielinski was ever willing to assist.

The Apurimac tested his talents as captain and teacher most severely on the fourth and last day of our shakedown run from the military bridge to Cunyac bridge, when we confronted our worst rapid. It was a series of rapids, in fact, all of them Class Five, which means something like "high degree of technical difficulty, and if a mistake is made, possible mortal consequences." Your basic "killer, no problem" sort of thing. (Class Five rapids are considered the upper limit of runnable water.)

We scouted that particular chain of rapids, about a half mile long, for two hours. Finally, Chmielinski picked a line of descent. Two boulders formed a narrow chute at the top of the rapid. As the river forced its way through the chute, it compressed from some fifty feet wide to fifteen. Then it exploded through the chute like gas exiting a carburetor, spilled over a short waterfall, and at the bottom built a "keeper," a wave that flows back on itself. Someone caught in a keeper makes several mind-altering spins before escaping. People who have experienced them also call such waves "Maytags."

Below all of this lay the kind of roiling mess that you knew, just by looking at it, could send you home in a wheelchair.

"It is a killer," Chmielinski said when we had finished scouting the run.

I knew the correct rejoinder: "No problem."

Then I let fly with an act of urination so wildly out of proportion to my liquid intake for the day that I felt my face begin to pucker.

Back at the raft, Durrant asked about the rapid.

"It is a part of a cake," Chmielinski said.

We backstroked out of the eddy and turned upstream. (By paddling against the current we maintained control of the raft, sort of.) We swung our nose slowly into the current, like a hand on a clock: upstream, cross-stream, downstream. Then we inched into the quickening water.

I remember, as we hit the chute, the roller-coaster-stomach, sick-sweet sensation of falling through air. I remember white walls of water rising around us, that we blasted into several boulders, and that the explosions we made when we hit them were louder even than the river itself. Once, my head snapped so violently I worried I had broken my neck. I remember the raft pinned to a boulder, up on its side about to flip, and us climbing to the high side while the rapid roared at our feet. I remember staring straight down at a knife-edged rock and watching it somehow shoot past my head. I remember the urgency of Chmielinski's screams, louder and more desperate by far than any I had heard from him before.

And then I remember calm sweet waters of peace and joy, drifting quietly in the raft in the wide easy river below the rapid. I remember that we were breathing hard but otherwise silent, and that in the slow water it seemed as if we and the river were one, motionless, while mountains and sky swept past us on their way upstream, to the source of the Amazon, or to wherever it is that mountains and sky might choose to go.

"Good, guys," Chmielinski said after a while. "Excellent. We almost made a bad turnover, but we did not." He shook our hands, and, exulting in the afterglow, Leon, Durrant, and I flashed the adrenaline-laced grins of fledgling river rats.

"The idea is not to beat the river," Chmielinski said. "The river always wins. It does not care. We try the river because we must try. White water is, how do you say it, like you are bleeding . . ."

"It gets in your blood."

"Yes. It is in your blood. It is a thing you are never forgetting."

With Chmielinski guiding us and then, for the hardest rapids, clambering back upstream to captain the Avon as well, we made the Cunyac bridge on schedule, four days after first putting in the river. The bridge, a sturdy wooden affair, is the most vulnerable section of the Lima-Cuzco road. We celebrated with a dinner of fried eggs and rice at a smoky, dirt-floored cantina tucked behind a military checkpoint. When we had finished, Odendaal asked me to step outside. We stood on the back porch, next to a sleeping pig.

"Piotr wants to take only the Riken from here on down," he said. "With Zbyszek, Pierre, and Jack. And you."

"Who will paddle?"

"You, Pierre, Zbyszek, except when Pierre is filming, then we let Jack use a paddle. I will kayak."

"What do you think?"

"It will be bigger water now. Bad rapids. Long portages. A strong chance you will swim. A chance you could die."

"Piotr is a good captain."

"Piotr is very ambitious. If he runs this section of the river on a raft he will be the first man to do it. He will be a hero in Peru once again. Tim and Jerome do not want to take a raft. They do not think it will be safe."

He said that Sergio Leon would go to Lima to try to extend our visas, most of which were about to expire. Leon did not enjoy rafting—he could barely swim—and had requested other duty. Odendaal said Durrant would go with him.

"You may have trouble separating her from Zbyszek," I said.

"That is not an expedition consideration," Odendaal said. "If there is a problem, they will be off the expedition." Relations between Durrant and Odendaal had not been smooth, which Durrant suspected had to do with her romance with Bzdak. The closer she had become to Bzdak, the cooler Odendaal had acted toward her. Nor had the situation been helped by the badgering Durrant had suffered from the Afrikaner film crew.

A soft rain fell. A roar from inside the cantina indicated that a bottle was making the rounds.

"Think about it," Odendaal said. "Let me know soon." He lit the homemade pipe he had taken to smoking. As he turned to reenter the cantina, he said, "This is starting to feel like an adventure again. Enough of this tourist crap."

I went to my tent, lit a candle, and tried to read *The Nigger of the Narcissus:* ". . . the solidarity in uncertain fate, which brings all men to each other. . . ." I soon put the book down. My mind was reeling. Before my taste of rafting, I had pushed hard to be included on the raft all the way down the white-water river. Now that I was being given that opportunity, I was not at all sure I wanted to take advantage of it. The river genuinely scared me.

I walked naked to the Apurimac and dove in. She ran broad and smooth there beneath the Cunyac bridge, her current strong but even. There were no rapids—that side of her was hidden around a bend, as if it were too rude a thing to be seen from the bridge—and the water was pleasantly cool.

In the dark night I swam across the river at an angle upstream (what the kayakers called "ferry-gliding"), and paddled just hard enough to hold even in the current, to prevent it from carrying me downstream. I was trying, I suppose, to feel the Apurimac, to test her, to see if I could trust her. I enjoyed the river life after the grime and sweat of hiking the high country—no dirt under the fingernails, a wonderful clean tiredness in arms and chest and shoulders after a day at the paddle. I had slept well those last few nights, except for the nightmares, in which I seemed to drown forever without actually dying.

Chmielinski was waiting at my tent, wearing, as always, a serious expression.

"What do you think about the raft?" he asked.

"I'm not sure."

"Tim does not want it. I think it is a personal thing against me, he is protecting François. I think it is important to have the raft. This is a chance to record history, Pierre with his filming, Zbyszek with his camera, and you with the book."

"Do you think it will be safe?"

"No problem. I will ask you to paddle in the back again, next to me."

He said that if I went with the raft, I would be assigned Leon's role as quartermaster. The lowliest work on the team, sticky, fly-ridden, thankless duty. First man up in the morning to outfit the cook of the day, last man to sleep after counting and repacking provisions, all free time spent checking for rot and insects.

My options? Return to Lima with Leon and Durrant and be

effectively off the expedition. Or go with the raft and travel country that few if any people had seen.

We left the Cunyac camp under a hot midday sun, the three kayaks ten yards in front of the raft, and bobbed for an hour on the slow, flat river. Then, with Jourgensen wedged between Chmielinski and me, Bzdak, Van Heerden, and I put paddles to water and bent our backs to Chmielinski's "Stroke . . . stroke . . . stroke . . ."

Within a few miles we passed the site of what had been the greatest of the Inca hanging bridges, the key link in the highway between mountain and coast. In 1533 the Inca burned the bridge in a futile attempt to stop the Spanish on their march to Cuzco, and the Spanish later built their own wood-and-stone span on the site (upon which Thornton Wilder based his *Bridge of San Luis Rey*). In all, the bridge is said to have been in continual use longer than any other in the Americas, but today the chipped white-mortar Spanish abutments, the only significant mark the *conquistadores* made in the Apurimac canyon, loom like ghostly portals to a dark, forbidding slash in the Cordillera Vilcabamba. The surrounding terrain is hot and stark save an occasional glimpse of a craggy snow-covered peak.

In mid-afternoon the headwind increased, blowing hard upriver as heat rose from the deep canyon below. It blew so hard, in fact, that even as we strained at our paddles it drove us backward, against the current, into an ugly whirlpool from which we extricated ourselves only when Chmielinski counted stroke in a desperate rage. We hid in the lee of a cliff while Biggs and Truran kayaked across the river with our bow line and planted themselves on shore. As they hauled on the line we paddled the raft. To cut wind resistance we knelt on the floor, bent to our task like supplicating monks.

Exhausted, we pitched camp in a thorny clearing near a hot spring presided over by a stout *mestizo* woman, her frail, toothless husband, and their teenage daughter, a shy, barefoot beauty in a short, tattered cotton dress. A cement pool captured water from the spring, and the crumbling cement buildings nearby, where the family lived, suggested that the place may once have been a kind of resort.

"If you swim naked in the pool," the matriarch said, "you will have twins." But she did not want her theory tested—she shooed the girl away.

Biggs was cook of the day. While I helped him set up his kitchen, the old woman rattled about the camp raising dust and shouting advice: "Put more wood on the fire." "Your pot is too small." Biggs cut her a slice of cheese. She walked away from us to eat it, returned, and asked, "Where are you going?"

"To where the river ends," Biggs said.

She considered this. "Europe."

"No," Biggs said. "Europe is across the Atlantic Ocean."

"What is the Atlantic Ocean?"

She left when the rest of the team returned from the pool. We built a fire and ate in silence. Afterwards, Odendaal said, "Without a woman I feel like I am in the land of the dead." He paused to light his pipe. "Now Zbyszek is one of us. Now he is among the dead."

If not intentionally cruel, the remark was certainly insensitive. Odendaal had dismissed Durrant from the rafting team in a way that she had not considered exceptionally gracious, and he had told Bzdak, in a patronizing tone, "I am sorry to have to break you two up. It is a very nice relationship, and it lends a good feeling to the team."

"The issue is not the relationship," Bzdak had replied angrily. "The issue is Kate is part of this expedition. She has earned the right to be on the raft."

Now Bzdak ignored Odendaal, who, having failed to elicit a response, turned to the rest of us. His favorite activity on the river seemed to be playing the pipe-in-hand storyteller, the sage. "How do you catch an alligator?" he asked. No one spoke. "Well, you take tweezers, field glasses, a boring book . . ."

"Scorpion!" Bzdak yelled. A three-inch-long bug glowing gold with reflected firelight poised on a rock two feet from his right leg.

"Zbyszek," Odendaal began again, this time in a harder voice, "how do you catch—"

Bzdak jumped up on a boulder and perched above the rest of

us, laughing his high, squeaky laugh and jabbing at the scorpion with a stick. The firelight glanced off the underside of his huge red beard and the front of his broad head and threw the rest of him into dark relief. He looked and sounded like some sort of wild Polish wizard.

Dazed from the afternoon's battle with the wind, we watched his thrusts and the scorpion's tentative parries. One step back, two forward, stinger cocked . . .

"Zbyszek!" Odendaal said. "I am not impressed." When Bzdak continued to ignore him, Odendaal said, "That lady's daughter is very pretty. Maybe I will ask her to come for a swim with me." He stood up and left the fire.

When Odendaal was gone Bzdak crushed the scorpion and kicked it into the flames, as if casting a wizard's spell.

The next morning, fearing the wind would rise by mid-afternoon and end our day, we launched our boats at first light and ran four fast miles, the kayakers in the lead, the raft trailing. Then the river widened to about fifty yards and the rapids began to show not just chutes and turns but waves and troughs. Some of these waves, as high as eight feet, loomed over the raft's bow like green walls and inhibited our ability to track the kayakers. At one point we ran right over Biggs, trapping him underwater, beneath the raft, and raking him over submerged boulders until Bzdak managed to reach under and yank the kayak free.

Biggs was not happy, to say the least, and claimed that he had heard Chmielinski yelling "Forward! Forward!" as we ran him down. Chmielinski vehemently denied this, and sitting next to him on the raft I had heard no such thing. But we agreed that Biggs and Truran would ride at least fifty yards ahead of the raft, scouting the river and signaling with upraised paddles to stop or come ahead. Odendaal would try to keep up with them.

This system worked well until Odendaal suffered two punishing swims and Biggs and Truran abandoned their scouting duties to rescue him. "He's shattered," Truran said when he caught up with us. "Badly fazed. He'll lose all his skills. Tim's worried."

Over the next few hours the river was rough but predictable, and we paddled as hard as we could until the headwind roared up. To either side of us the dark canyon walls rose vertically for hundreds of feet, perhaps more—who could see up that far? They were fragile walls, without vegetation, all boulders and granite slabs tucked into soft dirt and scree and shale. The boulders clotting the river were not the smooth, water-sculpted stone we had seen so far but jagged blades honed by detritus hurtling down from above.

A plume of smoke curled far downriver. When we arrived at the spot hours later it was still rising, but it was dust, not smoke. Hundreds of feet of wall had simply collapsed en masse into the river.

Suddenly the Apurimac narrowed so dramatically that we were all struck silent. It squeezed into a gorge a quarter of its previous width, perhaps forty feet wide, which so concentrated the headwind that paddling our hardest gained us only a standstill. We had to make camp, but we saw no beaches, no flat ground, nothing but the gorge's sheer vertical walls.

Finally we found a cluster of boulders along the left bank, and in between them small patches of sand just big enough to hold a tent or sleeping bag. Across the river, a waterfall tumbled in four long cascades down five hundred feet of slick rock. Jokingly, but presciently, Chmielinski named this "Last Hope Falls."

Nerves were short and so was dinner, for no sooner had we begun to eat than it started to rain hard. We ran for our tents. I drifted off to sleep but awoke to a horrible, thunderlike *crack.* Lightning flashed, but the *cracks*—I heard several more after I climbed out of my tent to investigate—were rain-loosened boulders tumbling down the wall.

I slinked naked down to the food bags and tucked them beneath overhanging rocks. Lightning flashed again, and I heard amid the *cracks* the occasional thud of a boulder hitting sand. Jourgensen, Odendaal, and Van Heerden had found shelter in small caves. Chmielinski was next to the river, his tent tied to the raft. With even a slight rain in this narrow gorge the water would rise rapidly and sweep the raft away.

Bzdak was still in his tent.

"I stay in here, maybe I get hit by a rock," he reasoned from beneath his rain fly. "I go outside, maybe I get hit by a rock there, too, but for sure I will get wet. So I will stay in my tent."

Truran had made a similar decision, though he tried to sleep upon his side, figuring that limited the possibility of either crushed organs or a crushed spine.

I elected to do the same, and wore my helmet for protection. But the rockfall continued until dawn, and I did not sleep.

In the morning, bug-eyed and mumbling after the exhausting night, we asssessed our situation. Chmielinski guessed that in two days we had run eight to ten miles, and that we were thirty to forty miles from the point where, we hoped, Durrant and Leon would be waiting with supplies. "Could take one day," he said. "Could take one week."

To our surprise we ran well that morning, handling three hard rapids without a mistake, and regained some of the confidence lost during the night's rock bombing. But that memory hung close. Many of the boulders we now saw in the river were freshly fallen, caked with dust and mud hauled down from the walls. Finding a safe campsite now held priority over achieving distance.

Then the river took an abrupt left and entered a gorge so steep and narrow its walls appeared to close overhead. Though it was midday, no sun reached the water. The river itself was a mess—fast, mud brown, roiling from the rain and still rising, studded with boulders that towered over our little fleet.

This was the Acobamba Abyss.

8 *The Acobamba Abyss*

Below us lay three bad rapids, a short stretch of calm water, and then, where the gorge suddenly narrowed, a single, twenty-foot-wide chute through which the whole frustrated Apurimac poured in unheeding rage. The river was whipped so white over the next half mile that it looked like a snowfield. The thrashing cascades raised a dense mist, rendering the dark canyon cold and clammy. Their roar made my head ache.

"You swim in that,'" Bzdak shouted in my ear, "you don't get out!"

But the gorge walls were nearly vertical. We could not portage, we could not climb out, we could not pitch camp. Even had we found a relatively flat area, as the gorge cooled through the night boulders would pop out of the ramparts. The rock shower would be deadly.

We had no choice but to attempt to "line" the raft, a tedious, nerve-racking procedure in which we sent the raft downriver un-manned at the end of Chmielinski's one-hundred-fifty-foot climbing rope a length at a time.

While I stood on a boulder on the left bank and held the Riken in place by a short, thin line tied to its stern, the two Poles affixed the heavy climbing rope to the bow and worked downstream with it as far as they could. At Chmielinski's signal I dropped my line and kicked the raft into the first rapid. Within seconds the boat was hurtling through the rapid at what must have been twenty knots, leaping wildly. I shuddered when I imagined riding it.

In the middle of the second rapid, the raft flipped. As it passed the Poles, half the bow line snagged underwater, tautened, and though rated with an "impact force" of more than a ton snapped as if it were mere sewing thread.

Unleashed, the raft sped down the river.

Truran, who had run the first rapid in his kayak, was waiting on a boulder near the calm water above the terrible chute. When he saw the raft break free, he dove into the river, swam for the raft as it drifted toward the chute, and managed briefly to deflect it from its course. He scrambled aboard, and as the raft accelerated toward the chute he caught a rescue line thrown like a football by Chmielinski. The Pole arrested the raft as it teetered on the chute's lip, and slowly hauled Truran back from the edge of disaster. (Chmielinski later described Truran's effort as one of the bravest he had seen on a river.)

Draining as all that was, we still had to get the boat through the chute, somehow hold it to the wall and board it, and then run the ugly water below. The lower rapid could not be scouted. We could only hope that it held no surprises—no waterfalls, no deadly holes.

Jourgensen and Van Heerden slowly worked their way down to the chute, creeping along the boulders that sat at the foot of the gorge's left wall. When they arrived, Chmielinski told them to rest. Then he and Truran anchored the raft with the stern line while Bzdak took the bow line, now shorter by some forty feet, and climbed hand over hand up the two-story boulder that formed the chute's left gate. From the boulder Bzdak then climbed to a foot-wide ledge that ran along the left wall.

At Chmielinski's command I followed Bzdak. I ascended the boulder easily enough, but negotiating the wet, slick wall was something else. It was so sheer that I couldn't find a solid grip, and I quickly developed what rock climbers call "sewing-machine legs," an uncontrollable, fear-induced, pistonlike shaking. I felt cut off and alone. One misstep and I was in the river, which now churned angrily fifteen feet straight below.

Bzdak stopped on the ledge three feet in front of me and looked back. He shouted to me, but I couldn't hear him above the river's tumult. He inched his way back and put his head next to mine.

"DON'T LOOK DOWN!"

We wormed along the ledge until we could lower ourselves onto a one-foot-square rock at the base of the wall and a few feet in front of the gate boulder. We squeezed onto that small rock, each of us with one foot on it and one in the air, and braced ourselves as best we could, trying all the while to ignore the exploding river next to us.

Bzdak twirled the climbing rope up off the top of the gate boulder and tugged on it, signaling Chmielinski to send the raft. I wrapped my arms around Bzdak's waist and leaned back like a counterweight. The raft vaulted the chute. Hand over hand, Bzdak reeled in slack line as fast as he could. I tensed, anticipating the jolt we were about to receive. The raft approached us, shot past, and BOOM! the line straightened and stretched, the raft hurtled down the rapid, I tried to calibrate my backward lean—

"HOLD ME, JOSE!"

I couldn't. We were going in.

Yet somehow Bzdak was hauling the raft toward us, fighting it home inch by inch. Then the line was in my hands and he was in the raft, tearing a paddle loose from beneath the center net. The raft smashed up against the left wall. The river pounded through the chute, curled into the raft, knocked Bzdak flat, and buried him.

Trying to hold the raft was like pulling against a tractor. I couldn't do it. But the raft bailed itself quickly, and Bzdak rose from the floor and paddled toward the rock. When he was five feet away he leapt for it. How he managed to land on that tiny space I do not know, but we made our stand there, anchoring the bucking raft from what seemed like the head of a pin.

We watched Van Heerden help a ghost-white Jourgensen over the boulder and along the wall, then down the wall into the raft. The two men took up positions in the front of the raft. Then

Chmielinski climbed over the gate boulder with . . .

. . . I read Bzdak's lips: "Shit!" . . .

. . . Odendaal's kayak.

Its owner appeared behind Chmielinski and stared at us. Chmielinski took aim and shoved the kayak down the boulder's face, dead on into the center of the lurching raft. Then he signaled me into the raft, but the rope had sawed my hands to bloody pulp and I couldn't uncurl them. Bzdak shook the rope loose. I dove the five feet from the wall to the raft and crawled to the left rear. Chmielinski worked his way down the wall and took Bzdak's spot. Bzdak jumped into the raft. With Jourgensen squeezed between them, he and Van Heerden got their paddles ready on front. I reached beneath the center net and yanked out a paddle for me and one for Chmielinski.

"What are we doing?" I yelled to Chmielinski.

He yelled back, "François goes alone, he dies!"

Biggs and Truran had managed to traverse the river above the chute and sneak down the far side of the rapid, but it was too risky for Odendaal. Were he to make a single mistake during the traverse he would plunge through the chute and into what we could now see was a deadly hole a few feet below it. Instead, Chmielinski intended to mount Odendaal and his kayak on the raft and run the rapid.

Chmielinski had tried that strategy with an overwhelmed kayaker once before, in the Colca canyon. Like Odendaal's, that kayak had been almost as long as the raft, and with it strapped over the center net the wildly top-heavy raft had flipped moments after it entered the rapid. Everyone had taken a bad swim, Bzdak the worst of his life. If that happened here, we would drown in the hole. But Chmielinski reasoned that it was better that six men risk their lives than that one be condemned to a near-certain death.

I looked up at Odendaal, standing atop the boulder. His eyes were frozen. He looked paralyzed. I knew the feeling.

Chmielinski screamed at Odendaal. He inched his way to the raft and into it and mounted himself spread-eagled on top of his kayak, facing to the rear.

"Squeeze on that kayak like it is your life!" Chmielinski yelled.

Chmielinski could not hold Odendaal's added weight. He leapt and landed in the raft as it bucked away from the wall. Seconds later, even before I could thrust Chmielinski's paddle at him, we were sucked into the heart of the current. With Chmielinski screaming at the top of his lungs—"LEFTLEFTLEFT!"—we managed to turn hard and get the nose of the boat heading downstream. We skirted the ugly hole, but it shoved the raft sideways. We found ourselves bearing down on a "stopper" rock no one had seen, a rock that would upend us if we hit it.

Chmielinski screamed "RIGHTRIGHTRIGHT!" and we were sideways, then "ININININ!," a steering command intended for me, and I hung far to my left and chopped down into the water and pulled my paddle straight in toward me so the rear end of the boat swung left and the front end right. Then a wall of water engulfed me and all I saw was white.

Somehow we shot around the stopper rock's left side but we were still sideways in the rapid "GOGOGOGO!" paddling hard forward fighting in vain for control and the river slammed us up against another rock, this one sloping toward us, Chmielinski's side of the raft shot up on the rock, mine lowered to the river coming behind us, the water punched at the low end, drove it ino the rock and stood the raft up on its side, teetering, "UPUPUPUPUP!" and I fought to climb the high side, to push it back down with my weight, but Odendaal and his kayak had me blocked and I saw Bzdak trapped the same way on the front end, the water pouring in knocked me off my feet, the boat started to flip "GOGOGOGO!" and all I could do was try to paddle free of the rock digging blindly with my paddle "GOGOGOGO!" and BOOM! we were free and bouncing off the left gorge wall and then heading straight for the gentle tail at the end of the rapid and the calm flat water beyond.

Just above the rapid's last one hundred yards we found an eddy and put Odendaal out of the boat to walk along a sandy bank that ran almost, but not quite, to the end of the rapid. We ran the rest of it, two small chutes *boom-boom,* and met Truran in the softly purling water below. He pointed overhead, to the narrow crack of sky between the gorge walls. Storm clouds were snagged on a dark peak. We had to find a campsite quickly, before the boulder-loosening rain hit.

But Odendaal had run out of walking room and stood stiff as a statue thirty yards upstream of us, at the rapid's tail. Biggs sat in his kayak in an eddy near Odendaal, shouting at him to jump in the rapid and swim. Odendaal refused. The exchange continued for ten, fifteen minutes. Then, as the sky darkened, we all began to yell at the Afrikaner. He looked up. He slipped. He was in the river. He bounced through the rapid unharmed and Biggs fished him out at the bottom. After we put his kayak on the water Biggs escorted him downstream.

We got lucky—the gorge widened and we found a generous expanse of sandy beach. But after we unloaded our gear Odendaal lambasted Biggs over the scene at the last rapid, saying that as the expedition leader it was his right to have stood there two hours if he so chose. Disgusted, Biggs walked away and joined the rest of us around the fire. When Chmielinski had dinner ready Odendaal sat down but did not speak, choosing instead to play Biggs's harmonica softly to himself.

Chmielinski guessed that we had covered barely a mile that day. This was disappointing, but for the time being we relaxed. The storm clouds evaporated and we sat by the fire on that fine beach and watched a star show in the thin opening overhead, the river that short hours before had been a deafening monster now bubbling along tranquilly beside us.

During the morning run on our second day in the abyss the gorge walls closed in on us once again, narrowing to perhaps thirty feet. At first this was a shock, but the river ran smooth and fast, and we calmed down. Truran, Biggs, and Odendaal paddled their kayaks ahead of the raft and disappeared around a bend.

Fifteen minutes later a gnawing worry gripped the five of us on the raft. Four hundred feet ahead of us the river appeared simply to stop. The gorge turned left, and the wall that crossed in front of us seemed to swallow the river. We expected to see a white line between the river and the wall, a line of riffles, the tops of rapids. The absence of such riffles suggested a waterfall.

We drifted, tense and uncertain. In the front of the raft Bzdak and Van Heerden shipped their paddles. I used mine as a rudder, keeping the bow pointed downstream while Chmielinski stood up and studied the river before us. After a few minutes he said, "Okay, I see a white line." Then we saw it, too, but it looked strange, too hard and unwavering to be riffles.

Jourgensen, sitting between Chmielinski and me, asked, "What if that line is part of the rock formations on the wall?"

We drifted in silence. After about a minute, Chmielinski said, "Shit!" I had never heard him use the word. "It *is* a rock formation! To the bank, fast!"

We paddled urgently for the left wall, and when we gained it Bzdak and I dug in the slippery rock for fingerholds. While we held the raft Chmielinski stood up and tried to determine what lay below the natural dam we assumed we were now approaching.

"This is the thing you are always afraid of," he said. "You cannot go back, you cannot portage, you cannot climb out, the water is dropping away in front of you. Even if that is a waterfall, the only thing we can do is go."

We set off uneasily, no one speaking, all eyes on the water line. Where were the kayakers? Now the river ended fifty, now forty feet in front of us. We went to the wall again, found a crack, inserted fingers. Chmielinski climbed the crack, but when he was fifteen feet above us he fell, returning to the river in a dark blur that ended with a splash and his red-helmeted head bobbing toward the falls.

Bzdak and I paddled furiously. Van Heerden unclipped a rescue line and threw it downstream. We hauled the raft captain aboard just as we began to shoot over the falls . . .

. . . but it was not a waterfall at all, just a long, gentle rapid. Steep—hence no riffle tops—but straight, no boulders, all lazy, harmless waves. And luck.

Then our luck ran out. We reentered pinball country. We lined the raft through a cluster of gargantuan boulders, hour after hour of whipsawing rope, bloody hands, and bruised shins, and at the end of the day had to negotiate an ugly rapid that took an hour to scout and half a minute to run.

Something happened to me in that half minute. The rapid was a tricky one. It had three chutes and a dozen turns, the last around a broad hole. We handled the first two chutes well, but the third had a ten-foot drop—a small waterfall. At the top of that last chute Chmielinski yelled "OUT!," a signal to me to set the raft's nose straight, and I managed two correcting strokes before we hit the chute's left wall.

Then the raft burst through the chute, a wave broke over the top of the raft, I saw nothing but water, and I heard Chmielinski screaming "OUTOUTOUT!" I dug with my paddle and managed three more strokes before we hit the edge of the big hole and the force of the currents spinning around the hole jerked the raft and threw me into the center net.

Or had I *jumped* into the net?

I could not honestly tell. The rapid had been a difficult one, that much was clear, and when we completed it Biggs and Truran shouted congratulations to us. Chmielinski was jubilant, beaming, charged with adrenaline. "Perfect," he said as he shook my hand.

I wasn't so sure. I suspected I was beginning to crack.

In general, however, that run buoyed our hopes—perhaps we would break free of the abyss the next day. There was a good feeling in camp that night, except for my self-doubts and a blowup between Biggs and Odendaal over Odendaal's failure to follow Biggs's instructions in a difficult rapid.

"Tim's in a terrible spot," Truran said to me as we sipped tea before dinner. "He's like a veterinarian injecting his own dog. If Frans drowns, the responsibility is on Tim. People will say to him, you were the river captain, why didn't you take Frans off the water? But Tim really cares for Frans. He wants him to have a good outing, so he's reluctant to send him off. Maybe the lesson in all this is that if you can't do the job yourself, you don't put a friend in charge. You look for someone impartial."

That night Odendaal came to my tent. He was smoking his pipe and seemed pensive and subdued.

"Is my behavior on the river causing you rafters worry?" he asked. Speaking for myself, I said, I was concerned mainly with running each rapid, with getting through the abyss alive. He was an afterthought, except when we had to carry him on the raft.

"That's good," he said. "I was afraid . . . well, Tim's being too emotional. I am paddling at my best, but Biggsy is overworried. In a good way, of course. I know he acts as he does because he cares for me."

I said Biggs certainly did appear to care for him. Then he wished me good night.

Thinking about it later, I found his assertion that he was "paddling at my best" surprising. As far as I could tell he was portaging any rapid he could. However, I did not think less of him for this. If anything, I admired his prudence, and at times was envious that he could portage his kayak around many rapids that, with our much bigger raft, we had no choice but to run.

I worked on my notes, but this did not distract me from questioning my own behavior on the river, especially on that last rapid. I had always assumed (without ever really testing that assumption) that the one thing I had control over was my nerve, my ability to act under pressure. Now I wondered if I had misled myself.

We had advanced one mile our first day in the abyss, two miles the second day. Our third day started off with no more promise. A hard rain had fallen through the night, and by morning the river had risen six inches. Biggs estimated that it had come up 20 percent overnight, from four thousand cubic feet a second to five thousand. We were awake at dawn and on the water by 8 a.m. By 11 a.m., lining the raft through three unrunnable rapids, we had progressed a grand total of about four hundred yards.

And then we encountered a chute almost identical to the one at the entrance to the abyss. The Apurimac compressed to about twenty feet wide, and the walls rose not just vertically but in fact narrowed—the powerful river had cut its gorge faster than gravity could bring the upper ramparts tumbling down. The kayakers found what they called a "sneak" along the right wall, a small chute next to the main chute that was an easy run for them but too small for the raft. Meanwhile, we couldn't scout the rapid and we couldn't line the raft through it.

Once again Bzdak and I climbed the gate boulder, inched along a thin ledge on the left wall, and retrieved the raft after Chmielinski shoved it through the chute. Once again Van Heerden and Jourgensen worked their way down the wall and into the raft. Once again we bore down on a monstrous hole. In fact, it was the biggest hole I'd seen, a gargantuan churning turbine easily thirty feet across, its eye sunk a good five feet below its outer lip. With Chmielinski screaming furiously we managed to skirt the hole, but as we did I had the distinct impression of it as a demon lurking over my right shoulder.

We shot past the hole, bounced off both walls, and spun clockwise in a circle. With the portly Jourgensen riding on my corner of the raft we sat low in the water and the river pelted us constantly over the stern. Now, as we spun, he lost his balance and with an assist from the water beating me on the back sent me flying out of the raft. On my way out Chmielinski reached across and jerked me back in.

Just as I got back into position I saw that we were bearing down on Biggs, who was in his kayak, in a tiny eddy right in the middle of the rapid, poised to rescue one of us in the event of a spill. Bzdak screamed a warning, but in the narrow gorge Biggs had nowhere to go—we had come on him too fast. We ran him down, trapped him beneath the raft, and hauled him fifteen yards before his boat popped out, riderless, from beneath ours. Then Chmielinski managed to reach under the raft, grab Biggs by the life jacket, and yank him free, alive but distraught.

We broke for lunch exhausted and demoralized. After five hours of work we had advanced perhaps eight hundred yards. Food went down hard, because each man felt within his gut a stone of fear and fatigue. To our right, in the east, the sight of snow-capped 21,000-foot Auzangate hovering over the gorge brought little joy, for it reminded us that we were still some six thousand difficult feet above sea level.

After lunch Chmielinski, Truran, and I scouted downriver and discovered our worst rapids yet. Four thundering drops, each at least two hundred yards long, with so much white water that at first they appeared to be one continuous froth.

Truran broke the rapid down into distinct runs: "Ballroom, Milk Shake, Liquidizer, Dead Man." He turned to me. "Whatever you do, *keep paddling.* Keep control of the raft. And do *not swim.*"

Bzdak joined us on the rock and appraised the river. "What do you think?" I asked.

He shook his head slowly. "Don't swim. My god, don't swim."

He and I climbed back to the raft and sat on it, waiting for Chmielinski. From utter emotional exhaustion I fell asleep, and awoke to Chmielinski splashing water in my face. He ordered Van Heerden to accompany Biggs, Truran, and Odendaal, who had found a portage route too tight for the raft but adequate for their kayaks. The cover was that Van Heerden could film the rapid. The reality was that by now Chmielinski did not trust Van Heerden. The Afrikaner would not respond to Chmielinski's commands, and his habit of smoking on the raft, and of tossing the empty cigarette packages in the river, had already led to harsh words between the two.

After the kayakers and Van Heerden left, Chmielinski said to Bzdak, Jourgensen, and me, "Okay, guys, looks good. All we do is keep straight in the top chute." He paused. "If you swim, try to go to the right." I had never heard him suggest the possibility of swimming a rapid.

We paddled upstream, turned into the current, maneuvered above the chute, and slowed slightly as we dipped into it. Then the river picked us up and heaved us forward. We were airborne. The only time I had felt a similar sensation was as a teenager, when I had ridden a motorcycle off a small cliff.

The raft hit the water, jackknifed, spun one hundred eighty

degrees. We went backward into the Ballroom. Chmielinski and I cracked heads and then I was on my way out of the raft. I grabbed netting as I went over the side.

"Jack!" someone screamed, and for a split second I saw Jourgensen in the heart of the rapid. He was under, up, under again, helpless, his life jacket his only hope, for he could barely swim. His face looked bloodless and frozen, his eyes blank. But he wasn't struggling. It was as if he had resigned himself to the inevitable.

The raft pitched, heaved, scooped me up. Chmielinski lay sprawled across the net, and at first I thought the force of our collision had knocked him out. The raft bolted up, then down. Bzdak, standing in the bucking bow like a defiant warrior, reached into the river and with one hand plucked Jourgensen back from eternity. He dropped the big man on the floor of the raft as if he were no heavier than a trout.

Two seconds later we plunged into Milk Shake.

"FORWARDFORWARDFORWARD!" Chmielinski yelled as he scrambled back into paddling position. We paddled hard to try to regain control of the raft, but it was too late. The front right rose and we began to flip. Jourgensen struggled up from the floor, climbed Bzdak's back, and nearly knocked him out of the boat. Bzdak wrestled him off and threw himself at the high side with Chmielinski. The raft leveled for a moment, then started to spin left to right.

"SWITCH!" Chmielinski yelled. That was a new one. He and I turned on the tubes and became front men, Bzdak the lone driver.

We handled the third rapid, Liquidizer, but lurched out of control as we tumbled over a short waterfall into Dead Man. We bounced off the left wall, hit a rock, spun a three-sixty, hit the right wall—and somehow ricocheted right across the hole. I got one terrifying glance at its ugly swirling eye, and then we shot into the calm water below it.

We paddled to some boulders along the right bank, climbed out of the raft, and sat in silence. You could almost hear the nerves jangling. Then Bzdak said, slowly, "Those were the biggest holes I have ever run."

Chmielinski agreed but didn't elaborate, which was unusual for him. Jourgensen said nothing, but with shaky hands tried to light his pipe. After a while Bzdak said, "We call that Wet Pipe Rapid, Jackie."

And then the laughter started, nervous titters at first, then low howls, then wild insane roaring.

Having once again advanced but a mile over the course of an entire day on the river, we finally began to understand how long a distance forty miles could be. On flat land you could walk that far in two days. We might well need two weeks to travel it on water. We resigned ourselves to a long haul.

That night Chmielinski instructed me to cut our already-lean rations by half. We would fill out the cookpot with our one surplus ingredient, water. Nobody was happy with this, but none opposed it.

As bats wheeled above us we ate a thin gruel—three packages space-age chili, one package powdered soup, water, water, water, eight bowls—then huddled on a granite slab along the river, watching the stars in the slit overhead, following them down to the top of the gorge wall, which in turn was lit up with fireflies. It seemed as if the stars fell right to the river.

"I don't think I've ever seen a more brilliant canyon," Tim Biggs said. Grunts along the rock affirmed that all shared his thought. We were scared and tired, but those emotions concentrated our attention, told us that we were in a sacred place, a place untouched by humans and perhaps, until then, unseen.

"Rivers have their own language," Truran said. "Their own culture. We're not in Peru. We're in a place that speaks in eddies and currents, drops and chutes and pools. So we only made a mile today. Can you think of a finer mile?"

I walked back to my tent and worked on my notes. An hour later, when I crawled into my sleeping bag, I heard the heavy breathing of Jack Jourgensen, who had pitched his tent near mine. I could not forget the look on his face that afternoon when he'd fallen into the rapid, the blankness of it, the resignation.

Jourgensen was nearly fifty-two, and at a crossroads. He'd been reading Leo Buscaglia's *Personhood* and wondering, as he put it, "What does it mean to get in touch with the world and yourself?" He wanted to be more than a man who got rich selling highway paint. His presence on the Apurimac said he was a filmmaker, an explorer, an adventurer—"Viking" was the word he liked to use in the diary he kept for his seven children, the youngest of whom, Leif, was only five months old.

I think all of us were inspired by the fact that Jourgensen would attempt a journey that scared the wits out of men two decades younger and in much better condition, but I know that I, for one, felt guilty about his being there. The cold truth was that he did not belong on the river. He was overweight, with a degenerating disc, arthritic hips, and a history of gout, and the swimming and climbing taxed him much more than it did the rest of us. Back home, he had a huge family depending on him. Yet in Cuzco, when Durrant had said that as the expedition doctor she considered it imprudent to allow him on the raft—"What will you do if he breaks a leg, or has a heart attack? You could kill him trying to get him out of the canyon"—no one had responded. No one had wanted to lose the golden goose.

I slept fitfully that night, my body bruised from the bad rapids. At first light I got up and checked the food bags for mildew. Bzdak was up, too, on breakfast duty. He made a pot of instant coffee and poured me a cup, although anticipation of the impending confrontation with the Apurimac already had my stomach in knots. We ladled the rest of the coffee into cups and distributed them to the tents.

"Zbyszek," I said when we had finished, "if we have another rapid like those ones yesterday, will you run it?"

"If there is no choice. Otherwise, no. What if someone breaks his leg? No way out. We put him to the raft and keep pushing. Not so good."

That morning the river's gradient increased, and, supported by the rain that had fallen over the last three days, the water rose another six inches and grew more volatile. We encountered rapid after rapid that was off the scale of difficulty—Class Sixes. For five straight hours the kayakers portaged and we worked the raft downriver on the end of Chmielinski's mountain-climbing rope.

This time, however, Chmielinski added a new twist to the lining procedure. He directed Bzdak to ride the raft and paddle it as we tethered him from shore. Chmielinski provided the bulk of the brains and muscle, but it was Bzdak who took the brunt of the risk. These were rapids a man could not swim and survive. The velocity of the water, let alone the rocks and boulders into which it would drive one, would crush a skull as easily as an eggshell. Yet all Chmielinski had to say was, "Zbyszek, go there," and point to a boulder in the middle of the river, or to an eddy far downstream, and Bzdak was in the raft and flying, with no more response than a hand signal to ask, "At which eddy should I stop?"

During six years in some of the wildest, most unforgiving places in the Western Hemisphere, these two disparate men had learned to depend on each other utterly. Despite the terrible risks they were running, despite our dire straits, it was wonderful to watch them work the precious raft down the beastly river. The only sign of the tremendous emotional pressure they were under was an occasional frenzied exchange in Polish.

By the afternoon of our fourth day in the abyss (and our sixth since leaving Cunyac bridge), Bzdak was exhausted. His eyes were red and puffy and his paddle responded too slowly to the raging water. I felt I should spell him on the raft, but Chmielinski would not hear of it. "This is a special thing between me and Zbyszek," he said. "We have many years together. It is correct for me to ask him to go, but not to ask you."

Chmielinski's reply came as a relief. I was more than grateful to scramble along the boulders behind him, hauling in slack line, paying out line as the raft took off, anchoring him so the speeding raft did not drag him into the river. I preferred the feel of rock under my feet, for by now fear of the river dominated my thoughts. My nerves were so raw from the white water that each afternoon, when the word came down that we were stopping to make camp, a wave of gratitude, of recognition that I had survived one more day, washed over me with a feeling that was palpable—it felt as if my body, one big knot of fear the day through, had suddenly come untied. The simple act of sipping my evening cup of coffee gave me immense pleasure.

Part of my fear was due to the fact that I could not get comfortable on the raft, which was packed in such a way that the fifth, nonpaddling man, either Jourgensen or Van Heerden, was crammed into my left rear quadrant. When Jourgensen rode next to me, weighing down our corner of the boat, I always felt that I was about to be pitched into the river. Van Heerden rode in back when he wanted to film, and jumped around constantly. Once, as we bounced through a rapid, he hit me with his camera, knocking me out of the boat and stamping my right temple with a purple wound. The tiny Riken, the agent of my salvation, of my deliverance through the terrible river, now seemed dangerously overburdened.

In all, it appeared that we might never escape the abyss, that it would never end. There was simply no flat water. It was rapid after rapid, mile after mile, driven by what Conrad described as nature's "sinister violence of intention—that indefinable something . . . in unheralded cruelty that means to tear out of [a man] all he has seen, known, loved, enjoyed or hated . . . which means to sweep the whole precious world utterly away from his sight by the simple and appalling act of taking his life."

"What do you think, Tim?" I asked Biggs later that day.

"I don't know, mate," he said. "But I'd be lying if I didn't say the river had me a bit scared."

Rainy season had begun in the high Andes. Influenced by tributaries miles above us, the river changed color daily. At times she appeared a coffee-and-cream brown, at others emerald green, still others a glacial gray. In the early evening she might run smooth and unthreatening past the camp, yet by morning, having come up a foot during the night, be thundering and powerful. In some places she was studded with three- and four-story boulders, in others her banks were packed with crushed gravel. Given these changes in mood, in appearance, it was impossible not to think of the river as having a will and intent of her own. In the end, however, it was sound, a voice, that most gave her life—she roared as she charged through her canyon. She seemed not only willful but demonic, bent on the simple act of drowning us. You could shout at her, curse her, plead with her, all to the same effect: nothing. She barreled on indifferent, unrelenting.

And so, inevitably, we turned our frustrations inward. On the river a shouted instruction might end as a yell and a grumbled epithet. In easier times, choice tent sites had been shared or left for another; now, as soon as we found a camp each man scrambled for the best land. Food was eyed greedily and served in strict portions.

In the abyss the competition between Chmielinski and Odendaal festered into open hostility. The Afrikaner's insecurity over his titular role as expedition leader manifested itself as a kind of delight when the Chmielinski-led raft encountered trouble. This attitude, though hardly admirable, was understandable. Several times a day Truran, Biggs, and the raft team would run rapids that Odendaal couldn't, and his solitary portages seemed to set him apart, to isolate him.

Chmielinski, for his part, had no respect for Odendaal as a riverman, and did not go out of his way to hide his disdain. "He is afraid of the water," he would mutter on the raft as he watched Odendaal portage yet another rapid he considered easily runnable. He did not regard Odendaal as his equal, let alone his superior, in any way.

At the end of our fourth day in the abyss, when it appeared that both Odendaal and the raft team would have to make a long portage, Odendaal's face cracked in satisfaction. "I'll be in camp two hours ahead of you!" he said, and laughed. Then he clambered up a boulder, hauled his kayak after him, and set off.

This goading was more than Chmielinski could stand, for the raft carried all of Odendaal's food and most of his gear. After the Pole scouted the route, we portaged the food and equipment bags downstream in three backbreaking trips, heaving them up and over boulders and nursing them along jagged crags. Odendaal did not see us and did not know that we had managed to put the lightened raft on the river instead of portaging it.

Kayaking downriver ahead of us, Biggs had found a tiny cave with a soft, sandy floor. We reached this camp well ahead of Odendaal. He looked shocked when he arrived, and without a word left to set up his tent.

The next morning I awoke to the sound of Odendaal's voice at Biggs's tent, which was pitched near mine. Odendaal wanted Biggs, the river captain, to command Chmielinski to deflate the raft and portage it over the next few kilometers. This, he argued, would be faster than lining. Biggs was noncommittal.

On the face of it, Odendaal's was a strange bit of logic. We lined the raft much faster than we could portage it, and as we had demonstrated the day before, we portaged our equipment and lined the lightened raft faster than Odendaal portaged his kayak.

However, if it came down to portaging the raft without the option of lining—if we deflated the raft—Odendaal would certainly move faster than we. And for Chmielinski, there was a world of symbolic difference between carrying a deflated raft overland and working an inflated one down the river. Deflating the raft would be humiliating, an admission of defeat.

Biggs fetched Chmielinski, who had a mumbled exchange with Odendaal that quickly escalated into a shouting match. Chmielinski told Odendaal that he knew nothing about white water. Odendaal threatened to throw Chmielinski off the expedition at Cachora.

I left then, and went to the cave. Truran was making coffee.

"If anyone goes at Cachora it should be François," he said. He was silent for a moment as he filled my cup, then said, "It's a constant game of one-upmanship with those two. They've got to get over that, or we'll put ourselves in even more danger than we already are."

Chmielinski did not deflate the raft, but that morning, as we attempted to line it through a rapid, it lunged around a boulder and pulled up short, teetering on its nose. Using one of our rescue lines, Bzdak, Truran, and I lowered Chmielinski thirty feet down the boulder's face. He freed the raft by slashing the snagged climbing rope, but the rope then ricocheted into aquatic oblivion. Suddenly, all we had left in the way of rope was our five short, thin rescue lines, which were dangerously frayed from overuse. Soon, unable to line the raft, we would be forced to portage. It would be slow, difficult, nasty work.

By lunch we had not advanced five hundred yards. Chmielinski sat by himself and spoke to no one.

That afternoon the rapids got worse. We would fight through a few hundred yards of bad water, lining some rapids, running others, but always hoping that beyond the next bend we'd find a calm, clear stretch. Then we'd peek around the bend and think, "This is getting *ridiculous.*" The rapids only got bigger, meaner, and longer.

Late in the afternoon we faced yet another monstrous rapid around which we could not portage the Riken. Chmielinski picked a rafting route, and then, in an attempt at conciliation, consulted with Biggs and Odendaal, who concurred. "You'll do well," Odendaal said to us as he set off to portage his kayak along a thin ledge on the canyon's left wall. Biggs agreed: "You've run much worse." He and Truran shouldered their boats and went with Odendaal, and Chmielinski instructed Jourgensen to follow them. (He feared that Jourgensen's next swim would be his last.) Bzdak, Van Heerden, and I waited for Truran to reach the bottom of the rapid and position himself to rescue us. Then we took up our paddles.

No one had read the current moving left to right just beneath the top of the rapid. I'm not exactly sure what happened when we hit it. One moment I was in the boat, the next all was darkness and silence. I grabbed for what I thought was the raft and got river. The water grew cold, colder, frigid. I tried to swim, but I couldn't tell if I was going up or down, and in any case my flimsy strokes were useless against the powerful current. Something squeezed the wind out of me like a giant fist. Again I tried to swim, searching for light, and again I was dragged down and flipped over and over and over.

I had taken some bad swims before, but this one was different.

In a moment of surprising peace and clarity I understood that I was drowning. I grew angry. Then I quit. I knew that it was my time to die.

Suddenly, as if rejecting such sorry sport, the river released her grip.

I saw light. Kick. Pull. Pull toward the light. A lungful of water. Pull.

AIR!

Then the river sucked me back down again. Blackness, tumbling, head crashing off rocks.

AIR!

LIGHT!

I surfaced to find the gorge wall hurtling past me. I hit a rock, snagged for a second, and managed to thrust my head out of the water long enough to spot Truran in his kayak at the foot of the rapid, holding in an eddy.

"Swim!" he yelled.

A blast in the back and I was in again. Everything went black. I sucked water up my nose and into my lungs. I bounced off something hard and surfaced next to Truran.

"Grab my waist!" he shouted. I wriggled onto the stern of his kayak and clamped my arms around him. He deposited me near a sandy bank on the river's left side and told me to wait there.

I knelt in the sand and vomited. When Truran returned, I waded into the river, stopped, and turned back to shore.

"Get in the water!" he yelled. "*Now!*"

Then we were in the rapid, and I was hugging him with whatever strength I had left, and the river was beating over me, as if angry she had not claimed me. Long minutes later I stood at the foot of the gorge's right-hand wall.

Van Heerden was smoking a cigarette rapidly and shaking. Chmielinski looked at me as if at a ghost. When the raft had flipped the alert Poles had grabbed onto it again immediately and been yanked from the hole. Van Heerden had been tossed clear and driven toward a flat-faced boulder. The river went directly under the boulder. If Van Heerden had gone with it he would have been shoved under the boulder and killed, but as he was about to hit it

Truran, scouting in his kayak, had yelled to him. Van Heerden had turned and reached for the raft, which was trailing him. The raft had slammed into the wall and pinned him. Van Heerden had been sucked under, but Chmielinski had managed to grab a hand, and Bzdak his head. When the raft bounced off the wall they wrestled him free. They assumed I had gone under ahead of him.

Chmielinski said, "Guys, in the boat." Either we got right back in or maybe we would never have the nerve to get in it again.

It was dark when we made camp, on tiny patches of sand hidden among boulders. We managed to eat about half our thin dinner before Truran accidentally upended the cookpot. No one spoke, except Chmielinski, to announce that we had advanced all of one mile that day.

Cold, hungry, and scared, I doubted whether I, or any of us, would survive the abyss. And though I knew it was self-pity, I resented the fact that everyone in that sad little camp but me had at least one partner with him, someone who would have to face family and friends and say, *This is how he died.*

The skies opened up and rain fell hard. We bolted for our tents. I hurried into mine, lit a candle, and stared at it until it had burned almost all the way down. When I blew it out the darkness terrified me—it reminded me of the darkness inside the river. I searched frantically for matches and burned two more candles one after another. I lit a fourth, my last. When it burned out I lay awake in the dark, eyes open, and felt my body tumbling, tumbling, tumbling.

In the black night I had pitched my tent right behind the big one Odendaal and Van Heerden shared. In the morning I heard them speaking in Afrikaans. They switched to English when Biggs joined them. Odendaal was considering a plan to remove the raft from the river once we were into smoother water. Van Heerden had shot all the film he wanted, and had had his fill of white water. He would depart. Truran, who had a nonrefundable airplane ticket back to South Africa, would also have to leave the river soon. Jourgensen, too, was ready to go home. From Cachora Bzdak and

I would go to Lima with Leon and Durrant, and perhaps rejoin the expedition much later, in the jungle. Chmielinski would kayak with Odendaal and Biggs.

"Don't tell anyone," Odendaal said to Biggs. "I don't want a lot of discussion about this, one of those things where everyone gives an opinion."

I was stunned and then upset. The river scared me, but I hadn't decided that I wanted to quit, and I felt that I had earned the right to plead my case. Bzdak and I had put our lives on the line taking supplies through the hardest part of the river, and once, at great risk, had carried Odendaal himself.

Bzdak was angry when I told him what I had heard. "Why am I trying my life for that guy if he just wants to throw me out?"

We consulted Chmielinski. He spoke with Odendaal and returned livid. With the rest of us gone, he would be isolated with the two South Africans, and at Odendaal's mercy.

Odendaal saw us talking and came over quickly.

"Piotr," he said, "I told you not to discuss this with anybody."

"You're taking the raft out," I said.

"We're thinking about some changes," Odendaal said. "Just discussing them."

"I overheard your conversation this morning," I said.

"Yes," he said. "I knew you were listening."

If he had known that, of course, he would not have bothered cautioning Biggs to secrecy. But the truth or falsehood of his statement was beside the point. Until that morning Odendaal and I had maintained at least the pretense of shared endeavor. Now, under the pressure of the abyss, we had betrayed one another. He had plotted my removal, and I, in turn, had clearly cast my lot with the men by whom he felt most threatened. All illusions of neutrality had evaporated.

We stared in silence for a few tense seconds, and then he left.

Chmielinski was seething. "No matter what happens," he said, "the raft is going down the river. We make that deal a long time ago. It is stupid to change now."

Chmielinski responded to this latest crisis by working the raft with an intensity I had not yet seen. In barely restrained fury, he leaped from boulder to boulder and scrambled up small cliffs, manipulating the short lead line from the most precarious of perches. Often it looked as if the raft would yank him right into the river. Bzdak and I trailed him along the bank, hurrying to keep up, coiling what was left of our line as Chmielinski hauled it in, anchoring him as the raft rocketed downstream and the line whipped through his hands and pulled taut.

Impatient because Bzdak and I could not match his pace, Chmielinski tried to line the raft through one rapid by himself. I climbed to the top of a boulder in time to see the raft tearing past him, the slack line paying out furiously and about to wrap itself around his right foot. I screamed. Somehow—this took more strength than I could have summoned from my entire body— somehow Chmielinski managed with one hand to arrest the line for a split second, yanking its stampeding half-ton to a halt. In the same moment he flung his foot far in the air as the line tightened around it. The line caught his shoe instead and ripped it off. Seconds later the shoe surfaced fifty yards downstream.

Bzdak and I scouted the next rapid. It was bad news, most of the current veering left into a deep whirlpool.

"We get sucked to the left, we're dead," Bzdak said.

Chmielinski did not need long to decipher our thoughts. "Okay," he said with resignation, "we line it."

From his tone of voice it was clear that Chmielinski wanted badly to run the rapid. Bzdak and I knew that the raft's speed absolutely could not be an issue when the showdown with Odendaal came, but just when Chmielinski needed us most we were losing what nerve we had left.

"Look, Piotr," I said. "You say go, I'll go. It's up to you."

"Me, too," Bzdak said.

"No," Chmielinski said. "We took a big swim yesterday. Better to learn to run small water again and feel good."

We lined the raft through the whirlpool's left side. It flipped. When we righted it, we looked downstream. Two tiny figures waved to us: Durrant and Leon.

9 *The Middle Apurimac*

They were camped on the bank opposite us, five hundred yards downstream, but the Apurimac thundered and roared as if mocking that fact. At least once in the abyss we had spent a full day traveling five hundred yards. It would not be safe to join our teammates until morning.

We could see Durrant picking her way nimbly from boulder to boulder along the left bank. Truran kayaked across the river, spoke with her, and returned to huddle with Bzdak. Then the photographer hurried to where Chmielinski and I were setting up our tents.

"Piotr," he said, "may I have permission to go across?"

Chmielinski yelled to Truran, waiting in an eddy: "You can make it with him?"

"Maybe," Truran yelled back.

"Zbyszek," Chmielinski said, "go there. Do not come back. We will meet you tomorrow."

As nervous as I could remember seeing him, Bzdak thrust his camera case at me, which was something like a mother giving up a child. He waded into the eddy, hugged Truran about the waist, and arrayed his bulk along the kayak's spine.

They danced slowly into the current, edging in and out of boils and small whirlpools. When they hit the heart of the current Truran turned directly upstream. The boat's plastic nose jumped in the air like a rearing horse, and the stern went under. Bzdak disappeared with it.

The river tossed him back up, he gulped for air, and, still clutching Truran, went back down.

Truran struggled to a faint midstream eddy, the river howling and gushing to either side. Bzdak bobbed and went underwater. Only his yellow helmet, bursting through the froth every few seconds, indicated that he was still aboard the kayak.

Finally, they gained the far bank. Bzdak and the doctor embraced.

"Look at that Zbyszek," Chmielinski said.

That night, Chmielinski, Biggs, Jourgensen, Truran, Van Heerden, and I gathered around the campfire and listened to Odendaal make his proposal: Remove the raft now. It was too slow. Biggs endorsed the idea, as did Jourgensen, which made the raft's demise almost a certainty. Jourgensen represented the expedition's fiscal salvation. He had seventeen one-hundred-dollar bills pinned inside his parka, and would give the expedition more when he could get to Lima. No decisions would be made without his approval.

But even Biggs, an Odendaal loyalist, did not accept Jourgensen's subsequent argument. Jourgensen suggested that we could predict the raft's future speed based on how fast it had come through the abyss. (At that pace, we would arrive at the Atlantic sometime in the next century.) His stand appeared to be an excuse to leave the river without seeming to quit. An honorable Viking stayed with his boat. Unless, of course, there was no boat.

When his first argument didn't float, Jourgensen said, "The raft is unsafe. Piotr is taking too many risks."

"Let's ask the crew," Truran said. He turned to me. On one level I agreed with Jourgensen. For him, at least, the raft *was* unsafe. He did not belong on the water. But I didn't believe that the raft was unsafe per se. Risky, yes, but if there were no risk to running the Apurimac, we would not have been there.

"I want to keep going," I said. "So does Zbyszek. We'll take our chances. I think the raft would be safer with fewer people and less weight. I'm sure Kate will join us if we need another paddle."

Chmielinski, for his part, believed that Odendaal knew nothing about the logistics of running such a steep, nearly inaccessible canyon. Without the raft to carry supplies, the kayakers would have to paddle fully loaded boats, and this would greatly decrease their maneuverability in the water. Even then they would have to depend on the countryside for sustenance, but the canyon was nearly uninhabited. Further, the river had to open up soon, had to level out. When it did, raft support would increase the team's speed.

And then Truran, as was his wont, dropped a bombshell: "This expedition is not going to reach the sea according to its schedule. I suggest we just give up that idea right now. Slow down. Accept the pace. Or else get completely into racing trim. Go as fast as possible. And that means getting rid of François. He's the slowest man here. He cannot possibly keep up."

Startled, Odendaal looked up from the fire. This was not an argument easily dismissed—Truran was the team's most respected riverman. "Okay," Odendaal said. "Let us talk about that."

"If it's a question of speed, you must remove yourself," Truran said. "If you do not remove yourself, then you cannot remove the raft, either. Zbyszek and Joe have earned the right to stay on this river if they so choose."

"We agreed long ago that the raft was going on the river," Chmielinski said. "People have risked their lives because they believed what we said. They have worked hard. There is no question here. The raft is going."

If Odendaal forced his hand, he had a mutiny, and perhaps a race to the sea—he and Biggs against Chmielinski and whoever went on the raft. On the other hand, if Odendaal consented to keeping the raft on the river, he had lost the showdown. What authority he still retained aside from Jourgensen's financial backing would evaporate.

We agreed to discuss it again the next day.

I picked my way back to my tent by the light of the waning moon and listened to the rapids thunder in the cold night. In my mind I ran them again and again. Each run ended in a violent, suffocating tumble through water and rock and darkness.

In the morning, shivering from the cold, I walked downstream, searching for the source of all that aquatic thunder. I climbed a low cliff, looked down, and studied my nemesis: chute, drop, hole, stopper wave. It terrified me.

I returned to camp, packed my gear, and loaded it onto the raft. Biggs had breakfast ready, but I couldn't eat. I walked back to the rapid and studied it again.

Truran had followed me. He knew what I was thinking. "See that hole?" he said. "It's turning left. If you swim, try to make yourself relax. You'll go around that thing a couple of times. You'll be helpless. Then it will spit you out. See it?"

There: The river dumped into the hole and erupted in a wave, an explosion of white and silver. I looked closer. That swirl, running off the wave and into flat water—would that save me?

I hurried back to camp. I double-checked the raft's lines and netting, pumped up a soft side tube, strapped on helmet and life jacket. I sat on my tube impatiently. I wanted to get this over with. Finally, Chmielinski arrived, and Jourgensen and Van Heerden finished their morning smoke. They said nothing as they boarded the raft.

We splashed ourselves to wake up. Chmielinski barked orders. We turned upstream, into a back eddy, then into the current. The raft's nose swung into the rushing river. Something grabbed it. We rose up. The river spread below us as if we were poised at the top of a rollercoaster.

Chmielinski screamed "OUTOUTOUT!" I yanked hard on my paddle to correct and get us straight in the chute—

—and *boom-boom* we were through, into the flat water.

Only then did I realize how small the rapid actually was, a dinky thing that my imagination had amplified into a monster. My fear had fooled me completely.

When we reached the opposite bank we learned that although Leon and Durrant had managed to bring our supplies to Cachora in Edwin Goycochea's truck, and from there had packed them on hired burros down the precipitous trail into the canyon, one of the animals, piled high with provisions that were to last us for the next few weeks, had misstepped and bounced a hundred yards down the canyon wall. The beast had landed on the supplies mounted on its back, saving its life but scattering our provisions. Fortunately, Durrant had managed to retrieve some of the staples. We would breakfast on oatmeal flecked with dirt, leaves, and an occasional tooth-jarring pebble.

That night, as I sat against a guava tree and worked on my notes, Odendaal approached me with a proposition. He invited me to leave the expedition at Atalaya and work my way to the sea alone. He said that everyone deserved the chance to reach the sea and implied that in a better world he himself would prefer the sort of trip he was now proposing for me. I pointed out that I was broke, that I had given him the seven thousand dollars I had raised in the States. He said that this was not a problem. He would return two hundred dollars to me. He assured me that he had researched the subject thoroughly and that this was quite enough to cover my trip.

My first reaction was, Oh, come *on*. But then I realized that he was not trying to swindle me. He believed what he was saying.

All at once I understood both the brilliance behind the entire Amazon project and its terrible flaw. No matter how farfetched the words that issued from his lips, Odendaal believed them. He believed that I could travel thirty-five hundred miles of unknown country with two hundred dollars in my pocket. He believed that by cutting me out of the expedition he was selflessly doing me a favor. He believed that he had intended for me to overhear his conversation with Van Heerden and Biggs the day before. He believed, as the river thrashed him, that he was paddling well. And he believed, even now, not only that he could lead an expedition all the way down the Amazon, but that he was actually doing it.

It was horrifying, and it was wonderful. If Odendaal had not had that extraordinary ability to interpret the ugliest truths in such a self-aggrandizing way, there would have been no Amazon expedition, and none of us would have been in Peru. He was, literally, a visionary. He saw what others did not. He was also the perfect salesman—he could sell dross because he sincerely believed it was gold.

I refused his offer.

"Look," he said angrily, "Piotr has no money, either. If you go with him on the raft, you will never make it."

"I don't know about that."

"What do you know about *anything?* I have been on *twelve* expeditions. You have been on *none.* You know *nothing!* You and your ridiculous hat. We *laugh* at you!"

He was right about the hat. But by now I knew something about his so-called expeditions.

"Piotr and I have a business disagreement," he said as he left, "but we are friends. You and I, however, have a serious communication problem. If it gets worse, one of us will have to go."

Chmielinski and he were *friends?* I understood then how completely out of touch Odendaal was. The saddest part was that he really seemed to think that it all came down to a question of money, that as long as he held the purse strings, it was his expedition.

Our camp, on a hot, cactus-ridden slope a hundred yards off the cool river, was miserable. Away from the water the countryside simmered even in the shade, and our dust and sweat aroused an avaricious insect population. Killing the large blackflies brought a certain satisfaction. They were fat and slow, and once they settled onto a patch of flesh they took time to indulge. Their bite was not bad, and when crushed with a savage open-handed slap they disintegrated with a satisfying squish.

Far more insidious were the biting, gnat-sized flies Peruvians call *mosquito.* You didn't feel the bite, but minutes later a powerful itch set in. The bites infected rapidly. Each of us bore scars about the ankles, wrists, and, among those who preferred to take a full measure of sun, buttocks. (Durrant theorized that the bugs inject an anticoagulant, for the bites bleed and fester but do not harden into scabs for some time.)

There were other delights. I pulled a parka from the top of my equipment pile and a furry tarantula ambled out, angry but not the least frightened. The sharp, lancelike spines of the desert plants made each footstep an adventure, with or without shoes. And that night, asleep, I felt my knife cord sliding along my neck. I reached for it and in one motion flung into the night the slick, wriggling thing I found. I wanted to dismiss this as a nightmare, but the oath emitted by Truran seconds later when something dark and squirmy flopped onto his mosquito netting suggested it was not. We had that day seen two black-and-yellow snakes that Bzdak had identified as vipers, and there were said to be bushmasters and corals in the area.

That was the last time I slept without a tent.

Once we left the Cachora camp, we would have one more possibility of resupply before we entered the restricted Red Zone. According to our map, the only place there might be access to the river on what we estimated would be a ten-day, one-hundred-fifty-mile run from Cachora to the Red Zone was at the village of Triunfo. The next day, after arranging a plan to attempt to meet the river team at Triunfo in five days with new supplies, and after collecting our letters to home, Leon climbed out of the canyon with the mules. Van Heerden went with him. If the raft remained on the river, Durrant would take his place.

Meanwhile, Biggs refused to continue on the river until Chmielinski signed a statement recognizing Odendaal as the expedition leader and agreeing not to split the team. Biggs based his stand on a principle almost as old as men and boats: Water is no medium for democracy. When you signed on for a voyage you agreed to accept the leadership without question.

Chmielinski, of course, refused to sign anything, and he, Odendaal, Biggs, and Jourgensen spent most of that afternoon a hundred yards downstream from camp, arguing amid the thorns.

Meanwhile, Durrant, Bzdak, Truran, and I discussed the crisis among ourselves. Bzdak brewed a pot of coffee, and though we were sweltering in the midday tropical heat, Truran and I built a fire. The four of us sat around it hoping, in vain, that its smoke would discourage the pesky mosquitoes.

It was clear to us that if the "B" squad (as Durrant referred to Bzdak, me, and herself) were forced to leave the canyon, the chances of our rejoining the river team would be slim. In effect, we would be off the expedition. "If Piotr is serious about taking the raft alone and leaving Tim and François to continue on their own, I'll go with the raft," she said. Bzdak and I were prepared to do the same.

Much to our relief, Truran agreed to accompany the raft if the team split. Without a kayaker scouting ahead of us, and ready to rescue us in the event of an accident, the Apurimac would be even more dangerous than she had been so far. Truran's decision did not come easily, however. He would now be competing against one of his closest friends, and as he put it, "Tim doesn't finish second."

There were elements of tragedy in Truran's decision. Although he rejected Biggs's dogmatic Christianity, he respected Biggs as a principled man, one who acted with little regard for personal gain. But Truran disagreed with Biggs on the subject of François Odendaal, and the disagreement was as profound as the bonds of friendship. Biggs believed that Odendaal's strength was his ability to carry an expedition to completion. He also thought, however, that Odendaal would be better off traveling without people "who knew his past history." Truran, alone among the rest of us, knew that history, and he had concluded that Odendaal was fundamentally unfit to lead a river expedition.

"Frans lost a mate a long time ago," Truran said, "and he's been trying to make up for it ever since." He said that a decade before, when he and Biggs had been members of the kayaking team at the University of Natal, Odendaal had come to them seeking men for a source-to-sea attempt of Africa's Limpopo River. Odendaal had already tried the river once, but three weeks into that first expedition his entire team save one man, Johan Smit, had left. Odendaal and Smit pushed on alone and became trapped in a whirlpool. Odendaal lost consciousness; when he came to, Smit was dead. Odendaal quit the Limpopo.

"When Frans asked me to go back there with him," Truran said, "he told me his mate had died trying to rescue him, and that he had to 'beat' the river."

(Odendaal had never mentioned the accident to me, but months later, reading his unpublished Urubamba manuscript, I came across a passage describing his state of mind when he thought he was dying from altitude complications:

"Crazy, I thought. This happened to me once before. In the whirlpool with Johan Smit. When I saw no way out of my drowning and realized that the world concerned me no more, I had laughed. Under the water. I was unconscious when the water released me, he died. I was there again, alone.")

Truran, Biggs, and several other men returned to the Limpopo with Odendaal. According to Truran, two-thirds of the way down the river, just above its worst rapids, Odendaal got in a violent argument with them and left the expedition. The rest of the team went on to make the first recorded descent of the Limpopo's roughest water, only to be stopped at the Mozambique border. Without mentioning the split, Odendaal later wrote that political events in Mozambique had prevented the expedition from reaching the river's mouth, but that he was satisfied he could do it. Truran considered this highly disingenuous, and had never forgiven Odendaal.

Truran said that he had come to South America out of loyalty to Biggs and a love of white water, but as far as his relationship with Odendaal was concerned, he was a hired hand. He was convinced that Odendaal was on the Amazon for the wrong reasons. He was exorcising ghosts, battling the memory of Smit's death. "He's not a kayaker," Truran said. "He's terrified of water. He's a man with something to prove." Odendaal was free to do that, Truran said, until his behavior compromised the integrity of the expedition, as it now threatened to do.

Then Durrant raised another point. "François wants the raft off the river," she said to me, "because he wants *you* off the river. He's performing terribly, and he doesn't want you writing about it. He realizes he made a mistake bringing you here."

In the end we reached an uneasy truce. Odendaal, though

refusing to acknowledge that he had a mutiny on his hands, agreed to include the raft as part of the river team. Chmielinski signed Odendaal's agreement, primarily because he believed the film project a worthy pursuit. But the next day, as we loaded the raft and prepared once again to confront the Great Speaker, he said to me, "François is my enemy."

The Cachora confrontation led to at least one unexpected but welcome development: The raft team became a tight unit. Jourgensen, as was his prerogative, remained with the raft. But he was tired now, content to ride most of the time as a nonpaddling passenger, and he wanted friends. Durrant took Van Heerden's place at the right front paddle. Though not as physically strong as the departed Afrikaner, she was more confident. She was a swimmer, and she knew water. When Chmielinski yelled "Go!" she paddled hard.

After we executed our first rapid smartly, bending neatly through three sharp turns and catching a benediction of cold spray at the bottom, a wave of shared knowledge rippled through the raft: *This boat belongs on the river.* For the next three hours we shot rapid after rapid, maneuvering like a seasoned crew, whipping the blue balloon through a slalom of tight curves. We were in control, running backward and forward and sideways, through elevatorlike drops and rolling waves. We laughed and hollered in our exhilaration.

This river, this forgotten place, was ours now, and ours alone. No towns, no bridges, no roads, no huts, no gold panners, no peasants working postage-stamp fields. A *wild* river. "It's *running*," Chmielinski said, and we were running with it.

The canyon narrowed; again the walls rose sheer and slick. An unnamed river poured in from the left and mined the Apurimac with boulders, but we ran them without mishap. When we had beaten them Durrant looked up and shouted: To our right, above the canyon's east rim, rose the spectacular white-and-maroon peaks of the Cordillera Vilcabamba. We finished the day with a long, gushing seesaw of a rapid, three hundred yards of troughs and waves, at the bottom of which we were as wet and happy as ducks.

Truran and Biggs were waiting in their kayaks. As we waved in greeting Biggs screamed and pointed behind us. Odendaal's kayak was shooting along, overturned and riderless.

Its owner surfaced upstream, bloody and gagging and clinging to a boulder in the middle of the river. Biggs fought his way against the current and got Odendaal onto the tail of his boat and safely to shore, but the accident lent an eerie note to an otherwise wonderful day. With the exception of Biggs and perhaps Jourgensen, the rest of us had witnessed the Afrikaner's suffering with indifference.

We camped on a small, pretty beach at the foot of a granite cliff. Chmielinski made dinner. He was the expedition's most orderly cook. He took pains to prepare a kitchen, erecting driftwood-and-rock counters and a rock fireplace replete with chimney, laying out his utensils in a careful row, throwing a cloth over our waterproof food crate to convert it to a table.

When Chmielinski got down to the actual cooking, his philosophy was, as he put it, "I am a slave for that time." He served each person himself, moving rapidly from one to the next, refilling tea and coffee cups, dishing out seconds if there were any. He prepared the expedition's most elaborate dinners. That night, he cooked a pot of powdered mushroom soup, a thick stew of packaged beef bolstered with fresh onions and carrots Leon and Durrant had brought into the canyon, and two desserts—fresh bananas and chocolate bars, and a pudding made of instant rice, raisins, cinnamon, and evaporated milk.

After dinner, when the others had retired, I packed the food crate while Chmielinski cleaned dishes.

"It was good today on the raft," he said. "Good running. This is the way a river should be."

"We seem to have regained some confidence," I said. "And Kate is very good with a paddle."

"Confidence is the thing. We must be prepared to take the raft alone."

"Do you think it will come to that?"

"I do not know. But we must be ready to do it."

Early the next morning the kayakers shot a big rapid and signaled us to follow, which we did without scouting. After all, now we were *running*.

No one saw the hole. The raft bucked once and vaulted Chmielinski and me forward off the back tube like rocks from a slingshot. As I flew over Bzdak, paddling on the left front, our helmets cracked, and then I was underwater. I came up perhaps ten seconds later, punchy and disoriented, and forty yards downstream of the hole.

Jourgensen got the worst of it. He and Bzdak stuck in the hole, and it sucked him under three times before the Pole was able to haul him out. Later, his eyes dull as stone, Jourgensen said, "I thought I was dead for sure."

It had been a mistake not to scout the rapid. We could not afford an injury. We were traveling through unpopulated, impenetrable country. The terrain between the canyon floor and its rim was hot, dry, scrubby, and unforgiving, with no sign of people, not a single cultivated terrace, not a hint of a trail.

For the next two days we ran almost continuous rapids, and got battered in the process. Jourgensen's bad swim had given him the appearance of a zombie, and he never really recovered. Paradoxically, Odendaal's stubborn pride was emerging as his most admirable trait, but he had endured several punishing swims and wore an ugly gash along his right cheek. Once more we carried him on the raft through a rapid he could neither portage nor run, and it angered him. Biggs was worn down from the grinding internecine contention, and Bzdak, his heroism now quotidian, badly damaged his left knee. It was swollen and immobile. Chmielinski crumpled his right hand in a fall and could barely use it, and he developed a pain in his right foot that Durrant suspected was a fracture (though he refused to acknowledge it as anything more than an irritation).

My own nerves were shot: Every rapid was a terror. I lost two fingernails and most of the knuckle skin on my right hand, and badly bruised the heel of it, which made paddling extremely painful. Scouting the rapids, scrambling over one wet slick boulder after another, stumbling and falling so often that it now felt as common-place as walking, I had beaten both shins to pulp.

Durrant, to my amazement, was unfazed. The hole that had nearly killed Jourgensen she had found "somewhat exciting."

Truran, as ever, slid easily through the worst the river threw at him, as if the *apu* Rimac had designated him our guardian angel. He alone had yet to swim, he rescued those of us who did, and if he was ever frightened he did not show it. His presence boosted the raft team's confidence immensely; in an activity that depends to such a great degree on rhythm, hesitation induced by doubt can be deadly.

Meanwhile, the schism within the expedition widened. Odendaal all but stopped speaking with Durrant, Bzdak, and me, talked to Truran and Chmielinski only as necessary, and spent long hours huddled with Jourgensen and Biggs. Chmielinski insinuated himself into these sessions to the extent he could. Jourgensen was beat up—"I've had two close calls . . . and enough white water to last a lifetime," he wrote in his diary—and had decided to leave the river as soon as we found Triunfo. Whoever he gave his money to would gain material control of the expedition.

Each night, for the sake of future travelers, Chmielinski labored over his graph-paper notebook, sketching in the section of river run that day, consulting with Truran to corroborate his memory, marking the turns, the rapids, their class of difficulty, branding the worst with names ominous in their dry simplicity: "Broke Nose Here," "Jack Almost Drowns." The Peruvian military map we had actually to use was grossly inaccurate, but in the absence of anything better a convincing seductress. "Triunfo," it claimed with all the authority of the printed page. The gullible read the black dot below the name as a guarantee of hot food, cold beer, a cantina—life.

Late in the afternoon of our fourth day out of Cachora Biggs spotted a faint trail climbing the river's steep left bank. Two miles up the trail sat Triunfo ("Triumph"), which proved to be nothing but the ruins of a sugar mill abandoned more than a decade earlier in response to land reforms instituted by the radical general Juan Velasco Alvarado, who had seized power in a 1968 military coup (he was ousted in 1975). Instead of cold beer and dancing partners Triunfo offered crumbling mud-brick walls and scraps of rusting metal. Only the mill bearings, their stainless-steel races chipped but gleaming, suggested that Triunfo had ever been anything more than an elaborate hoax.

We had no choice but to climb out of the canyon in search of Leon and Van Heerden. Jourgensen had to leave the river, and we badly needed one last resupply before the Red Zone.

At dawn the next morning, leaving Bzdak and Durrant to attend the camp and the slower Odendaal and Jourgensen to ascend at their own pace, Chmielinski, Biggs, Truran, and I clawed up through unruly stands of mango and banana and about noon stopped briefly at a hut no larger than our raft. Inside it sat a grinning Quechua woman with a baby at her brown breast. She gave us *platanos,* like bananas but plumper and not as sweet, and we rested briefly at the door of her hut, chomping the fruit and admiring the view. The intense Andean light, the vast blue sky, the parade of humpy brown *cerros* atop the canyon rim, the white peaks of the Cordillera Vilcabamba receding into infinity like ocean waves—these were shocking after four weeks in the deep, dark canyon. I felt as if I had been released from a prison.

The river ambled along thousands of feet below, but all I could see was a silver-gray rock crease where the canyon walls seemed to have sealed her off. I was startled by how isolated the Apurimac was. She had nothing at all to do with life in these mountains. She was utterly alone.

We passed through a settlement called Marabamba with no word of Leon and Van Heerden and at sunset reached the village of Karquique, about halfway up the canyon wall, its sixty huts set around a network of neat paths, here and there a tin roof reflecting the evening light. The village teacher said that he had not seen any gringos, or heard of any being spotted on the mountain trails. He directed us to a crossroads three days' hike away. Perhaps our friends would be there.

As we readied ourselves to depart, a young girl ran toward us.

"Gringo!" she yelled, and pointed far up the mountainside. Two mules were easing down the trail, led by a man too tall to be a Peruvian. If we had left Karquique an hour earlier, we might have missed Van Heerden and Leon altogether.

Van Heerden brought disturbing news, gleaned from a BBC short-wave broadcast along the trail: Capetown had exploded. The riots were the worst in recent history, the death toll high. Biggs and Truran fell into a deep funk. This lifted slightly when the teacher induced Leon to cut his five-year-old daughter's heretofore un-shorn locks, thereby becoming her godfather. In return, the teacher cooked us chicken soup and guinea pig and let us sleep in the schoolhouse.

Jourgensen and Odendaal arrived the next day, having spent the night in Marabamba. Jourgensen would leave for Cuzco with Leon and Van Heerden and the mules, and proceed from there to the United States. "If you can't trust one another," he asked Chmielinski and Odendaal in a tired voice, "what's the point of the expedition?"

Still, Jourgensen believed that the expedition must have one undisputed leader, and in the end he backed Odendaal, who was also his business partner in the film. "Frans and I had become good friends in just a few weeks," he wrote that night in his diary. "We liked the way each other thought about things, and we both have a fairly even temper. Frans is a philosopher at heart and so am I. People who love adventure tend to love life . . . Frans is a VIKING!"

Chmielinski felt deeply betrayed. He and Jourgensen had been friends for years, and here on the Apurimac it was the penniless immigrant Bzdak who had twice risked his life to save Jourgensen's. Chmielinski told Jourgensen he was "crushed."

Then we gave letters to the battered rich man, said good-bye, and descended again into the dark canyon.

Below Triunfo the river grew with every mile, expanding remark-ably in width and depth, and the rapids grew with it. We ran them well, considering that our raft was laden with three weeks' supplies, but we had worn an irreparable hole on one of the floor tubes, rendering it floppy and unstable. As each rapid approached (that's how it felt, as if the rapids were charging up to confront us), I wondered, is this the one that we will underestimate, the one that will swallow us for good? On the biggest drops I found myself diving shamefully for the center net. I did not want to swim again, ever.

Two days below Triunfo we passed the mouth of the Pachachaca River and paused to bathe in its translucent green waters. A few miles farther we crossed the Pampas confluence. We had anticipated a raging beast (the Pampas is one of the Apurimac's principal tributaries), but we met a docile giant. And abruptly, right there below the Pampas, the fearsome Apurimac gorge appeared to end, opening into a valley filled with light. It was like sliding out of a cave.

That night the sun hung in the sky long after we had expected it to set, and though we were still a mile above sea level we dried quickly in the desert heat. We made camp on a stretch of fine white sand, and Chmielinski and Bzdak built a roaring driftwood fire.

In the morning we heard what sounded like small explosions or rockfall coming from somewhere across the river. Not for several days would we understand that this was small-arms fire, and that we were under attack.

10 *The Lower Apurimac (The Red Zone)*

When we entered the lower canyon that first day below Triunfo it felt as if we had finally escaped the dark, constricted underworld of the middle Apurimac, but by the following day we knew better. There was more light in the broader canyon, but it revealed only hot, steep, yellow-red dirt walls, barren of vegetation, that appeared poised to tumble into the river at any moment. The canyon's right-hand rim towered two miles above the river, the left almost that.

It was a ghostly, intimidating place, and the river herself seemed hell-bent to be somewhere else. The Pampas swells the Apurimac's volume by about 25 percent, and while the corrosive power of this added mass widens the river, it also increases its gradient. The roller coaster gets wider and steeper and longer and faster, until the river appears to be a single unbroken chain of white water. The noise of these rapids drowns out every other sound in the canyon. Down on the water, paddling the raft, we had to shout to be heard more than a few feet apart.

That second afternoon in the lower canyon we took a break near a thick wire cable that ran from a boulder high on the left bank to one high on the right bank, a distance of perhaps seventy-five yards. In the hundred and fifty miles of river between Cunyac bridge and the marine garrison of Lechemayo, just below the river's last major rapids, there are three such cables, or *oroyas*. Other than raft, they are the only means of crossing the river. There had been an *oroya* at the Cachora camp, and I had watched, amazed, as a Quechua man negotiated it hand over hand, his feet dangling high above the thrashing river, then hauled across behind him his wife, his child, and a bewildered cow affixed to the cable by ropes and two handcarved wooden yokes.

According to what we had learned in Karquique, from the right-bank terminus of the *oroya* under which we were stopped a vague trail climbed to a pass at about twelve thousand feet, and from there descended into a region known as Vilcabamba. It was here, in a rugged, isolated land of snow peaks, swamps, and steep gorges—and not, as is so often claimed, in Machu Picchu—that the legendary "last refuge" of the Incas once flourished.

The story, briefly: Shortly after they occupied Cuzco in 1533, the Spanish installed a compliant young Inca prince, Manco, as a puppet ruler. Three years later, after the *conquistadores* had chained him up, called him a dog, pissed on him, raped his wives, and stolen his gold and jewelry, Manco rebelled. He laid siege to Cuzco for eight months before being forced to retreat. He fled north and west, and in 1539 settled in the remote Concevidayoc valley, near the eastern lip of the Apurimac canyon. There, he turned the sleepy village of Espíritu Pampa into a capital worthy of an Inca, building palaces and temples, fountains and bridges, canals and plazas. He called his city-state Vilcabamba.

It took the Spanish thirty-five years to conquer Vilcabamba. By then, Manco was dead, and his son Felipe Tupac Amaru ruled. The Spanish led Felipe from Vilcabamba at the end of a gold chain. The final chapter of the Inca empire closed in Cuzco's main plaza, where Felipe was hanged and his body mutilated. After his execution the Spanish settled in Vilcabamba and profited from its sugar, coca, and silver for almost two hundred years. When those resources were gone they abandoned the valley.

Hiram Bingham, the American archeologist who in 1911 discovered what has become South America's most famous ruin, Machu Picchu, also passed through Vilcabamba several times, but missed the city buried there. He went to his grave believing that

Piotr Chmielinski   Zbigniew Bzdak   Tim Biggs

Joe Kane   Jerome Truran   Kate Durrant

François Odendaal

"El Condorito."

At 15,000 feet on the approach to the source. From left: François Odendaal, Tim Biggs, Pastor.

Portaging the Upper Apurimac:
Piotr Chmielinski, Tim Biggs,
François Odendaal, Jerome Truran.

Dr. Kate Durrant and the author in San Juan.

Kate Durrant consulting patients near the
Hanging Bridge.

Jerome Truran on the upper Apurimac.

Left: The last Inca hanging bridge, woven
entirely of hammered grass.

Tim Biggs executing an Eskimo roll.

Right: Tim Biggs on the upper Apurimac.

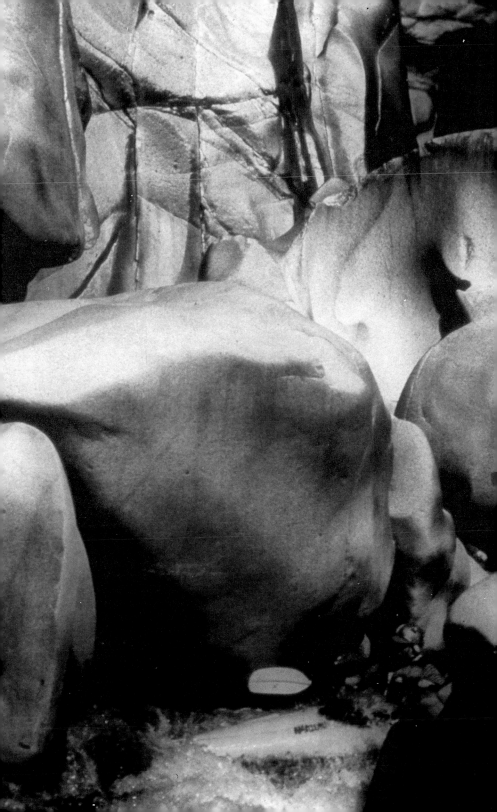

Bottom to top: Piotr Chmielinski, Jerome Truran, Tim Biggs.

Quechua man and son.

Shakedown run on the Apurimac. From
left: Piotr Chmielinski, the author, Sergio
Leon, Kate Durrant.

Left: Jerome Truran in the Acobamba Abyss.

In the Acobamba Abyss (note high-water mark).

Lining the raft through the Acobamba Abyss.

Right: Jerome Truran in the Acobamba Abyss.

Cloud forest in the Red Zone. From foreground:
Jerome Truran, Tim Biggs, François Odendaal.

Asháninka man.

In the Red Zone. Left to right, on raft: Jerome
Truran, the author, Kate Durrant.

On the lower Tambo, from left: Kate Durrant
and Jerome Truran on native raft; Piotr
Chmielinski and the author on *Gringo* equivalent.

Piotr Chmielinski (left), Kate Durrant, and the author with sea kayaks and the *Jhuliana* in Pucallpa.

Machu Picchu was the fabled lost city of the Incas. Not until another American, Gene Savoy, led expeditions to the region in 1964 and 1965 was Vilcabamba correctly identified. The ruins have largely been ignored since Savoy's discovery, and the region itself is nearly uninhabited, a ghostly adjunct to the ghostly lower Apurimac canyon. According to Gregory Deyermenjian, an American who visited the site in 1986, only one thatch hut stands at Espíritu Pampa, and the nearby ruins are so overgrown that he, too, would have missed them had not a local man pointed them out.

As we departed the *oroya* we heard three sharp reports. We dismissed these as rockfall set off by the northwesterly headwind, which now blew so fiercely we were forced to kneel in the raft and paddle with heads lowered while Chmielinski counted stroke. After half an hour of this penance I glanced up and saw the canyon walls moving slowly past us in the wrong direction. The wind was blowing us upstream. When Bzdak and Durrant came to the same realization and collapsed in laughter, Chmielinski had no choice but to call it a day. The kayakers agreed, we pitched camp, and Chmielinski announced that we would wake at three-thirty the next morning and be on the water by dawn.

Which, bleary-eyed, we seemed to be. Light was just beginning to filter into the canyon as we loaded the raft and prepared to put it into the river at the top of a good-sized rapid. Chmielinski and I heard several whizzing sounds, followed by a series of the now-familiar reports. Suddenly Biggs shouted and pointed across the river, toward the canyon's right wall. A few hundred yards above us six men were descending the wall. One of them knelt and put a rifle to his shoulder. A bullet zipped into the river two feet from where Truran sat in his kayak adjusting his spray skirt.

"Go!" Chmielinski yelled.

Never had I been so grateful to enter a rapid. At first I wasn't so much frightened as overwhelmed. I had never been shot at, never watched a person try to kill me. It took a few moments to digest that idea. *Then* I was frightened, but at that point we were hidden in the rapid and hurtling away.

We ran the rapid, found fast, smooth water below it, and glided swiftly down the right side of the river. Half an hour later, we heard a deep rumbling directly opposite us, and turned to the left bank to see dozens of boulders and small rocks plummeting into the water. A plume of golden dust arched skyward. Had it been a natural avalanche? Or one deliberately set off?

Now the brown, barren canyon walls had eyes. Now they teemed with a life unseen but vividly imagined. As we paddled down the river we surveyed the walls for a trail, for any sign of man. We found none, but, distracted from the discipline of rafting the river, we shot a rapid without scouting it and vaulted sideways into a hole. The raft flipped and threw all four of us into the river.

As I reeled through the underwater turbulence I thought, "Hold on to the paddle," for we were down to two spares. However, when my tumbling ceased and I began to rise to the surface, I thought something else altogether: Was I about to come up to a bullet in the head?

A shadow loomed above me. I reached up, grabbed the up-turned raft's center net, and pulled myself into the black, cavelike air pocket between river and floor. The raft dragged me along swiftly, my legs colliding with submerged rocks. I heard coughing and hacking, some of it my own, some Bzdak's. The sounds caromed eerily off the raft's rubber skin, and at first I didn't realize that he was right next to me.

"You okay?" I asked.

"Yah, yah," he sputtered. He hacked twice to clear water from his air passages. Then, in a hoarse, urgent voice, he asked, "Where is Kate?"

"I don't know."

"Have to get out."

I reached under the tube and groped for the safety line on the outside of the raft. When I found it I went underwater, reluctantly, crossed under the tube, and popped out into daylight, the roar of the rapid, and canyon walls rushing past.

"Quickly up!" Chmielinski yelled from the top of the raft and extended a hand over to grab me.

Bzdak surfaced next to me. "Where is Kate?" he yelled.

"Up!" Chmielinski yelled back. He hauled me aboard, then Bzdak. When we had climbed onto the raft Bzdak asked again, more urgently than before, *"Where is Kate?"*

"There!" Chmielinski said. He pointed upstream, to the heart of the rapid, where a small round object was spinning around in the hole. Durrant's head. Truran, who had worked his way upstream in the slower water along the right bank, kayaked into the froth, grabbed her, turned, and raced down to us. We paddled the raft behind a boulder and then, nerves jangling, yanked and tugged with our remaining rope until we righted it.

Biggs and Odendaal caught up with us a few minutes later. "Everyone all right?" Biggs asked. Our murmurs of assent were hardly emphatic. "Then we best move as quickly as we can," he said. Odendaal said nothing, but he was smirking.

At the next rapid he spilled out of his boat and took a bad swim, and Truran, Chmielinski, Durrant, Bzdak, and I did a little smirking of our own.

Though the river was thick with fourth- and fifth-class rapids, that day we ran more of them than we usually did, and the few we lined we lined as quickly as we could. We ate lunch furtively, in a hidden, rock-walled nook, wondering if we had outrun our attackers, if we were safe. "I know I risk my life in my kayak," Truran said, eating quickly from a can of tuna, "but at least I have some control over the situation. The river's not an *aggressor.*"

Having entered the Red Zone, we assumed that the men who had attacked us that morning were members of the Sendero Luminoso. Over beers in Cuzco we had joked about the war between the government and the Senderistas, as the movement's members are called, but none of us had taken it very seriously. In my notes I had commented only on the "poetic symmetry" to be found in the political history of the Apurimac canyon, whose rugged natural boundaries had protected the fledgling Inca state, formed one critical flank of Vilcabamba, spawned Tupac Amaru II, and now nurtured Peru's bloodiest uprising since she won her independence from Spain in 1824.

We were not alone in our ignorance. In the nearly six years since the morning in 1980 when the guerrillas had announced their war of revolution by hanging dead dogs from lampposts in Lima (to protest China's treatment of the Gang of Four), Peruvian authorities had failed to penetrate the group. The guerrillas had volunteered almost nothing about themselves, publishing in that time only three pithy communiqués. They were regarded as the fiercest and most uncompromising of the myriad guerrilla factions then operating in South America. The movement is the brainchild of Abimael Guzman Reynoso, who came to the National University of San Cristobal in Ayacucho (as it happens, Quechua for "corner of corpses") in 1962 as an assistant professor of philosophy and founded the Sendero Luminoso a few years later. He is believed to have spent time in China in the mid-sixties and to have returned to Ayacucho convinced that Mao's revolution could be replicated in Peru. Considered a brilliant, scholarly man, he built a strong following at the university, and by 1968 Senderistas were running the administration. Guzman, the director of personnel, instructed his supporters to learn Quechua and to spread the Maoist doctrine in the rural highlands. He went underground in 1978 and has not been seen since.

By 1985 Peruvian intelligence estimated the guerrillas' numbers at two to four thousand armed soldiers and as many as fifteen thousand sympathizers, mostly rural Quechua in the highland departments of Ayacucho and Apurimac. At least six thousand people had died as a direct consequence of the war.

The Red Zone, which was under martial law, included most of the Apurimac canyon below the Pampas confluence. In late 1985, shortly before we began our navigation of the river, Peru's minister of war announced that 80 percent of the Red Zone had been pacified and that the Senderistas had been isolated. Almost no one we spoke with in Peru believed this. The popular belief was that the conflict was intensifying, and that support for the guerrillas had spread nationwide. It appeared to be particularly strong in Lima, which in the year before we arrived had suffered over a thousand bombings. (Government figures would later show the hostilities claimed more than three thousand lives over the next year.)

As could be expected, the government maintained that the guerrillas were thugs and that they recruited mainly through intimidation and terror. According to the *New York Times*, however, a confidential national police report said that while one-third of the conflict's victims could be described as "communist terrorists" and two-thirds as "civilians," few were soldiers or police. This was a strong suggestion that many of the war's atrocities were perpetrated not by the guerrillas but by agents of the state. Indeed, according to the report, most relatives who had witnessed abductions attributed them to national security forces. Several mass graves found in the Andes in 1984 held bodies later identified as those of people who had last been seen being detained by the police or military. According to a United Nations report, there were more "disappearances" in Peru in 1983 and 1984 than in Chile during the first six years of the Pinochet government. The worst abuses occurred in those rural areas controlled by the Peruvian marines, including the Red Zone.

For their part, in a rare public statement released in 1986, the Senderistas claimed responsibility for "more than thirty thousand actions in six years of popular war, five thousand actions each year, more than thirteen military actions daily. Every two hours, somewhere in Peru, there is a military attack."

After lunch we resumed our travels at a furious pace, until, in mid-afternoon, we encountered a rapid that Chmielinski thought imprudent to run without scouting. We stopped the raft at a small beach on the right bank. While Bzdak and Durrant stayed with the boat, Chmielinski and I scurried through the cactus along the bank. We climbed a boulder and spotted the kayakers waiting in the calm water below the rapid, gesturing frantically for us to come ahead. Something was wrong.

I turned and ran for the raft.

As I leapt past Durrant and Bzdak, into the boat, two men

charged from the bush. One of them held a submachine gun, the other what to my untrained eye looked like an ancient carbine.

Machine Gun was dead silent, but Rifleman screamed wildly, put his gun to Bzdak's head, and demanded the raft's lead line. Chmielinski stepped out from behind a boulder, hand outstretched as if to shake, but Machine Gun trained his weapon on him and Rifleman confiscated his watch and hunting knife.

"We are the Shining Path," Rifleman yelled, as if challenging us to do something about it. Barefoot, wearing camouflage baseball hats, torn khaki fatigues, and holey soccer jerseys rolled up over hairless bellies, both men looked far more like working *campesinos* than a crack military cadre.

A dozen men emerged from the bush, several armed, all wearing the same sort of patchwork rags.

Machine Gun spoke for the first time. "Have you heard of us?" he asked.

"Yes," Chmielinski said.

Machine Gun smiled and nodded to Rifleman. Then he turned back to Chmielinski and said, "Our captain attacked your camp this morning."

Speaking Spanish in a low, easy voice, Chmielinski said, "We are not soldiers. We are not here to harm you." He said that we were of more use to them as propaganda than as corpses, and that they should let us go.

Machine Gun, to whom the other men clearly deferred, appeared willing to be persuaded. He, Rifleman, and Chmielinski climbed the bank and sat down, out of earshot of the raft.

Durrant, Bzdak, and I remained on the raft, its nose drawn up on the beach. I sat in the back left corner, Durrant in front of me, Bzdak in the right front. Another guerrilla held the lead line. Bzdak asked him if he had heard the score of the Peru-Chile World Cup soccer game that was to have been held that day.

"Soccer [*fútbol*] is an American capitalist plot," he said.

Three young women and six small children emerged from the bush. Giggling and blushing, the women approached the raft. Unlike the men, they wore traditional Quechua clothing—woven skirts and blouses—accented by gaudy plastic earrings. One carried a transistor radio tuned to a Cuzco station playing Andean folk music. Shyly, she offered the radio to Durrant. After Durrant indicated that she enjoyed the music, they negotiated an exchange of earrings. Emboldened by the trade, two of the women reached down and felt Durrant's breasts. ("To see if I were made from the same model," she said later.)

A solemn boy of perhaps ten surveyed all this from shore while fondling a haftless shiv and staring at me with what I could not help but regard as a warrior's eyes. After a few minutes, several very old women walked out of the bush. And then the whole scene seemed cockeyed. On the one hand, it was hard to believe these men would butcher us in front of their mothers, wives, and children. On the other hand, by what could I gauge the ridiculous? The entire history of this region was drenched with senseless bloodshed.

Then I heard someone yell, in rough Spanish, "I am a communist! I am a communist!" I turned to see Odendaal standing twenty yards down the bank with his hands over his head. Nervously, Rifleman signaled him to sit down across from Chmielinski.

Minutes later Chmielinski hurried down the bank, into the raft, and dug for papers that identified him and Bzdak as Polish citizens.

"What's up?" I whispered.

"Stay on the raft," he said under his breath. "If they find out we have an American with us I think we are in big trouble."

Chmielinski returned to his negotiations. The boy with the knife climbed aboard the raft. I handed him a paddle. He maneuvered the tethered raft up and down the bank, his eyes wide and pinned to mine, his mouth firm and serious. Satisfied, he thanked me. He walked away with the grim pride of a man who had confronted the enemy on the enemy's turf.

Suddenly Rifleman jumped up and started shouting at Chmielinski and waving his gun.

Durrant whispered, "I feel like I'm reading a novel about myself."

As Chmielinski later explained it, when he had handed Machine

Gun his and Bzdak's papers, he had delivered a line that usually worked magic in Peru. He had said that he was from the same country as the Pope. *Big* mistake. Rifleman had been on a team that had attempted to assassinate *El Papa* when he had visited Peru.

When Rifleman cooled down, Chmielinski started again. From time to time Odendaal appeared to say something. The discussion continued for about an hour or so. Finally, Chmielinski led Machine Gun and Rifleman down to the raft, Odendaal following.

Machine Gun said that they would let us go, but they wanted a donation.

Rifleman asked about Durrant's sturdy waterproof watch, which had hands but no numerals. Bzdak explained that to use the watch, one had to approximate the time, divide by four, add the quotient to . . . Rifleman no longer desired the watch.

We undid our bags. Chmielinski extracted our fishing net, with which we had caught not a single trout. Machine Gun nodded in appreciation and accepted it. But when Chmielinski withdrew the film crew's boom microphone, Machine Gun's eyes widened and Rifleman raised his gun. Slowly, coolly, Chmielinski mimed its function. Machine Gun and Rifleman relaxed.

"Fish," Rifleman said. Chmielinski had agreed to give him five cans from our stores. I removed them from the food box.

"Six cans," Rifleman said.

"Five cans," Chmielinski said, with surprising vehemence.

"Six."

"We agreed on five. That is what I will give you."

"Give him six!" Durrant hissed.

Chmielinski stood firm. I thought I would faint. I could not see the wisdom of getting shot over a can of tuna.

Rifleman accepted the five cans. He smiled. Machine Gun smiled. We smiled. We shook hands all around. Machine Gun gave Odendaal a poster of their presidential candidate. And then we closed up our bags, tied them under the net, jumped in the boat, and paddled like hell for that big rapid, which we then ran without scouting. Once into the flat water below it we stroked for all we were worth. We did not look back.

Below the rapid the river bent sharply left and delivered us into a translucent mist. Twenty minutes later the mist lifted, unveiling, to left and right, mountainsides covered with rain forest. The air, an hour before dry and brittle, now hung thick and moist and pungent with balsam. Parrots and parakeets sounded off overhead, and above them circled two hawks. Brown balls that looked like oversized coconuts revealed themselves to be monkeys as they looped through broad, leafy trees and swirling liana vines. We had emerged from the land of the dead.

In the flat water Odendaal paddled ahead of us, and an hour after sunset we found him, Truran, and Biggs in their kayaks, hidden behind a rock. With the kayakers in the lead, our fleet drifted silently under the light of the rising half-moon until Biggs spotted a creek protected by a rock wall. We pitched camp on a high sandbar near a grotto bursting with tropical ferns. Chmielinski cooked dinner, but when he started to serve it by candlelight we put the candles out immediately. Better to spill our stew than to make ourselves easy targets for a sniper.

As we sat in the darkness and ate, Odendaal gave his version of the Sendero confrontation. After instructing Biggs and Truran to kayak ahead in search of help, he said, he had sacrificed his own safety to race back to the guerrilla camp and offer himself as a hostage if the guerrillas would set the rest of us free. He believed that he had rescued us.

Chmielinski, of course, did not remember it this way. Later, he told me that the guerrillas had referred to Odendaal as "that crazy guy." Whatever the case, Odendaal's return to the guerrilla camp had been bold but unneccesary, and he did not fully comprehend the gravity of the situation—though he knew that our captors were something called "Sendero Luminoso," he believed they were unrelated to "the violence that exists elsewhere in Peru." The explanation that seemed better to fit the facts of his behavior was Truran's: The memory of his partner's tragic death on the Limpopo

River drove Odendaal to seek redemption through feats of bravado that he interpreted as heroic.

After dinner we stood watch through the night in one-hour shifts. Each lookout wore Chmielinski's rescue whistle, which he was supposed to blow loudly at the first hint of strange activity. At the sound of the whistle Biggs and Truran, who slept with their kayaks in a place removed from the main camp and close to the river, would sneak away and paddle through the night until they could find help.

Bzdak and Durrant kept a two-hour watch together and shook me awake at eleven o'clock.

"Kate thinks every shadow is a Sendero," Bzdak whispered.

Durrant said, "It's creepy."

I took up my position atop the rock wall. The river gurgled at my back, and on the slope facing me fireflies illuminated the shadowy slanting bush. As I stared at those flickering dots I thought, *Is that one there a bug? A match? A candle? A flashlight? Why does it continue to flash in the same place?*

At midnight I went to Odendaal's tent.

"François," I whispered.

He jumped up and shouted, "All right all right! Everything okay! No worries!"

When he was fully awake and had quieted down I said, "Your watch."

Then I retired. At 4 a.m. Chmielinski said softly, "Joe," and left a mug of hot coffee at my tent.

About noon the next day we landed at the marine outpost of Lechemayo, across the river from the charred remains of what had been a settlement called Villa Virgen. Two dozen shirtless, crewcut young men in khaki pants stared at us from the bank. When we beached they brought bananas and pineapples and beer. The garrison commander, an older, serious man, was not happy to see us. We were in the Red Zone without permission, and he had trouble swallowing Chmielinski's description of how we had descended the river. No boats that he had seen could handle the Apurímac above

Lechemayo. At first he was suspicious when we said we had not met any guerrillas, but then his face cracked in a lurid grin. "You were lucky," he said. "Last week they hanged five civilians up there."

Below Lechemayo new rivers entered the Apurimac every mile or so. The Great Speaker swelled and picked up speed, but she ran smooth and deep. Her voice fell to a whisper. Every few miles on either bank crude log watchtowers loomed over the thick green canopy. Rural irregulars used them in the campaign against the guerrillas, but I was certain they were also useful to protect the dozens of coca-bush plots we now began to see. They were everywhere, not hidden at all, planted in hundred-square-foot patches carved out of the bush, their bright greasy leaves twinkling in the sun like green coins.

We arrived at Luisiana the day after Lechemayo. Although there is a small village there, Luisiana was, or had been, better known as a cacao plantation and resort hotel run by a godfatherlike figure, or *patrón*, named Pepe Parodi. We found a state of riotous entropy. The guerrillas had bombed the guts out of Luisiana. Its gardens and patios and swimming pool were cratered and charred, the resort compound overrun with jungle vegetation. Pepe Parodi had fled to Lima. All that remained of any consequence was a small distillery run by a shifty-eyed *mestizo* who offered to sell a bottle of what the label described as "Luisiana Brandy" but tasted like cheap cane alcohol.

The *mestizo* did grant us permission to camp in a mud patch near the mouth of the stream that carried the village's refuse into the Apurimac. The night was clear, but the stars, veiled by jungle humidity, lacked the brilliance they had displayed in the high Andes. We built a bonfire and Odendaal called a meeting.

We had planned to pick up four sea kayaks some two hundred and fifty miles farther down the river, in the village of Atalaya. Leon would be bringing them there by jungle plane. Three of these boats were to be manned by Odendaal, Biggs, and Chmielinski. Because we were so far behind schedule (at least two months), Truran had no choice but to leave the expedition to return to

England for what would probably be his last shot at a berth on the British national team. Nor did he have any great desire to paddle the flat water. There had been a tacit agreement that I would use the fourth kayak if I wanted to. Chmielinski did not want to be isolated on the river with Biggs and Odendaal and had strongly urged me to paddle the fourth boat, as had Truran, Bzdak, and Durrant.

There in the Luisiana mud, however, Odendaal announced that he was changing the plan. He would not allow me to kayak the first leg of flat water below Atalaya. Instead, Bzdak, Durrant, and I, together with Leon when he rejoined us, would form what Odendaal called a "free-lance" team. We would be on our own. However, if we were able to move ourselves and the extra kayak the four hundred miles from Atalaya to Pucallpa in time to rendezvous with Odendaal, Biggs, and Chmielinski, I would then be permitted to paddle the fourth boat. Odendaal gave as his reasoning that if I kayaked that first leg, I would slow the river team.

"Why don't you give Joe a chance?" Truran said. "Let him paddle from Atalaya to Pucallpa. If he can keep up, you haven't broken his journey. If he can't keep up, take him off the river in Pucallpa."

"No," Odendaal said.

"He has an opportunity to be the first North American to travel the entire Amazon under his own steam," Truran said. "That would be a real feather in the cap for this expedition."

"I am acting in the best interests of this expedition," Odendaal said.

"Speed has nothing to do with it, François," Durrant said. "You are the slowest person here at everything you do. You are acting out of personal animosity. You don't want anybody on the river now but you and Tim."

"This is what the expedition needs," Odendaal said, his voice rising. "It has nothing to do with my personal feelings."

"We help you through the bad water," Bzdak said. "Now you are going to push us out."

Odendaal denied this.

"Your plan is for the benefit of François Odendaal," Truran said, "not for the benefit of this expedition."

Odendaal exploded. "This is my expedition!" he yelled.

"This expedition belongs to all of us!" Chmielinski shouted back. "We are all working. You, me, all of us."

The atmosphere was so tense that we ignored the headlights that had suddenly sliced through the night. Jeep doors opened and shut and we were surrounded by Peruvian marines who trained their weapons on us. A young captain demanded our passports. He studied them for several minutes while his men searched our tents. Satisfied, he smiled. "There is a curfew at six o'clock," he said. "If you leave your camp, you will be shot on sight." Then he wished us a safe journey and left with his men.

When the marines were gone Durrant asked Odendaal, "Are you saying that you can remove an expedition member at your whim? For no reason other than that you are in a bad mood?"

"Yes!" Odendaal said. He glared at her. "If I so choose I can remove *two* people!"

"So Joe goes now," Truran said, "and then Kate and Zbyszek, and then Piotr. And then it's just you and Tim."

When Odendaal did not respond, Truran continued. "I don't think the question here is how fast someone can or cannot paddle the river," he said. "The real question is whether François Odendaal is fit to lead this expedition."

"Are you saying you have no confidence in me?" Odendaal asked angrily.

"Yes," Truran said.

Odendaal leapt to his feet. "Then that is the question!" He turned to the rest of us. The fire glinted off the underside of his face, throwing it into reverse shadow. "Do the rest of you agree with Jerome?" he demanded. "Do you? Do *you?*"

"What do you want, François?" Durrant said.

"I demand a vote! I demand to know exactly what each of you thinks of me!"

"Then you are asking us to commit ourselves either for or against you," she said.

"I will not leave here tomorrow without a vote!"

"And if we vote against you," Bzdak said, "then you will try to throw us out any way you can."

"I give my solemn vow that if the vote goes against me, I will turn the leadership of this expedition, and all its remaining resources, over to whomever you select to replace me."

Tim Biggs quietly tended the fire and kept his peace.

"François," Chmielinski said, "do you know what you are doing?"

"Jerome!" Odendaal shouted.

"Frans," Biggs said, "maybe this isn't the time."

"I will be damned," Odendaal shouted, "if I will go down this river with an expedition that does not want me as its leader!"

"Then let it be," Biggs said. He sounded tired, resigned to the inevitable.

"Jerome!" Odendaal shouted again, pointing a finger at Truran.

"No confidence!" Truran shouted back.

"Joe!"

"No confidence!"

"Tim!"

"Yes. Confidence."

"Zbyszek!"

"I vote no."

"Kate!"

"Really, François," she said. "This is childish. Be reasonable."

"How do you vote!"

"Don't make me do this. We're in this together. We don't want to remove anybody."

"Confidence or no confidence?"

"All right, then. If you intend to remove Joe, no confidence."

"Piotr!"

"Frans!" Biggs yelled.

"Piotr!"

"François," Chmielinski said, "you do not understand what you have done."

It appeared to be true. Odendaal looked from one to another of us with a blank stare. Either he did not comprehend what had just happened ("He hadn't done his sums," Truran would say later), or he was startled to find his bluff called. Even without Chmielinski, the vote was four to one. He was out.

Biggs jumped up and stood between his friend and the fire, shielding him from the rest of us.

"Look, why don't we leave this until the morning?" he said. He smiled nervously. "Everyone needs a good night's sleep. What do you say, mates? Let's do this in the morning, eh?"

He led Odendaal away from the fire, into the darkness.

Biggs was on breakfast duty the next morning. Before we ate he asked for a prayer.

"It's Sunday," he said. "The day we speak with our God. If we ever needed his help, we do now."

"Tim," Truran said, "it's Saturday."

Biggs said his prayer nonetheless, and we ate in silence, scratching at mosquito bites, until Odendaal spoke.

"There will be no vote," he said. "Last night I failed to consult with my co-leaders. By putting myself in a position to be removed as leader, I abrogated my agreement with them. Anyone who has a problem with my leadership may speak to me about it in Atalaya. I will permit Joe to kayak from there. When we reach Pucallpa, we will decide if he shall continue."

"Who will decide?" Truran asked.

"I will," Odendaal said. Then he excused himself, saying that the *mestizo* had promised him a bottle of brandy. He walked up the mud beach to the ruined estate.

When Odendaal was gone, Biggs said, "That was really a courageous thing Frans did last night. He really put himself on the line."

"Courageous?" Durrant said. "You call that courage? He flushed us out, and when he lost, he went back on his word. It was the height of cowardice."

"We voted, Zulu," Bzdak said. "He lost. He is out."

"That's it, Tim," Truran said.

Biggs was solemn. "If you throw Frans over, a stink will settle on this whole expedition. I don't want any part of it."

"It stinks now," Durrant said. "It has to change."

Biggs saw Odendaal returning, ran along the beach, and stopped him before he reached camp. Truran joined them. He told Odendaal that we were prepared to stick by our vote.

When Odendaal sat down with the rest of us his eyes were vacant and his face ashen. He spoke slowly and would not look at anyone.

"It is apparent," he said, "that this expedition no longer trusts me. I understand that you intend to remove me as leader, and that my word is no longer enough to maintain my position. I don't want to end this expedition, and I don't see a way to divide it cleanly. I apologize to Joe and to each of you who feels I have plotted against you." He said that if we would allow him to remain as leader he would agree "not to put my personal goals ahead of the expedition's."

No one spoke. After a few moments I realized that the others were watching me as if to say, right now you have the most to lose, so what do you want to do? But the looks on their faces were undeniable. Nobody had the energy for any more fighting, not then, not in that suppurating mud patch, not with the marines peering over our shoulders, not with all we'd been through over the last few days.

"It's fine with me if you call yourself the leader," I told Odendaal, "if you'll agree to open your decisions to veto by simple majority vote."

"I'll do whatever you want."

"That sounds fair to me," Biggs said, and the others agreed. At Odendaal's request we put the agreement into writing and signed it.

When we had finished Odendaal walked over to me and shook my hand. I was amazed. For such a proud man, his was an enormous effort.

"One day," he said, "we will laugh about how stupid we have been."

I said that I hoped we would do just that.

An hour later we all stood in the mud and jungle heat and said good-byes. Odendaal and Biggs, who had yet to secure Brazilian visas, would kayak the two hundred and fifty miles to Atalaya ahead of us and try to establish communication with the consular offices in Lima. We would meet them in Atalaya in a week to ten days. We wished them luck. Then they mounted their boats and paddled into the heart of the current, Biggs tense and alert, Odendaal listless and glassy-eyed.

Two hours later, the raft packed, the kayak tied to the stern, Bzdak, Durrant, Chmielinski, Truran, and I set off.

Returning to the river was like coming home from a bad vacation. The tropical heat was blistering and the humidity a dead weight, but after the turmoil of Luisiana we found it immensely relaxing to drift back into the bosom of wild country. That evening we camped on a long, clean beach, its glistening white sand warm late into the night. Across the river, throwing down a gentle chorus of birdsong and cicada buzz, the forest rose in a green wall of broad leaves and snaky vines so dense it looked like a single plant. Behind our camp, bushy hills climbed through a skirt of clouds to a high ridge. White puffballs hung above the ridgetop, and when the sun dropped between cloud and mountain, the sky lit up crimson, violet, and gold. It was the first real sunset we had seen in six weeks.

A post-catharsis peace reigned in camp. Truran cooked, Bzdak read, Durrant and I bathed in the cool Apurimac, here emerald green, fifty yards wide, and running smoothly but so swiftly that to stay abreast of camp I had to swim against the current as hard as I could. Chmielinski, reviewing his hand-drawn maps, looked up and said, "Something is wrong here." He paused, then concluded, "Ah—François gone. No one is watching who I am talking to."

Later, sitting around the fire while Truran dished out beef burgundy, we tried to decide what exactly had happened at Luisiana, and what we would do next. None of us believed the confrontation with Odendaal had been our last, not with almost thirty-eight hundred miles of river still to run. We agreed that one reason

Odendaal behaved as he did was his insecurity with his role as the expedition leader and with the river itself. "He hates the river," Truran said. "He wants to have done it, but not to do it." He also said that it would be a mistake for us to trust Odendaal's word. "He's an Afrikaner, you know, and they have a tendency to destroy anything that doesn't work according to their terms."

Chmielinski seconded this, and added that while he had once considered Odendaal a smart man shackled by an inability to control his emotions, he now considered him simply "stupid." He thought the best thing to do would be to humor Odendaal until we gained control of the remaining expedition supplies.

Durrant ventured that Odendaal might benefit from "positive reinforcement," but added that "he started this trip in a better position than any of us to get on well, and step by step he has squandered those advantages."

Bzdak was blunt and succinct: "The river has broken him."

I did not trust Odendaal, but I did consider my own insecurities similar to his. In fact, that afternoon, just before he left Luisiana, we had sat by ourselves and had a brief talk, an attempt at hatchet burying. He had agreed when I said that we were alike, that we had both arrived in Peru unsure of ourselves. He had been worried about his ability to lead an expedition of such magnitude; I had lacked confidence in my ability to fit in with a group of strangers, and to travel the river and write about the experience.

And deep down in my stomach, the place where, as a child, I had believed my soul could be found, burned the knowledge that what I despised in others was that which I feared in myself. Looking over my notes a little later, I found an entry made during the Cachora-to-Triunfo run, after Odendaal had taken a bad swim. "Admit it—a certain satisfaction watching FO bloodied—this is ugly stuff." It confirmed that I was capable of exactly what I detested most about Odendaal, the pleasure he seemed to take from the suffering of those with whom he shared a common purpose. As the wise old French admiral says in *Lord Jim*, "One talks, one talks, but at the end of the reckoning one is no cleverer than the next man, and no more brave."

11 *The Ene*

Chmielinski and Truran insisted that I use the Luisiana-to-Atalaya leg to get in shape to paddle a sea kayak. They designed a regimen that kept me in Truran's white-water boat for an hour the first day, two hours the second, three the third, and so on. In theory, when we finished the ten-day run to Atalaya I'd be able to sit in the kayak all day. Meanwhile, they, Bzdak, and Durrant paddled the raft and amused themselves by jeering at my efforts, mocking my fear, and fishing me out of the cool brown Apurimac.

The kayak terrified me. It wasn't much longer than I, and compared to the lumbering raft it seemed a tippy, skittish insect. The raft rode above the river, but the kayak sat right down in it and vibrated with the rumble of distant rapids long before my ear picked them up. Also, I found myself utterly incapable of judging the river's myriad new currents. The rapids were smaller than the upper Apurimac's, but the river was pocked with frothy white *remolinos*, or whirlpools, up to forty feet wide, with outer lips that rose as much as four feet above their vortex eyes. My bladder gauge said these could easily swallow a kayak.

Drowning was my most immediate concern, but I had others. According to Durrant and Truran my most serious problems on the three-thousand-five-hundred-mile haul from Atalaya to the sea would be fatigue and tenisinivitis (a painful, debilitating inflammation of the tendon sheaths in the wrist). The only cures for tenisinivitis are complete rest for six weeks or surgery. To prevent it, one must learn to wield a paddle properly, but as with paddling the raft, proper technique is the opposite of instinct.

To simplify gravely, the key to manipulating the quarter-turn, two-bladed paddle is to regard the arms as fulcrums. For example, to execute a left stroke, one does not pull the blade toward the body with the left hand. Rather, one extends the left arm, hand loosely gripping the paddle shaft, pushes with the right hand from the waist forward, and at the end of the stroke retracts the left arm.

Repeatedly, I found myself concentrating so hard on technique that I forgot to look where I was going, only to discover myself hurtling toward a whirlpool, a bank, or a boulder. I then tossed technique to the wind and paddled furiously. Too often the result recalled my first time on ice skates, when my eyes, frozen in fear, had locked on the skating-rink wall even as I slammed into it.

One soggy accident built on another, and I couldn't help thinking, as I hauled myself back into the kayak: Three thousand five hundred miles of *this?*

"Tell yourself two things," an exasperated Truran said to me again and again. "Don't tighten your fingers on the paddle, and think *push*, not *pull*."

"You will have a lot of time to practice," Bzdak yelled from his safe perch on the raft, and laughed in his squeaky way. He enjoyed my flailings immensely and teased me without mercy until the day I called him a talking *pierogi* (a sort of ravioli I had once eaten in a Polish restaurant). He was stupefied: "Where did you learn this word?"

Late in the afternoon that first day out of Luisiana I heard Chmielinski shout. I looked up from my paddling to see the raft about a hundred yards downstream. Chmielinski was standing up, his hands cupped into a megaphone.

"Joe, what is that?" He pointed toward what appeared to be a half-submerged rock in the reeds along the left bank.

I paddled out of the main current, toward the rock. A vulture had perched on it but took flight just before I banged the rock with my paddle. It felt as if I had struck a heap of wet rags. Only then, shocked, did I focus on the blue feet bulging through sandal straps, the swollen gray thighs, the oozing hole that had once been a stomach, the torn gold sweater and crimson chest, the pecked-away face framed by black hair.

Choking back nausea, I turned and paddled downstream as fast as I could.

"It was a body," I said when I caught up with the raft.

"Anyone we know?" Truran asked.

"I don't think so. It looked Peruvian."

Shaking, I tied up the kayak, climbed aboard the raft, and made myself a nest amid the food bags in the center. I lay down and shut my eyes. A couple of hours later we stopped at a marine checkpoint, but the lieutenant greeted the news of the corpse with no more concern than he would that of a dead dog. He did not even ask where we had seen it.

San Francisco, the largest settlement on the Apurimac, consists of a score of one-story buildings of wood and cement and a boxlike marine headquarters. If San Francisco were in the high country it might be quaint, all whitewashed colonial architecture and cobble-stone streets, but the jungle eats the quaint, and San Francisco is not so much a town as a slum. The two main streets are mud, the buildings are dank, moldy, and starkly industrial in design, and the people look tired and defeated.

About fifty locals gathered around the raft the afternoon we arrived. They were loud, as if noise could hold back the encroaching jungle rot, but they seemed more bored than mean, their lethargy the weariness of the besieged—San Francisco sits well within the Red Zone, at the end of a jagged dirt road that winds down out of the mountains from Ayacucho, fifty miles southwest.

"Hey, Whitey, you want to buy some marijuana?" a grizzled *mestizo* yelled out, his T-shirt identifying him as a member of the "California Yatch Club" [sic]. Another man urged us to sample his "*oro blanco*" or white gold—cocaine.

Leaving the others to guard the boat, Chmielinski went to register with the base commander, and I investigated the marketplace. Not since Cuzco, a month earlier, had I had the opportunity to shop for fresh food. Now that simple act overwhelmed me. Blindly, without bothering to haggle over prices, I grabbed lentils, tomatoes, onions, garlic, carrots, parsley, bananas, ginger, chilies, evaporated milk, cooking oil, *avena* "Quaker," cinnamon, a plastic pail for water and one for a lunch bucket, a machete, and, with First Mate Bzdak in mind, three bottles of *pisco* and a case of beer.

Exhausted, I shouldered my treasure and walked into the street. I heard a loud epithet and turned to find myself face-to-face with a dozen rifle barrels—I had wandered right into a marine flag-raising ceremony. I walked another block and sat down in the shade. A burro stopped and stared at me and unleashed a superb volume of urine, then galloped up the street scattering women and children. A dwarf and a young boy with a deformed right leg chased the beast. The boy wobbled like a bowling pin until he slipped and fell in the urine puddle.

When Chmielinski found me we hauled our supplies down to the river. The crowd had doubled in size and pressed in on the boat. A drunk lunged for Durrant, she whacked him with her paddle, soldiers dragged the man away. We departed as fast as we could.

We lost sole possession of the river at San Francisco, where the Ayacucho road crosses a bridge (the first on the river below Cunyac, and the last until the Atlantic) and slops to a muddy end. At that point the traffic has no choice but to slide into the river itself, where it is serviced by a fleet of ragged boats often called *yonsins*, or Johnsons, after the Swedish manufacturer of the outboard motors of choice in the area.

The dorylike Johnsons are designed to traverse the broad whirlpools and flat but deceptively strong rapids of the lower Apurimac and the Ene River, which begins thirty-five miles below San Francisco. The typical boat is about forty feet long but only a couple of feet wide, with a shallow draft and low gunwales that rise barely to the hips of the seated and invariably terrified passengers. Studied from a distance, a Johnson beating along the river looks like an enormous motorized pencil.

Near the right bank, where the current was weakest, a Johnson lumbered upstream. It veered toward us. A shirtless man balanced like a bowsprit at the top of the prow, his brown chest bared and thrust into the wind on this bright, suffocatingly humid day. He held a thin pole about twelve feet long and studied the river intently. Behind him, strung along the boat one by one, sat the sort of farrago one expects to see on a Peruvian bus: dark little men in bright straw hats and gaudy shirts, fat women with chickens clutched snugly in the laps of their crisp white-cotton church dresses, children half-naked, goats in harnesses, drums of kerosene and gasoline, bushels of bananas and pineapples.

The Johnson chugged alongside our raft. A second bare-chested man sat at the stern, working twin forty-horse outboards. His nonchalant expression contrasted sharply with the looks of lugubrious determination on the faces of his passengers, who were not happy to be bouncing around in the middle of the river. They were bound for church—this was Sunday—but not at all sure they'd arrive. The boat's utter lack of life preservers was a matter of economics, not confidence.

"Where are you going?" Bowsprit shouted.

"Brazil!" Chmielinski shouted back. "To where the river ends!"

At this a great cheer erupted from the Johnson, and the worried faces gave way to gap-toothed grins that said, Now *there* is a ship of fools! We had painted our noses and cheeks white with zinc oxide against the sun, and for insect armor we wore our black-and-gray-striped, chain-gang long underwear. With his loud red bandana tied over his head Bzdak looked like a gypsy, and Truran had fashioned a garish, sun-blocking nose plate from cardboard and silver duct tape. Durrant wore a bathing suit, unheard of on the river, and all four men sported scraggly beards. We were a motley crew, if not a disgusting one, but the locals waved and wished us luck. As we did them, in the sincere belief that at this moment, with the Johnson beginning to climb the rapid we had just descended, their cause was the needier. The men clutched their hats, the women clutched their chickens, and their faces reverted to that mask of hardened resignation.

The pilot attacked the rapid head-on. Water gushed up and over the low gunwales. The propellers jumped out of the water and the pilot gunned all eighty *caballos* to no avail—the blades caught only air and foam. The boat stalled, the river beat on it, Bowsprit planted his pole and struggled to drive the boat forward. He failed. The frantic pilot maneuvered to keep his nose straight in the rapid—if he went broadside the boat would capsize immediately— and the passengers screamed.

Slowly, however, the prop caught water, gained fragile purchase, held its own. Bowsprit strained mightily. The Johnson earned a foot, four feet, ten feet. Then it burst through the top of the rapid and another great cheer rose up and the boat hurtled toward San Francisco, Bowsprit silhouetted defiantly against the wind.

The knowledge that such everyday heroics, and heroic tragedies, are part of the river's rhythm should have put my struggles with the tiny kayak in context, but pain has a way of destroying perspective. The day we left San Francisco I managed two hours in the cursed thing, and got out of it in a state of extreme discomfort. The vessel offered no back support, and, with my legs crammed into the hull, I could not move at all. When Durrant said she was not feeling well, and fashioned herself a sickbed atop the food bags, I gladly tied the kayak to the raft's stern and took her position at left-front paddle.

It was the first time I had worked that part of that boat. I asked Bzdak for advice.

"Best thing," that veteran long-distance paddler said in a low whisper, "is take it easy." He had perfected a grandiose, elegantly inefficient paddling technique, one that required almost no work but gave the appearance, to the ever-vigilant Captain Chmielinski, of extraordinary effort.

An hour later I had the Bzdak Stroke down cold, and sat happily on the raft and watched the jungle slip by. As we pulled away from the smoky outlying huts of San Francisco the vibrantly green bush grew dense and thick. The low jungle wall ran unbroken along the banks, but in the sloping hills beyond it were neat squares of a duller, more orderly green—coca plantations and grazing meadows and the odd banana orchard. Every half hour or so, to break the grip of the incessant tropical sun, we dove into the still cool Apurimac, now a hundred yards wide and running slowly, at perhaps four knots.

At high noon (Chmielinski called out the exact time) we shipped our paddles and dug avocados, cheese, and a pineapple out of the plastic pail stored on the raft's cool floor. After lunch we paddled in shifts, Chmielinski and I working in back while, in front, Bzdak and Truran slept, read, and teased Durrant.

Two hours later we traded places. Chmielinski went immediately to sleep. I, too, started to drift off to the earnest cadence of Truran and Bzdak paddling behind us, their every sharp thrust timed to Truran's authoritative "Stroke!" But after one particularly strenuous sequence I sneaked a glance from under my hat and saw their paddles lying unused on the raft floor. Each man had a beer in hand, and at each count they gave a little jump on the back tube, which felt enough like a stroke to keep Chmielinski slumbering.

About four o'clock the flat green Mantaro River entered from the left, or west, signaling the beginning of the Ene River. In the late afternoon light, the most beautiful of the day, we waved goodbye to the Apurimac, our home those last two months. Above us, puffy cumulus clouds turned gold and crimson, and the sun, on its downward arc, reflected softly off the jungle wall. In midday the bush had been an indecipherable monochrome, a solid block, but at dusk each tree, each vine, each broad plant leaf glowed with its unique shade of green, and the river, as it ambled through that happy republic of foliage, seemed for the first time a gentle place.

Promptly at five we searched the banks for a campsite, soon found a broad, sandy island, and quickly enacted our domestic routine—unload the raft, pitch tents, gather firewood. I took a swim, which included my semiweekly shampoo, and stood naked in the setting sun to dry and marvel at the jungle's fecund splendor. Then into cotton pants and shirt as the *mosquitos* and blackflies came out, and off to the campfire to marvel again, this time at cook-of-the-day Chmielinski's impeccable kitchen: utensils laid out to hand, bowls and spoons and cups in careful rows, coffee poured, dinner simmering away in the stew pot.

"Piotr," Truran asked as we sipped coffee, "have you always been so . . . *neat?*"

Chmielinski thought about this while he cut carrots into the stew. "Yes," he said finally. There had been no choice. He had been raised in a family of nine children, and without order they would have been lost. He added that he had an identical twin brother, and that he had not seen any of his family since he had left Poland in 1979. Then he stopped. "Where is that Zbyszek?" he asked suddenly. "He never misses his coffee."

It rained hard during the night, a dense, tropical rain, and in the morning fog curled upward in soft plumes toward a patchwork-gray sky. A fine mist hung over the water, then swelled to rain.

Late in the day we drifted into a *pongo*, where narrow rock walls compressed the Ene and increased her velocity to about six knots. The river rolled and boiled. The locals called this the *pongo* of the Seven Devils, for the seven furious whirlpools that are said to be capable of swallowing a Johnson. Nervous, flustered, I struggled to master the kayak before meeting the demons. But they were only my fear, and the *pongo* spit me out unscathed.

Below the *pongo* we entered Campa Indian territory. From the left, or northwest, bank of the Ene steep hills clotted with stands of rain forest and open, rolling savanna rise to about five thousand feet. These roadless highlands, called the Gran Pajonal, include some of the least-penetrated areas of Peru, and are inhabited mainly by Asháninka, as the Campa speakers call themselves. The four thousand or so Asháninka who live in the Gran Pajonal's roughly one million acres are one of the last peoples native to the upper Amazon basin who retain to a noticeable degree their traditional ways. In part this is because they were long considered exceptionally savage. Unlike many of their indigenous neighbors, they had the foresight to massacre the early Franciscan missionaries. In fact, in 1740, under the messianic half-breed Juan Santos de Atahuallpa, they drove missionaries completely out of this part of Peru, and the difficult terrain and their fierce reputation kept their territory free of outsiders for the next one hundred and fifty years.

At the turn of the twentieth century, however, the rubber boom brought prospectors flooding into the Amazon, this time armed with sophisticated weaponry. By 1935 the Franciscans had built three missions and an airstrip in the Gran Pajonal, paving the way for colonization after World War Two, particularly by Europeans. The newcomers established themselves along the rivers, which offered the best agricultural land. (Despite the Gran Pajonal's apparent fertility, less than one half of 1 percent is considered arable.)

Many lowland Asháninka have since settled around the white colonies and missions, and though they often display the outward signs of their traditional life—they wear long, dark cotton *cushmas*, paint their faces with bright orange achiote-seed rouge, and draw dark, cat-whisker lines about the eyes, cheeks, and foreheads—they have for the most part built an existence around handouts, odd jobs, canned milk, white rice, and the Christian god. They provide the work force for the colonist farms (according to a Danish anthropologist studying the area, there has been an active trade in Asháninka children, and it is not an uncommon practice to whip an upstart Asháninka with a dried bull's penis), but the intricacies of white law often prevent them from owning land.

Meanwhile, the Peruvian government, faced with an enormous international debt, is anxious to tap the Amazon basin's oil, timber, and minerals, and as part of an ambitious colonization program has encouraged a variety of missionary groups—Roman Catholic, Baptist, and evangelical—to "educate" such native peoples as the Asháninka. Such efforts, however well-intentioned, are devastatingly insidious. Traditionally, the Asháninka lived in small family-group clusters, but as missionaries have gathered and herded them into larger settlements, communicable disease has increased enormously. As, in consequence, have medical clinics manned by people long on the Word but short on real medical ability.

Until recently, the dense forests of the high Gran Pajonal offered refuge for the Asháninka, who continued to survive there by hunting and gathering and slash-and-burn agriculture. As settlers have pushed into the highlands, however, conflicts have naturally increased. It is unlikely that many Asháninka will remain "uncivilized" for more than another generation or two.

The Ene River is considered frontier, although the government has established a beachhead of sorts at the six-shack village of Puerto Prado (store, whorehouse), near the Ene's confluence with the Perené River, at the southern foot of the Gran Pajonal. Judging by the few we met, the *mestizo* colonists who have fled to the Ene from Peru's cities, which are generally horrible, have worked hard literally to carve a life from the virgin bush and cannot afford to look back. Luis, a twenty-six-year-old from the city of Huancayo (his thatch hut was decorated with a Beatles poster), proudly showed us a recently planted grove of avocado seedlings that would not bear fruit for at least four years, assuming floods, insects, and weak soil did not do them in first. "I had more fiestas in the city," he said, "but here I have a future."

Later that same afternoon, after we had pitched camp on the Ene's muddy left bank, I waded up a clear-water creek and met three men who were naked except for their soapsuds. When I asked in Spanish to use their soap they found the question uproariously funny, laughing and poking one another and pointing at me, but in the end they said yes. I lathered up until we shared the same uniform. They were short, dark men with strong, fatless trunks, broad chests, shoulders knotted with muscle, and stubby, slightly bowed legs. With the exception of the thick black growth on their scalps and pubic regions they were completely hairless. One of them reached out and tweaked my chest hairs. I gasped. They laughed again.

The tweaker introduced himself as Mikele. The other two men, who appeared to be his age, were in fact his sons. They said they were Asháninka, and that they had a farm farther up the creek. We dressed—they wore cotton pants cut off at the knees—and hiked to their land.

Mikele and his sons appeared to be prospering. Their three families had cleared and planted about five acres with banana, papaya, pineapple, avocado, lemon, guava, mango, and yucca. (Yucca, or sweet manioc, is to the Asháninka what potatoes are to the Quechua.) Chickens shared the clearing with a pig ripe for butchering. The main building, a large, sturdy log platform, looked like an outdoor stage. A loft had been built at the back and covered with mosquito netting and a thatch roof.

Mikele's youngest son, ten-year-old Jesus, had studied at the Franciscan mission at Puerto Ocopa. "Ow are jew, meester?" he asked me. "Are jew clin?"

Mikele sold me a dozen mangoes, three yucca roots the size of my forearm, and ten eggs. With the money I paid him he would buy salt and kerosene in Satipo, a one-hundred-forty-mile round-trip that would take him three days in his dugout canoe, which was powered by a seven-horse outboard motor. He would have to make the trip within the week. The Ene was rising. In a month the river would be too high to travel, the farm cut off. They would be isolated for three months.

I asked Mikele about the *colonos*.

"Our people have always been near the river, " he said. "There is not much hunting anymore, but the soil here is good. We are doing well. Our farm is big. We are not hungry."

"How do you get along with the whites?"

Mikele smiled. "That is our land, too," he said. "We will let them stay until we need it." As is the custom, he did not wave or say good-bye when I left. Hiking back to our camp, I found myself wondering what he would think of snow, or the ocean.

After two and a half months of river travel we had finally returned to sea level. What a homecoming. The jungle floor was, in a word, wet. Always, everywhere. Mud collected in every dark hole and crevice, wood didn't burn, sweat didn't dry, cuts didn't heal. The acrid odor of jungle rot gained purchase in our clothes, and in the thick jungle humidity the stink simmered and our clothing disintegrated. Sand infested the food, the drinking water, the tents. It wore holes in the raft's rubber skin and rubbed blisters on our shanks.

And, everywhere, bugs: spiders, cockroaches, moths, bees, wasps, ants, chiggers, ticks, and, of course, mosquitoes. They buzzed and hummed around our eyes and ears, bit our feet and ankles, and embedded their greedy little snouts in our skin, which soon erupted in sores that festered constantly. Even the most angelic of these pests, the butterflies, collected in such swarms that they became a nuisance. They descended on the raft hundreds at a time, in vast fluttering clouds, and hung upside down from the bill of my baseball cap.

In an odd way, the troubles we had faced almost daily in the high country—the cold, the altitude, the deadly white water, the guerrillas—had helped keep us going. Progress had been a matter of overcoming immediate and often mortal obstacles. If nothing else, those dangers had focused us. The jungle was a different matter. Entropy is the law of the bush; one wallows in it and slowly sinks. In the soggy jungle funk we grew languid and sluggish. We argued and complained about trivialities: Who should fetch the firewood, what to cook for dinner, when to wake up, how hard to paddle the raft in the slow-running river, where to make camp. We threatened to destroy ourselves by anomie.

"Look, guys," Chmielinski said our third day on the Ene, after some silly squabble. "What are we going to do? We can argue and be rude, or we can learn manners. We can stick to our rules. An expedition is easy when everyone is feeling good. When you are feeling bad, rules tell you what to do. If it is my turn to cook, it does not matter how I feel. I do not have my own life."

"But you must allow for bad luck," Durrant said.

"Luck does not matter. The firewood is wet, there is not enough food, the stove is broken. Does not matter. You must perform your duty."

This was a code Chmielinski had brought with him from the Old World. It had seen him through six years of adventuring in South America, and was reflected even now in the careful attention he paid to every task he performed. As Chmielinski told it, in his Poland everyone had a specific role, a place, well-defined duties within the structures of family and community. In that poor and troubled country one's dignity was found in the performance of those duties.

Chmielinski's was not an attitude I initially endorsed. From my corner of the New World, from my culture of abused abundance, I regarded the preoccupation with duty and manners and pre-scribed social roles as a weapon of the powerful few, the invoking of arcane forms for the purpose of intimidation.

I had to admit, however, that life as I saw it lived in the jungle tended to support Chmielinski's view, at least in a visceral way. The mountain homes of the Quechua had been chaotic affairs, smoky black holes with animals underfoot, entrails drying on the walls, pots and pans and corn husks scattered about. Order had been exter-nal, in the ceaseless *puna*, which rolled on barren and unchanging for as far as the eye could see and the heart could bear to imagine. On the jungle floor, however, domestic life was an exercise in stark minimalism. Home was a platform, four poles, a thatch roof, a hammock, and a mosquito net, surrounded by a rapacious verdant chaos. Every day the jungle had to be chopped back, disciplined, bent to man's order, or the illusion of it.

12 *The Tambo*

Late in the afternoon on our fourth day on the slow green Ene we began to look for Puerto Prado, near which the Ene would join the Perené to form the Tambo River. I let the raft drift ahead and paddled the hundred yards from the middle of the river to the left bank. Two men were fishing with line thick as a pencil.

"How big are the fish here?" I asked one man.

In answer he pointed to his friend. "One of him," he said. They were after *zungaro*, a catfish that can exceed a hundred pounds.

The second man said, "Yesterday we saw two gringos with plastic canoes." Biggs and Odendaal.

"Where is Puerto Prado?" I asked.

"*This* is Puerto Prado." I raced after the raft and caught it just before the Ene bent sharply right and due east. We beached the boats and climbed a small sand-dune island.

There, below us, was an absolute monster of a river—the Perené in full flood, engorged by rainy-season runoff from the central Andes. Roiling, mud brown, flecked with frothy white whirlpools and swirling currents, she charged along at a good ten knots, roaring like gravel falling out of a dump truck and carrying a flotilla of uprooted trees the size of small tugboats. On the far bank, perhaps four hundred yards away, hundred-foot chunks of earth collapsed into the river in silent explosions, taking with them fifty-foot trees that shuddered as they fell.

We made camp there on the dune's crest. The news that Biggs and Odendaal had passed through the day before surprised Chmielinski. "They should be going faster," he said. "Something is not right."

That night the Perené's roar filled the air, making sleep difficult, and as the river meandered ever closer I heard the percussive collapsing of the near bank. By morning our island had shrunk to about two hundred square feet, or a tenth its previous size. On one side the Perené was still in flood, and on the other our once-gentle friend the Ene had overnight become a blustering brown giant chortling along at two to three times her former speed and volume.

Meanwhile, running from the flood, the whole world seemed to have climbed aboard the dune. Under my pants, discarded in the sand the night before, I found a frog the size of an apple flanked by a dozen offspring. A snake slumbered in the raft, lizards crawled among the food bags, and, in the tent Durrant ran screaming from, clutching a towel about her breasts—

"Get out, Zbyszek! There's a huge spider in there!"

"Yah, look this," Bzdak, not fully awake, mumbled from inside the tent. "Lot of small ones, too. I think—I think he reproduced on me!"

Durrant stuck her head back inside and shrieked. "He did! Bloody hell! There's thousands of them!"

"He reproduced pretty good."

On one side the Ene sidled ever closer, from the other issued the continuous thunder of terra no longer firma tumbling into the wild Perené. We loaded the raft quickly and sloppily, tied the unmanned kayak to its stern, and put in at the tip of the island, where the two rivers met.

At first that fast new river was frightening. Though considered a "headwater" of the Amazon, the Tambo is twice the size of the Sacramento, the biggest river in California, and comparable to the mighty Columbia. She would barrel along straight and fast for a quarter mile, lulling us with a bouncy joyride, her rolling boil drumming lightly on the raft's underside and only hinting at the force at work below. Then she would slam into a curve and snap us awake with powerful turbulence and huge whirlpools that surfaced and sucked and disappeared like some kind of carnivorous aquatic giants. We escaped their grasp only by paddling hard to Chmielinski's urgent cadence.

An armada of uprooted trees sailed in and out of the frothy brown devils, some of them chugging along harmlessly, others threatening to puncture the raft with their sharp branches. We parried with our paddles, fending them off as if they were marauding pirates.

By noon, however, we had adjusted to the brown Tambo's charged rhythms, learned to read her swift currents and skirt her voracious whirlpools, and simply by riding her current we traveled faster than at any time since we had stepped off our respective buses in Arequipa, and twice as fast as we had on the Ene.

Chmielinski lashed a paddle to the stern. While one of us worked it like a rudder, the rest drank beer and relaxed. I scribbled in my notebook, Durrant settled onto the food bags and read, Bzdak took pictures and slept, Chmielinski studied his Portuguese Berlitz.

Truran dove into the Tambo, swam to a runaway log raft with a hand-carved wood paddle lashed to it, and rode it downriver twenty yards ahead of us, flirting with the whirlpools.

"Great stuff!" he said when he returned to the big raft an hour later. "Give me a little money for food and one of those rafts and I'd be happy here for months."

Late in the day the Tambo took a sharp left turn and headed due north. Behind us, the peaks of the Andes had faded to small gray shadows; to our left, low clouds hid the hills of the Gran Pajonal. I took my turn at the rudder enveloped by green bush, brown water, and the bright blue sky overhead. Now and then, in a thin clearing along either bank, a ghostly, *cushma*-clad Asháninka stood stiffly as we approached, then offered a wave that escalated from tentative to frantic as we sped out of his life. Here and there I spotted a hut, smoke curling from a fire, or a dugout canoe hauled up on the muddy bank by a path leading into the dark bush.

Despite the flood, despite the fact that in that roadless country the rivers are the only highways, I saw no trash, no bottles, no cans, no plastic, no Styrofoam. No power poles, no billboards, no neon signs. And heard no sounds but the voices of my friends— "José, *cerveza* please"—the Tambo's insistent lapping on the rubber raft, and the occasional anguished roar of a tree dying a natural death.

In a day and a half on the swift Tambo we covered almost seventy miles. About noon the second day Chmielinski spotted, along the right bank, a white clapboard house atop a grassy hill with a clear, sweet-water creek running below it. Up the creek, squatting amid the bush like misplaced Andrew Wyeth paintings, were acres of rolling pasture, a whitewashed schoolhouse, a pump house, a grain mill, a herd of fat cattle, a manicured soccer field, and a dozen neat bamboo huts.

Chmielinski estimated that we were ten miles short of Atalaya, which we now envisioned as the threshold to the civilized world. We decided to stop at the idyllic *hacienda,* clean ourselves and our abused equipment in the clear creek, and arrive in Atalaya clean and refreshed. But we received an odd reception at that neat white house. A skinny, nervous *criollo* glanced at the papers Chmielinski presented him, said we could make camp next to the soccer field, and slammed the door shut.

We set up camp and did our wash. While Bzdak mixed cocktails from *pisco* and a powdered fruit drink, Chmielinski spoke briefly with two shy young sisters, one of whom said she was the *hacienda's* schoolteacher. We saw no one else until a few hours later, when a squat, barrel-chested Indian man showed up with a soccer ball. As we kicked it around another half dozen Indians materialized, and soon we had a game, big, strong gringos versus small, fast Indians. Our opponents said nothing, but they played with wild abandon, exploding with shrieking laughter at every errant shot, goal, bad pass, or tackle. The game ended suddenly, when my knee popped—it felt as if a nail had been driven into it—and the Indians disappeared as mysteriously as they had arrived.

Durrant and Bzdak carved me a walking stick, and at sunset, in pain, I retired to my tent, lit a candle, and read Conrad for a few minutes. I soon found myself distracted. Something about the *hacienda* felt strange. Everywhere else we'd been we'd attracted crowds of curious locals, but here in the middle of this fairly large settlement we were being left completely alone. It was eerie. In the morning, as we packed to leave, Truran and Durrant echoed my thoughts. "It feels like we're in some sort of religious camp," Truran said. "You know, where they tell you when you can eat and when you can talk and when you can take a leak. Gives me the creeps."

We saw no one as we paddled down the little creek and turned right into the muddy Tambo.

We smelled Atalaya several miles before we saw it. The breeze wafting up the Tambo mixed the stench of Atalaya's ordure, kerosene, and diesel with the sweet-sour odor of jungle rot, producing the first sign that we were emerging into the modern world. Then, on the left bank, we saw corrugated tin roofs glinting amid the green jungle wall, and a flotilla of log rafts, dugout canoes, and leaky aluminum flat-bottom skiffs. Little dun warts grew into thatch huts, and farther on, raised on stilts, stood shaky structures of plank, twine, leather, and cardboard. Their open pipes dripped effluvia into the river. Rats and pigs ambled along the mud bank and paused beneath the pipes to anoint themselves. Brown faces darted through the bush and stopped at the single cement ramp that is Atalaya's port.

Atalaya sits a mile above the Tambo's confluence with another great jungle river, the Urubamba. To the west, cutting the village off from Lima, rise the dense gray-green hills of the Gran Pajonal, and, behind them, the Andes. To the north and east is the Amazon basin. No roads leave Atalaya; she is serviced only by sporadic river traffic and an air taxi that splats onto her soggy grass landing strip once a week or so. Other than tiny Satipo, sixty miles southwest by air, she stands alone, isolated, the only real town for hundreds of miles in any direction. She has perhaps a thousand inhabitants, and a mud plaza and mud streets, and, along the river, a commercial center—a row of precarious lean-tos and stalls, not one of which looks older than yesterday, or as if it wouldn't topple in a good storm.

This was the face of our Oz. It had been six weeks since we put the raft in at the military bridge near Cuzco. Wallowing in Atalaya's mud meant deliverance.

To our surprise, Atalaya did have a clean, two-story cinder-block hotel whose dollar-a-night rooms included bed, shower, electric fan, sink, and refrigerator. There was electricity from six to ten at night, but the fans did not work, and a refrigerator that is cold only four hours a day is a peculiarly Peruvian notion. Still, the beds and sheets were clean, and with some creative gymnastics beneath the water that dribbled from a hole in the bathroom wall I approximated a shower.

That night, having stored the raft and kayak in the hotel courtyard, Chmielinski, Truran, Bzdak, Durrant, and I took to Atalaya's streets. The air was humid but cool, and from the hills that rose beyond the last shack in town the scent of night-blooming jasmine slipped down and rode gently above the mud. Young couples strolled arm in arm, sidestepping puddles and flushing chickens and pigs before them. A mufflerless motorcycle carrying three passengers skidded past us. A gas-powered generator rumbled in the church next to the plaza. Sticking my head through a side window, I saw a standing-room-only crowd of about a hundred and fifty, watching Johnny Weissmuller in *Tarzan the Ape Man.*

A bearded leprechaun slouched up the street: Tim Biggs. He appeared happy to see us, but distracted. He said that he and Odendaal had arrived in Atalaya only two days before us—"Frans was pretty sick, man, he could hardly use a paddle. He floated most of the way"—and that their visas were still in limbo. Having failed to secure them by radio, Odendaal had hopped the air taxi out of Atalaya and gone to Lima. Biggs did not know when he would return, but he accepted this mess with some relief. "Even if the visas come through now, I think I'll head on home. I'm not too excited about spending another three months without Margie, you know?"

With Biggs gone, the kayaking team would be Odendaal, Chmielinski, and me. That was a shocking notion, to say the least, and one that needed more thorough digestion, but we agreed to drop expedition talk for the moment and get on with a decent celebration—it was Biggs's thirty-fourth birthday. We found a bar, and because we were now broke borrowed money from Biggs. This we invested in beer, keeping Biggs busy while Bzdak lifted his room key and snatched the pair of khakis I had loaned Biggs in Arequipa, and which had become his river uniform. These we wrapped in a towel and gave him as a birthday present. He seemed delighted.

After we had weaved our way back to the hotel that night the manager handed Chmielinski a note he'd forgotten earlier. Truran and I accompanied Chmielinski to his room and sat with him as he read the note by candlelight. It was from Odendaal. Though there was still a chance his visa would come through, he had decided to give up his dream of kayaking the Amazon. He said we should continue without him.

When Chmielinski had finished reading the letter we sat in silence for a moment. Then Truran squeezed me with one arm and shook Chmielinski's hand with the other. "Good luck, gents," he said. "Looks like it's up to you."

Up to us? Up to Chmielinski. My short stretch in the whitewater kayak had convinced me that it would be absurd to attempt to paddle such a beast thirty-five hundred miles. I had already decided to travel instead with Bzdak and Durrant on a Johnson, carrying Chmielinski's supplies and rendezvousing with him as possible, but this idea I kept to myself. We were not going anywhere soon. Odendaal had said he would be returning to Atalaya to complete his filming, but he had neglected to indicate what would happen to the remaining expedition assets, which were now at his disposal and without which we could not hope to continue our journey. The money we had borrowed from Biggs gave us a budget of about two dollars a day per person for one week. We decided to wait for Odendaal.

The next afternoon the heavens opened up with a blinding deluge, a foreshadowing of the rainy season that within a few weeks would leap upon us with all claws bared. The streets flooded, and as I stared down at drowned chickens, I was happy not to be on the Tambo. Two hours into the storm the river was strewn like a lumpy stew with tree trunks, derelict rafts, half-sunk canoes, torn-up thatch roofs, and every weird sort of jungle debris, all of it literally hurtling along. I shuddered as I studied the river. Caught up in that mess in a kayak, I would be squashed like a water bug.

The two young women from the mysterious *hacienda*, the teacher and her sister, tracked us down in Atalaya, where, as it turned out, they lived. Their names were Wendoly and Rosa Torres, and they took the five of us to their home and introduced us to their father, Alejandro, the chief custodian at the village school and the father of four other daughters and two sons. The two-story home he had built on the outskirts of town, of bricks baked in his kiln, was the tallest building we had seen since Cuzco. "Who wants to marry one of my daughters?" he asked when we visited. "I will build you a house right here, myself!"

While we sat and talked with him beneath the shade of a mango tree, near the creek that ran behind the house, Wendoly and Rosa shyly served platters of papaya, mamey (something like a cross between an apple and a plum), and small, exceptionally sweet mangoes out of which Torres had bred the teeth-separating fiber that can make eating the fruit such a chore.

Bzdak asked Señor Torres if he knew any mysteries of the *selva*, as the jungle is known. We had witnessed the horrible work of one, the bushmaster or *shushupe*, which is the largest venomous snake in the world. (The bushmaster and the fer-de-lance are considered the deadliest vipers in the Amazon.) Thirty-six hours after being bitten by a bushmaster an Asháninka man had walked down out of the high country into Atalaya's tiny medical clinic. Durrant had assisted the two clinicians in an unsuccessful three-hour attempt to save the man's gangrenous left leg, which had looked like a cocoa-colored balloon oozing yellow axle grease. (The facility, sponsored by the Save the Children foundation, had no electricity and no running water, but it was the only place within several hundred square miles that could legitimately be called a medical clinic.)

As soon as the jungle taxi returned the man would be sent downriver to the city of Pucallpa, where his leg would be amputated. Despite this tragedy, Torres dismissed our worries. "You sound like people from Lima," he said. "They expect to be attacked by ferocious animals and snakes and insects. Ask Rosa about that. She is twenty-four years old, she has lived in the jungle her whole life, and she has never seen a jaguar. She has never been bitten by a snake. Every day we make the schoolchildren swim across the Tambo. Piranhas have not eaten them."

Far more dangerous, Torres said, were the *narcotraficantes*. The *selva*'s major export is coca paste, most of which is shipped by plane or boat to Colombia to be refined into cocaine. Atalaya sits right in the heart of the action, and certainly seemed to have a druggy tone. One night, for example, I had a beer with an American (the first American, I realized later with mild shock, that I had seen in three months) who was staying at our hotel. He was a blond young Southern Californian—he looked like a fraternity boy. He said that he had been arrested trying to smuggle five kilos of processed cocaine out of Peru and been sentenced to ten years in a prison colony on the Urubamba River. After serving several years he had been released on a kind of probation and been allowed to buy a four-hundred-acre farm next to the prison, including a house, two power boats, and a shortwave radio, and to live there while he served out his sentence. He grew vegetables, which are hard to find in the *selva*. He was particularly proud of his tomatoes. He had a Peruvian wife, and he was permitted to visit Atalaya every few weeks—"got a side-squeeze here." In all, he said, it was not a bad life, but he could not leave Peru.

His room was right below mine. Each night when he had returned he had played American rock and roll on his tape recorder, very loudly, into the wee blue hours.

Two men staying in a room next to Biggs on the hotel's first floor had identified themselves as narcotics police. They left their door wide open, so that anyone walking past saw the half dozen guns resting on their beds.

On the second floor, sharing one room and a single bed, were four peons whom Truran and I recognized from the soccer game at the *hacienda*. It was to discuss these men that Rosa and Wendoly had brought us out to the Torres house. They said that the *hacienda* was in fact a coca-paste factory, and that we had inadvertently landed at the factory an hour after a plane loaded with five hundred kilos of paste had taxied down the grass runway hidden behind the schoolhouse, hit a cow, caromed into a tree, and sheared a wing.

If what the Torres sisters said was true, and we had no reason not to believe them, the peons had been working frantically to unload the plane even as we blissfully ignorant gringos paddled up in our strange blue boat. The *patrón*—the nervous man who had answered the door of the neat white house—had not known what to make of us. Were we DEA? CIA? He and the plane's pilot had kept us under gunsight surveillance while several of his men distracted us with the soccer game. Meanwhile, other men had dismantled the plane, dumped it in the river, and sent the paste downstream in a motor boat. The four peons in the hotel had been assigned to watch us in Atalaya.

This news disconcerted us for several reasons, not the least of which was that we had seen the peons and the police shooting pool together in Atalaya's one dingy hall.

"Be careful," Torres said as we left to return to the hotel. "In the *selva* nothing is quite what it seems." As for his daughters: "That hoodlum can find himself a new schoolteacher."

We spent the next six days trading mean stares with the *narcotraficantes*. They shadowed us everywhere but did us no harm, although one night, as Truran and I went in search of beer, one of the peons popped up out of the dark, drew a finger across his throat in a cutting motion, and hissed the name of our hotel.

Finally, Odendaal returned, with Van Heerden and Leon. He

wore crisp new clothes and carried a roll of one-hundred-dollar bills. The good news was that the expedition now had a treasury of about five thousand dollars, courtesy of Jack Jourgensen. The bad news emerged during a meeting at the hotel, when Odendaal, armed with charts and graphs, explained why he was passing but a third of the money along to the four of us who would continue on the river. He concluded by saying that he and Van Heerden would be filming in Peru a while longer, and that when he was done he would fly back to the United States, go on to London to present an account of his descent of the Apurimac to the Royal Geographical Society, and return home to South Africa for Christmas. He said that despite the present circumstances he was still the expedition leader, that Chmielinski, Bzdak, Durrant, and I were to continue on the river under his name, and that when he returned to the States from his Christmas vacation to begin the spring term at his university he would contact us in Brazil and issue instructions for completing our journey.

There was no point in arguing with Odendaal. He controlled the money and could do with it as he pleased, and the idea that he could lead an expedition from thousands of miles—indeed, continents—away appeared to make perfect sense to him.

The next day Odendaal left Atalaya, accompanied by Biggs. Minutes before their hired motorboat was to leave Biggs rushed into the hotel lobby, where Chmielinski and I were packing our kayaks.

"Nothing personal, right, mates?" he said, and then, as we shook hands, he wished us luck.

Sergio Leon also left with Odendaal, to help with translations and filming logistics. He was tired. He and Van Heerden had had a rough time transporting the sea kayaks from Lima to Pucallpa—they had been confronted by guerrillas but not harmed—and I felt sorry for him. He had enjoyed our hike in the Andes, but he had quit his job and spent all his money mainly to explore the Amazon rain forest, and now it looked as if that experience would be denied him. However, he did not appear to have in him the emotions of sadness or regret. My last image of him is dominated by his wide smile.

That day Durrant, Bzdak, Chmielinski, and I also said good-bye to Truran, as he waited for the air taxi. Up until that moment he had debated whether to continue down the river with us, but in the end he still couldn't handle the idea of kayaking all that flat water. Also, he had turned thirty in Peru—old for competitive kayaking—and owed himself one last try at a world championship. He had to begin training almost immediately.

It was strange, and hard, to stand there in the jungle and try to offer proper thanks to Truran. He had saved my life more than once, had blocked Odendaal's attempts to drive me off the river, and, above all, had inspired me with his courage. But Truran didn't want to hear my thanks. He spent his last hour on the Amazon instructing me in paddling technique (*"Push*, not *pull"*), and told me that if Chmielinski tried to travel too fast, as he almost certainly would, I must refuse. If I didn't, my wrists would give out and I'd have to quit the river.

Then, with a grin and "Cheers!," he boarded the tiny plane and escaped.

Chmielinski and I would make the four-hundred-mile trip to Pucallpa in the white-water kayaks Biggs and Odendaal had left in Atalaya. (The irony of my paddling Odendaal's boat did not go unmentioned.) Chmielinski estimated that we could paddle that distance in ten days. Durrant and Bzdak would wait in Atalaya until the river went down and boat traffic resumed and they could negotiate a ride to Pucallpa. No one in Atalaya knew when that would be possible.

We washed out the boats behind the hotel and then hauled them into the lobby and began to pack. For me this was a charade. I still had not told Chmielinski that he would be kayaking alone. Having failed to find a graceful way to express my cowardice, I proceeded to pack the boat as if there were nothing else I would rather do.

A blond man of about forty sat down on the floor beside us and watched us work. He had checked into the hotel the day before. He was Italian, but in Spanish he said that he had been in Atalaya a year ago, with his wife and young son.

"We wanted an adventure," he said. "We bought a dugout canoe and some food and things and put the boat in the Ucayali. Two days later we were sucked into a whirlpool. The canoe turned over." He paused to light an "Inca" cigarette. "I went around and around, and then suddenly I shot down the river. I swam for I don't know how long, maybe ten minutes, maybe an hour. When I reached the bank I had nothing left, not even my shirt.

"Some Indians were fishing there. They walked me to their village, and then a couple of days later they took me to a mission with an airplane landing strip. I got free rides all the way to Lima, but the Italian consul would not help me—I had to beg in the streets. Three months later I was back in Italy, but I had lost everything."

"What happened to your wife and son?" I asked, and regretted the words immediately.

The man began to cry, softly, and said only, "Everything." Everything but the memories that had called him back to Peru.

That was enough for me. When the Italian left the lobby I stopped working on the boat. The time had come. I had seen the mountains, I had seen the jungle, I had endured more close calls than I cared to remember.

"Well, Piotr," I began, "I've been thinking."

"What have you been thinking?" he asked, and looked straight into me, his unflinching, ice-blue eyes holding my own with an unbreakable grip. That look held no emotion, no bullying, no prodding, nothing but an even measuring of the spirit that asked, *What exactly are you made of?*

My answer was: hesitation, doubt, weakness. I experienced a

blind, overwhelming desire to be in my own country in my own home in my own bed, curled up with my girlfriend, a glutton's feast spread out beside us, the present secure, the future bright, the Amazon and Chmielinski, that Polish drill sergeant, thousands of safe miles away.

Chmielinski continued to stare at me.

I said, "I was thinking about how exciting this is going to be. You and me and our little kayaks and that big river. You know, exploring and all that."

"Good, Joe," he said. "That is the rightful thing."

THREE

THE RIVER SEA

13 *The Upper Ucayali*

Chmielinski and I left sleepy Atalaya in mid-afternoon. Bzdak, Durrant, and Wendoly and Rosa Torres saw us off. Spurred on by the Torres sisters' encouraging squeals, Chmielinski began the journey of three thousand five hundred miles with a flurry of quick strong strokes, but my attempt to imitate his performance was a fraud. My stomach hurt; I felt the flu coming on. The sun was intense, the humidity suffocating, the Tambo a maelstrom.

We paddled into the middle of the river and let the strong current sweep us away. Minutes later the jungle had reasserted itself. Verdant walls queued along either side, marching to the river's edge. The flooding Tambo had undercut her clay banks, and one four-story tree after another had collapsed into the river. Their tops were submerged like the heads of drowned corpses, but their trunks stayed rooted to the earth and vibrated with the current. Every hundred yards or so one of these trunks would suddenly spring back up, breaking the river's surface with a roar and launching a volley of spray from its shuddering branches.

That was the brutality of the jungle—its anonymous, threatening mass. The high Andes had been brutal but transparent, showing themselves plainly to the eye for miles in every direction. In the jungle, however, everything hid behind a lurid green barricade.

The bush seemed to be one many-limbed, conniving beast.

The tropical sky, by contrast, presented itself boldly. Concocted from an intense mix of tropical heat and humidity, it was never all of a piece, but its theaters were distinct. We were ten degrees south of the equator and heading due north. The sun was directly overhead, the sky blue and blinding. Though I wore sunglasses and a hat, I saw spots before my eyes and my head burned. A few miles north, however, a haystack of deep purple storm clouds dropped a steady, sharply defined column of rain that looked like a cyclone's tail. To our left, sanguine cirrus feathers hovered over the bush. Behind us, the dark ridges of the Gran Pajonal faded to gray behind a thick skirt of low fog.

A mile below Atalaya the Urubamba River joined the Tambo from the right. These two big jungle rivers form the Ucayali, which at the confluence is about half a mile wide. We would follow the Ucayali for twelve hundred miles, more than twice the distance we had traveled since reaching the river's source three months ago. Those twelve hundred miles would deliver us only to the Ucayali's confluence with the Marañón River, near Iquitos. From there we would paddle four hundred miles to the Brazilian border, and from the border another two thousand miles to the Atlantic.

Swollen from the week-long rain and mined with floating trunks, the Ucayali plowed through the bush with intimidating strength. Pockets of turbulence swirled up from the deep, erupted in spinning mushroom caps, and spun off in unpredictable currents that grabbed my kayak and pushed it back, sideways, in circles. Trunks thumped my boat, and I saw the bloated carcass of a drowned pig, its hooves in the air. My shoulders and forearms ached from working the paddle.

The river offered no sign of people until dusk, when a fat barefoot woman in muddy rags signaled us from shore, near the mouth of the tiny Unine River. She hooted our efforts to climb the soupy, fifteen-foot left bank. Dragging our boats behind us, Chmielinski followed her into the bush and I followed him, walking in this duckling fashion along a path that opened to neat rows of coffee, corn, peanuts, and tobacco and a trim thatch-roofed shelter mounted on bamboo stilts.

A short, bare-chested *mestizo* sat in the middle of the shelter, wearing a self-satisfied expression beneath tiny dark eyes that sparkled like a panther's. His thick hair had gone to silver, but his belly was hard and flat, his shoulders and arms thick with muscle. Though shoeless, he had a regal air. He introduced himself as Don Rafael Machelena, *patrón* of Unine. ("Don" connotes power and respect.) He rapped Chmielinski's kayak, threw his head back, and snorted.

"Where are you going in this contraption?"

"To the Atlantic Ocean," Chmielinski said.

"In this? You are crazy. You will not make Pucallpa." He snorted again. "Do you want a cup of coffee? It may be your last."

In the middle of that desolate bush Don Rafael served us a thick, delicious brew in elegant china cups, the first real coffee we had tasted in months. (Like many poor coffee-producing countries, Peru exports its best beans and serves instant.) He shaved tobacco from a club that looked like a green salami and rolled us each a strong smoke.

"I grow this stuff," he said. "The coffee, too."

The woman was his wife, Elsa. She cooked us a dinner of rice, eggs, yucca, fried bananas, and a piquant paste made from peanuts and chilies.

"I grew all this, too," Don Rafael said as she served it. "And chocolate! I sell it to the Russians. Those idiots need it. It is cold over there!"

Chmielinski heated a serving of our beef burgundy. Don Rafael turned up his nose and said, "How barbarous."

He had never left Peru—"How can I? That is for rich men"—and he had been to Lima only once, but as the night wore on and we burned one log after another we discussed Lech Walesa, Ronald Reagan, François Mitterrand, the Dalai Lama, and whether Swiss watches are as good as they're said to be. He read us a letter from a man he had met on the river who now lived in Nepal. "It is some world," he said when he finished, and we agreed.

By then I had a sore throat and my head ached. I excused myself and rolled out my air mattress and listened to Don Rafael and Chmielinski. I was glad that we had stopped in Unine. Contented and self-sufficient, Don Rafael gave the anonymous bush a wise face.

In the morning the *patrón* brewed more of his coffee and Chmielinski boiled a pouch of chicken cacciatore. "This is crazy," Don Rafael said as he ate it. "Plastic food." When he finished he gave us a clump of bananas and two clubs of his tobacco. "If you do not smoke, hit some vagabond over the head with it!" He advised us to travel as fast as we could. The floods would begin in a matter of weeks.

Then he marched into the bush, machete in hand, and we slid down the slick bank into a cold fog.

In all my imaginings of the Amazon I had never thought about fog, but there it was, cold and clammy, just like fog anywhere. Chmielinski and I paddled side by side, our boats perhaps six feet apart. The fog was spooky stuff to kayak in. It seemed to smooth the water into a glass sheen, to hush it, but every few minutes I heard a loud farting sound and a slapping at the river's surface. An hour later, when the fog burned off, Chmielinski hissed at me and nodded toward the mouth of a creek. Something surfaced, I heard the farting sound, it went under. I counted. At forty-one seconds it breached again.

I paddled over to investigate. A blast behind me startled me so badly that I almost tipped out of my boat. I turned and waited. About a minute later a pink-and-gray blob bubbled up and voided a blowhole the diameter of a large marble.

It would be several days before Chmielinski and I convinced ourselves that those flatulent schmoo-heads were dolphins, which we hadn't expected thousands of miles from the Atlantic. In fact, freshwater dolphins as primitive as those pinks, or *Inia geoffrensis*, are found only in one Chinese lake, the Ganges River, and the Plata, Orinoco, and Amazon rivers in South America. With their dorsal humps, thick elongated snouts, and doughy bodies they more closely resemble beluga whales than the common marine bottlenose dolphin.

However, the Amazon also has a close freshwater cousin of the bottlenose, the "black" dolphin, or *Sotalia fluvatis*. From what I would see, pinks and blacks share habitats (some marine biologists would disagree). In demeanor, however, they cannot differ more. A black cavorted in the space I had so hurriedly paddled away from after that blast from the pink. Leaping out of the water again and again in a smooth arc, it appeared to be about three to four feet shorter than the pink, and the grace of its performance seemed to mock the lumbering ancient, who surfaced indolently, barely nudging its blowhole out of the water.

Neither freshwater dolphin possesses any loudly exotic talents (although the pinks are fond of rubbing one another, and of hanging out in large cuddling clusters), but together they occupy a significant niche in the sexual folklore of the Amazon. A dolphin eye, dried and grated into a woman's food, will drive her mad with desire. If a man views a woman through the ring of a pink's dried eye socket, she will be unable to resist him. A dolphin ear worn around the wrist guarantees a prolonged genital tumescence. Intercourse with a female dolphin is so intense a man will die in the act. According to the most pervasive bit of lore, a male dolphin can assume the appearance of a young man. Dressed all in white and wearing a hat over his blowhole, he appears in river towns and seduces virgins.

Pink dolphins do have a gymnastic, Gumby-esque ability to turn around completely within a space the length of their body, which enables them to follow shallow, flooding rivers into the jungle floor and to maneuver around the debris that clogs the river in flood season. However, this provides little defense against *Inia's* sole predator, *Homo sapiens*. The pinks are nearly fished out in the lower Amazon, and increasingly rare on the upper river.

Once I had adjusted to their snorting, the pinks were, like Don Rafael, an avuncular, reassuring presence. If something that goofy could handle the Amazon, I thought, maybe there was hope for me.

The upper Ucayali is an intestine of a waterway, twisting and turning more than any other major river in the Western Hemisphere. By plane, Pucallpa is about a hundred miles from Atalaya, but by boat on the Ucayali it is four times that. There are no reliable maps of the river—it floods every year, changes course by many miles, and wipes out entire villages in a single swipe. The survivors move on, and a year later the village pops up somewhere else entirely, a collection of thatch huts where before there had been only bush and bank.

"Where is Tabacoas?" one asks in Iparía. "Tabacoas?" comes the response. "It used to be one day from here, but it is farther than that now."

The river divides into dozens of channels, and it is often impossible to know which of them to follow. The sun provides no clues. One moment it shines in your face, the next on the back of your head, and two turns of the river later it is in your face again. You plunge blindly ahead, trusting in the direction of the current.

Though maddening, the Ucayali is also sublimely beautiful, most visibly so within the tight confines of the narrow side channels we so often found ourselves plying. In these canals (seldom more than ten yards wide) we easily approached parakeets, large crowlike birds of neon blue, parrots, darting golden finches. Where two canals met, dolphins and flying fish whipped the surface, and a few yards farther on a muddy log might rise up on stubby legs. As we closed in, these heavy-lidded caimans would slide off the bank and disappear in what only my naive sense of trust told me was the opposite direction.

The upper Ucayali is a river of loners. A few grizzly *mestizos*, such as Don Rafael, work small plantations to which an Indian settlement may be attached, but for the most part the river is peopled by Asháninka who continue to live traditionally, in small, isolated family groups. Our second day on the river we saw only one other boat, a dugout canoe paddled by an Asháninka boy moving stealthily through the shadows along the bank, a hundred yards behind us. After three hours of this we stopped, hid in a creek, and surprised him.

He was not alarmed. He wanted to make a deal. He said, "You need a turtle," and held out a specimen the size of a man's hand, with a hole punched in its shell and a piece of yarn threaded through the hole. Holding the yarn like a leash, he set the turtle down on the floor of the canoe and whistled. The turtle huffed to the front of the canoe, teetered on the edge, and stopped. The boy whistled again, and the turtle returned.

"You need a turtle," he said a second time. Chmielinski explained that if we took the turtle it would surely die. The boy sighed and said, "Then eat him."

Chmielinski paid him for the turtle but did not take it.

I felt like the turtle—teetering on the brink of escape but trapped at the end of a leash. To overcome my fear I had taken to throwing myself into the warm, silty Ucayali every couple of hours, and had begun to enjoy swimming in it. But we had to get down the river before the floods, and to that end Chmielinski had established a staggering regimen.

Each day we rose before dawn and from then till noon paddled fifty-five minutes of every hour and took a five-minute floating break in the kayaks. (Chmielinski called these respites "five minutek.") At about noon we stopped paddling for a half-hour lunch. The first two days out of Atalaya we tried to eat on land, but the mosquitoes forced us to return to the boats and drift with the current. After lunch we paddled fifty minutes of every hour until sunset, then made camp.

Twelve hours a day in the boats, seven days a week. Fifty strokes a minute, thirty-six thousand strokes a day, two and a half million strokes to the Atlantic. At times the existential chasm suggested by the execution of a single stroke paralyzed me, and I had to set down my paddle and drift until Chmielinski, realizing I was no longer at his side, paddled back and prodded me into a sort of life.

After three days on the Ucayali my wrists were painful to the touch, inflamed with the tenisinivitis about which Durrant and Truran had warned me. I had flu and a gastrointestinal complication picked up in Atalaya. ("One hundred percent of the population here has parasites," the clinician had said.) I could not hold food, and I was so tired I couldn't sleep. The heat and humidity were awful, the sun so relentless that I continued to see spots.

But I was not lonely. Or, I was not as lonely as I wanted to be. That may have been the worst burden of all. On the raft we had been a family of five, the days filled with jokes and conversation and camaraderie. The real advantage to such numbers, of course, is that it is easier to hide in a crowd. Now it was just Chmielinski and I. I did not mind that we were strangers. In fact, I welcomed it. I am a selfish person, and prefer to wallow in my own company. No, the problem was quite the opposite: You cannot live with someone around the clock for months on end, in relative isolation, and not expect him to share the most intimate details of your life. You cannot spend all of your time hiding behind baseball talk (in fact, with Chmielinski, I could not spend *any* time talking baseball). With nowhere to hide, I saw, to my horror, that this stranger would come to know me inside out.

Here I must give Chmielinski his due. He brought to our enterprise an attitude exactly opposite to mine. He acted as if he *wanted* the company, and made every effort to keep me on the river. He carried all our tonnage—the canned food, the kerosene stove, the water jug. He crammed far more than his share of the supplies into the nose of his kayak and down into its tail, strapped them on his deck and affixed them to the hull with elastic cords. Water jugs, pineapples, fuel cans, stove, spare paddles—his boat looked like a floating junk shop. And with all that weight it rode low in the water, which meant he had more resistance and had to paddle that much harder. When the afternoon wind came up the river lapped into his cockpit.

By our fourth day I was embarrassed at how little I carried. "Give me something," I said.

"I give you something, Joeski. When we get to Pucallpa, I give you the biggest ice cream you can eat."

He selected our campsites, persuaded the Asháninka that we were of the same species and not hostile, cooked breakfast and dinner, made sure I took my malaria pills. Once, overcome by fever, I passed out in my kayak. When I came to he was towing me. He sang songs, mainly Polish marches, and he sang them loudest at dawn. His voice rocketed across the river and into the trees, where it ignited flocks of parrots and set howler monkeys to roaring.

One afternoon he said, "Joe, you sing now."

"I can't sing."

"Sing anything you like."

There was no way out of it. "*They call it Stormy Monday,*" I began, "*but Tuesday's just as ba-a-a-a-d—*"

He cut me off. "I sing," he said. "You write."

That night we camped with an Asháninka family, two young men dressed in holey *cushmas* and a bare-breasted old woman in a ragged skirt. They lived in a thatch-roofed hut raised on ten-foot stilts (the matriarch indicated we were to sleep in their chicken hutch), and the sum of their possessions was two tin pots, a machete, some fish hooks, a bow, and assorted arrows, though there were mosquitoes and fleas in abundance.

One of the young men showed us the arrows. The shafts were of wild cane, the fletching parrot feather, the tips a hardwood further hardened by flame and lashed to the cane. One arrowhead was round and bulbous, for knocking out of trees what was, I believe, an exceptionally stupid turkeylike bird. Another, for taking fish, had barbed serrations, and a third, broad as a fist and sharp enough to draw blood when tapped, was for *sachavaca*, or tapir. The man said that five years ago you might have seen a hundred or more cross the river in a single day (a memory shared by Alejandro Torres in Atalaya), but now he was lucky to see two or three. He did not know what had happened, but the hunting was terrible.

Three logs smoldered in the middle of the muddy, forty-foot-wide clearing. Their smoke was supposed to keep the mosquitoes at bay, as was our repellent, but the welts on my face, neck, arms, and legs indicated otherwise. I rubbed my hand with repellent and held it out at eye level, palm up, over the fire. Within perhaps thirty seconds it was black with mosquitoes, about a quarter of which displayed the raised wings of *sancudos*, or malaria carriers.

Our hosts cooked their sparse evening meal, fish boiled with *platanos*, and said that although there was not enough to share, we were welcome to use their second pot. Chmielinski prepared a batch of *comida plástica* (here I will hazard the claim that our meal marked among the Asháninka the first appearance of beef Stroganoff), and as we ate we joined the family in a kind of Zen walking meditation, circling the fire in an attempt to outwit the mosquitoes. When this failed, the stoic Asháninka were content to be bitten, but Chmielinski and I threw down our bowls and commenced a frenzy of swatting.

When Chmielinski went down to the river to wash the cookpot I tried to open my water bottle—the fever had given me a terrific thirst—but my wrists were too sore to twist the top. The old woman saw my predicament, squeezed the bottle up against her floppy breasts, and loosened the lid, but this was only a temporary solution. We erected our tents in the chicken hutch, and later that night I awoke to find my hands so swollen I couldn't unzip my tent to let myself out to urinate. This wasn't just painful, it was humiliating—I felt like a baby in a crib. It was time to stop kidding myself. Chmielinski was an explorer, but I was a masochist. I decided that if we reached Pucallpa I would quit the river once and for all and go home where I belonged.

I lost track of the days. Chmielinski woke me in the morning, I followed his boat's wagging tail, I collapsed at night. At the town of Bolognesi—huts, chickens, pigs, bugs, mud—Chmielinski went in search of fruit while I crawled onto a grassy knoll overlooking the river and vomited. I rolled over to look at the blistering noon sky and saw five old peasant women staring down at me.

"Where are you going?" one asked.

"Brazil. "

"You should fly."

To reach Iparía we paddled through a stinking swamp expecting "all the things in which we do not believe" (as John Steinbeck once wrote of skin diving). We hauled our kayaks up a thirty-foot sandstone bluff by rope, and found six slatted huts and a gentle, middle-aged *mestizo* woman named Flora, who was terribly frail except for her strong bony fingers. She lived with her half-blind father, Guillermo, and her quiet adolescent grandson, Elvis Presley.

Where had Elvis Presley gotten his name? He shrugged and

made a desultory display of playing air guitar. He was not proud of the name. He led us to a thatch-covered patio and helped us prepare a camp. He dreamed of being a lawyer: "They are smart men." Later that night we would hear him reading aloud to his grandmother and great-grandfather.

On her prized possession, a two-burner kerosene stove, Flora cooked us a spirit-reviving soup of cilantro and rice. She, Elvis, and Guillermo grew rice in the swamp. For many years they had farmed near Iquitos, but every rainy season the floods had wiped them out. They had been in Iparía two years. It was higher ground, Flora said, and life was better. Guillermo agreed. "We have the moon and the river, and plenty to eat. Sometimes no money, but the people are good. Not like those bums in Lima."

Flora's husband had gone away to Iquitos three months ago and not returned. She did not know what had happened to Elvis's parents—it had been years. In the morning she said she would like to have a rice-harvesting machine, "so I can grow old with all of my fingers."

Elvis and Guillermo helped us lower the kayaks back into the swamp. As we paddled away, Flora cried out, "How you suffer!"

It was late November. The Pachitea River had flooded, and where it entered the Ucayali it looked as if a man could cross it on the floating trunks. The village at the confluence, also called Pachitea, is the largest Shipibo settlement on the Ucayali. Julio Caesar Gomez, the government teacher who taught the village's school, estimated that there were about two hundred families in the village, though it was difficult to say with certainty, for the Shipibo were always coming and going. Given its proximity to Pucallpa, Pachitea is visited by representatives of the Summer Institute of Linguistics, a nondenominational coalition of evangelical missionaries devoted to translating the Bible into the indigenous tongues. Gomez said that when the missionaries were in Pachitea, the Shipibo stayed in the village, because the missionaries brought them presents. The Shipibo, he said, were very attentive at the religious services, and particularly enjoyed the singing. But when the missionaries returned to Pucallpa, "the Shipibo forget every-thing." It was Gomez's opinion that the majority of Shipibo had not been converted to much of anything beyond an appreciation for plastic jewelry and canned milk. "The children especially are afraid," he said. "Their parents tell them that if they are bad, the white men will steal their skin and shrink their heads."

The chain-smoking Gomez and his young wife, who hosted us for the evening, were overfond of neither missionaries nor Indians, and escaped downriver to Pucallpa whenever possible. Gomez owed the government one more year of teaching, and then they were going to travel.

The Shipibo speak Chama, one of some thirty surviving languages indigenous to the Peruvian jungle. They wear their black hair in a bowl cut, and the women also grow it long in back, to their waists, and adorn themselves liberally with jewelry, particularly through the nose and ears. The women dress in traditional woven skirts and blouses, but most of the men have adopted the modern trousers-and-T-shirt trappings of the average starving *mestizo* in Lima.

The Shipibo were aggressively curious, crowding around our boats, giggling and elbowing one another and pointing at us. Most wore a sort of knowing grin, as if they were about to pull off an elaborate practical joke. We watched a soccer game between two teams of adolescent girls. The field was huge, larger than a regulation pitch, but they covered it with amazing speed. They played barefoot but kicked the deflated ball ferociously—one girl launched a bullet of a shot—and they tackled often, their bones crunching with the sound of chicken wings being torn apart.

As for the *lingüísticos,* as the Summer Institute missionaries are known, they have had a base in Pucallpa since 1947, and their influence in the upper Amazon basin is pervasive and controversial. Their defenders point out, rightly, that for decades the *lingüísticos* have been the only outsiders apart from the Roman Catholic mis-sionaries to have an interest in the welfare of the Indians, and that by teaching the Indians to read and write they help to prepare them for their inevitable clash with the forces of so-called progress. The *lingüísticos'* critics point out, also rightly, that their work with the natives, and most particularly their translating of the indigenous tongues, is inspired by the simple fact that it is the most effective way to replace the indigenous cosmologies with such Christian doctrines as guilt and hell. (The only missionary I met on the Amazon who claimed to be affiliated with the *lingüísticos,* a Baptist dispatched by the U.S.-based South American Mission, was also the only English-speaking person I met who referred to the Indians as "savages"; in Atalaya, as a prelude to a ceremony arranged for our benefit, he had forced a hungry, embarrassed, "saved" Asháninka boy to sing "Nearer My God to Thee" in his native tongue before permitting him to eat.)

The moon was coming full and the river running strong, and I was starting to recover from my illness, whatever it was. The next morning, our tenth since leaving Atalaya, we decided we would push on straight into the night until we reached Pucallpa.

We paddled steadily through the day, and late in the afternoon hitched a ride on a raft built of some two hundred mahogany logs, manned by six ragged fellows from a village several hundred miles away, near the Brazilian border. Afloat for almost three weeks, they looked like shipwreck survivors. They planned to sell their logs in Pucallpa. Because the most accessible hardwoods in the upper Amazon basin have long since been cut, their load would earn them sufficient cash to get them through the next year.

As we drifted I brewed coffee on our stove and one of the men built a fire on a log, stuck a branch in a plucked chicken carcass, and cooked it over the fire. We ate and drank and watched the moon begin its ascent. I tried to recall where we had been the last time it had come full. The Acobamba Abyss. I had almost drowned.

When Chmielinski mentioned that he was Polish, the raft's captain, a huge man the others called Gordo, or Fatso, asked if he was the Pole who had run the Colca River. Chmielinski said he was. The men gathered around and pumped him with questions about Lech Walesa. Chmielinski admired Walesa and had no trouble speaking about Solidarity, which he did for the next twenty minutes.

When Chmielinski had finished, Gordo said, "But they put him in jail."

"The communists did that," Chmielinski said.

"And well they should have," another man said. "He was disrupting the government. You cannot have that."

"Why not?" a third man asked. "Look at us. What do we have to lose? These logs?"

"I don't think communism is so bad," Gordo said. "Peru could use a change. The generals and the drug dealers own Peru."

"Communism sounds good until the communists take over," Chmielinski said. "Then everything changes. People disappear, there are shortages. Everyone suffers."

"We already have that," the second man said. "I cannot imagine it getting any worse no matter who runs the country."

Gordo opened a papaya and passed it around. It was perfectly ripe, glowing red and orange as the sun now settling into the jungle wall. Another man gave us sugar cane stalks for our journey.

"We will meet you in town," Gordo said. "I know a place"—he named a cantina—"the women have melons like *this*." He held two papayas to his chest. The other men laughed. We put our boats in the water and left the men coasting on their fortune.

The sun set and the bank and the river melded into one. The full moon cast only enough light to show us we were traveling through an alien world. I heard dolphins breach and snort. In the blackness, the *whoosh* of whirlpools forming and disintegrating seemed much louder than it had during the day. Invisible mosquitoes attacked. We cleaved to the middle of the river to the extent we could find it, and Chmielinski devised a system of flashlight signals that we would use if we became separated.

I heard the slapping of paddles and, almost too late, saw a shadow twenty yards behind me and gaining. I shouted. No answer.

"Go!" Chmielinski yelled.

We outpaddled the shadow, but when we stopped, an hour later, my chest was heaving and my wrists felt as if someone had cracked them over his knee.

When my breathing slowed I smelled something awful, heard a low thrumming, and noticed that the water dripping off my paddle and across my thighs left an oily film. Then we rounded a bend in the river and I was blinded by the industrial lights of the port of Pucallpa.

There is one good thing I can say about Pucallpa: There are very few mosquitoes. They cannot survive the foul air. Most jungle towns stink, but into the usual mix of excrement, urine, dead dogs, pigs, rotting fruit, fish, kerosene, and diesel exhaust Pucallpa weaves the emissions of a lumber mill, an oil refinery, and boom-town avarice.

As recently as 1960 Pucallpa was a sleepy jungle town of thatch huts and a few thousand people. Today it is not only the legislated administrative capital of the department of Ucayali, created in 1982, but also the de facto capital of the Peruvian Amazon. Pucallpa, linked to Lima by road, has wrested that title from Iquitos, eight hundred miles downriver, even though its hundred fifty thousand inhabitants make it twice Pucallpa's size. Until the 1970s the road washed out in rainy season, and the jungle was connected to Lima only by foot through the Andes, by small plane, or by boat down the Amazon and through the Panama Canal, a journey of seven thousand miles. Now surfaced in the washout areas, the road permits the steady trucking of the huge machinery necessary to tame the jungle, and the quick export of the natural resources harvested there—from oil and timber to rare birds and animal skins.

Indians, mainly Shipibo, were a common sight in Pucallpa, though as in Cuzco their role seemed limited to selling trinkets in the streets. In the middle of the city, in an area of perhaps one square mile, were a few paved roads, several expensive air-conditioned hotels, pizza parlors, a movie theater that showed *Blue Thunder* during our visit, and sturdy modern banks managed by young men from Lima who knew the daily dollar exchange rate by heart. Most of the buildings were one-story, bunkerlike exercises in steel and cement. Farther out, on the east end of town, near the river, the pavement ended and the road turned to rutted dirt and slipped past the candlelit shacks of the poor, who are the bulk of Pucallpa's permanent population.

Cuzco has its Inca walls and Spanish churches, Lima its chipped colonial architecture, Arequipa its volcanoes and quiet isolation. Pucallpa has no such distinction. It has grown too quickly, and has no real connection to the land around it beyond simple greed. It represents the apotheosis of the modern law of the jungle—open season for anything one can get one's hands on, or one's machines under.

At any rate, that's how I saw Pucallpa. As in Cuzco, however, my discontent was to a degree a result of fatigue. I was still fifteen pounds underweight, beat up, and foggy headed, and my wrists and forearms creaked painfully. While Chmielinski worked Pucallpa's arcane public telephone system in an ultimately futile attempt to hustle more funding from the United States, I slept long hours in our cheap hostel, trying to regain my strength.

After three days I had recovered sufficiently to spend time in a cafe next door run by a transvestite from Lima named Roberto. He had a knack for the restaurant business—his food would not kill you, which in Pucallpa was an achievement—but what he really wanted to do was sing.

"Peelings, Señor Cho," he said. "You will be hearing my peelings?" And as Barry Manilow bleated through the loudspeakers ("*Feeeeliiings . . .*") Roberto lip-synched the lyrics—incongruously, for he was wearing a sequined dress—while I sipped coffee and nodded feebly at his tortured, and torturing, efforts.

Everything about Pucallpa struck me as false, and in that light my own motives for being in the Amazon seemed less than worthy. The notion of traveling the Amazon source to sea under my own power loomed as a colossal stunt. Paddling the kayak was so demanding that I wasn't really *seeing* anything on the river. I was ready to quit.

Three things changed my mind.

First, Chmielinski. He was an iron man. He did not need me on the river. But when I suggested that I was a hindrance, which I most clearly was, and that it was only proper that I stop kayaking, he was indignant. This, he said, was out of the question. He would continue regardless, but would prefer if I went with him. He said this so sincerely I believed him.

Second, Bzdak and Durrant. They had waited nearly a week in Atalaya for a Johnson, and had arrived in Pucallpa a few days ahead of us. I was overjoyed to see them, and not only because they had all our food and medical supplies. They were family. We were in this together.

And, finally, I came face to rude face with my options. For the trip from Pucallpa to Iquitos Bzdak and Durrant had booked passage on the *Jhuliana*, one of the elegant, turn-of-the-century passenger ships Werner Herzog flung about the Urubamba River in his film *Fitzcarraldo*. With her fine hardwood paneling, gleaming brightwork, and well-scrubbed cabins, the *Jhuliana* stood out in Pucallpa's suppurating port like a diamond.

That was how I felt on the lower deck, anyway. The upper deck was more like Pucallpa. The odor drifting from shore stung my nostrils. On the stern of a dilapidated launch moored upstream of the *Jhuliana* a man unzipped and pissed right into a group of swimming children. One of the kids, covered from the neck down in river muck, waddled to shore. As he did, a vulture, the closest of the perhaps two hundred I could see at that moment, looked up briefly from the dog carcass into which it had buried its beak, considered the child, and returned to its prize.

In the Amazon you expect parrots, macaws, parakeets, toucans, but the vulture is the bird of the Amazonian future. It is the one indigenous species that thrives in man's slobby wake.

That scene was enough for me. I suspected that by motorized boat, even as fine a ship as the *Jhuliana*, the trip to the Atlantic would be a pogo-stick hop from vulture nest to vulture nest, Pucallpa to Pucallpa. I owed myself the chance to see the places in between, the real Amazon.

That night Chmielinski and I packed our kayaks, and in the morning we set off for Iquitos, eight hundred miles downriver.

14 *The Lower Ucayali*

Beep-beep-beep *godDAMN!* At exactly 4 a.m., according to the whining Japanese alarm clock Chmielinski had bought in Pucallpa, I bolted awake to find a dark, fist-sized blob squatting atop my mosquito netting. It was almost on my face, its underside thrown into shadow by the half-moon.

I jabbed at it.

"*Cricri,*" it said, for that is what a Spanish-speaking frog says. (A Spanish-speaking dog says *guau* and a cat *miau.*) It didn't move until I punched its soft belly, launching it into the shadows.

Then I shut off the alarm and crawled out of my tent. A knee-high mist had settled onto the sand, and a faint odor of dirty armpits drifted down from the mud skin early floodwaters had deposited on the grass shelf above the beach.

We had left Pucallpa the day before. On the occasion of our departure I had resolved to maintain a positive attitude toward our endeavor. The Chmielinski Method, as I thought of it. Attention to order and faithful execution of duty would get us to the sea. And so, as cook of the day, I set forthrightly into the matutinal routine one of us would, we hoped, execute daily for the next three thousand miles. I dunked myself in the Ucayali, boiled drinking water, woke Chmielinski, boiled coffee, boiled breakfast, packed lunch, boiled more water, watched the sun sneak up over the grass, packed my gear. At 5:35 the air temperature was about 85 degrees and rising. Cursing the mosquitoes and chasing Chmielinski, I dragged my kayak to the river and put in.

Two miles downstream, in the morning light, the river and the horizon blended into a solid silver-blue canvas, and I felt as if I were paddling inside a cloud. I would not say that I was joyous at that moment, for the blue sky signaled a long, hot day, but neither was I tormented. I had something new working in my favor on this leg of the trip—my kayak.

Chmielinski had sold the white-water boats in Pucallpa, and we had continued our journey in the sixteen-foot Aquaterra "Chinook" sea kayaks Sergio Leon had stored there for us. The new boats were a deliverance. The white-water kayaks had been highly maneuverable, but now we were navigating a river that day by day became more oceanlike. The obstacles we would face included tropical storms, hard winds, rolling waves, and extreme distances. The sea kayaks, longer and wider than the white-water boats, were sturdy and fast. They held a straight line in all but the strongest currents, and they were equipped with pedal-operated rudders, which greatly reduced the strain on my aching wrists and forearms.

And this was *my* boat. Unlike the white-water kayak, no one else had used it. I took a captain's pride in my new craft. On its tail Chmielinski had painted "S.S. Elyse," after my girlfriend back home (his boat was the "S.S. Joanna"). The good ship *Elyse* was about as comfortable as a thing can be if you have to sit in it twelve hours a day. Its broad, open cockpit allowed me to bend my knees, and I had glued foam-rubber padding to the plastic seat. It had deck straps fore and aft and storage pockets in the cockpit. As we left the beach that morning I had, within arm's reach, my Swiss Army knife, a water bottle, a pineapple, a dozen bananas, two papayas, sunscreen, lip balm, T-shirt, rain gear, baseball hat, spare sunglasses, mosquito repellent, an emergency medical kit, and my waterproof briefcase with pens and notebooks. For the first time in a long time I felt comfortable, and in control.

In the swift new boats we traveled the one hundred twenty

miles from Pucallpa to Contamana in two days. *Conta*, in the Chama language, is "palm tree," and *mana* is "hill." There were no palm trees in Contamana, or, as far as I could tell, any Indians, but there was a hill, a five-hundred-foot sandstone bluff that is the last significant rising in the land all the way to the sea.

Contamana was about the size of Atalaya, but by Amazon standards much wealthier. It had timber nearby, gold in the surrounding creeks, a healthy rice industry—growers and brokers had packed the town for selling season—-and a state-owned PetroPeru refinery. (It is said that eleven thousand PetroPeru employees earn as much as 175,000 schoolteachers.)

Along the waterfront soft electric lights lit a neat wooden promenade, and beneath the lights smiling men in clean shirts walked arm in arm with pretty women in long cotton dresses. Duckwalks lined the graded, well-drained dirt streets, and behind them stood sturdy wooden houses. Every fluorescent bulb in the ice-cream parlor worked. Smooth new felt covered the pool hall's three tables.

And Contamana was connected with the beyond: It had a satellite dish, a television store, and a steel-and-glass church. In this last we made camp (rice brokers had filled the lone hotel), though only with reluctance did the Italian priest allow a Pole to sleep in his vestibule.

We walked to a waterfront restaurant and ordered fried chicken, hearts-of-palm salad, and rice. A man named Raoul joined us there. A mutual acquaintance from Pucallpa, a pilot, had radioed Raoul and asked him to keep an eye out for us. Raoul was wide and dark, with a serious stomach, thick black hair, and a goatee. Though fifty-six, he looked much younger. An engineer, he had come to Contamana from Lima ten years before to work on a potable-water project, but funding had disappeared. He had stayed in Contamana to build irrigation systems and broker rice. Now he was waiting to see what would happen under "Alan."

That was how most Peruvians referred to their new president, Alan Garcia. The accent falls on the second syllable, so the name ends with a rising, optimistic tone: a-LAN. Ninety-two percent of the electorate had turned out for the vote, which Garcia had won handily, receiving more votes than the next eight candidates combined.

For Peru, after twelve years of military rule and six years under a conservative president, Fernando Belaúnde Terry, Garcia's election represented a peaceful revolution. He was young—only a few years before the election he had been singing for his rent in the cafes of Paris—and left of center. In his inaugural address he had announced a cap on the interest payments for Peru's staggering $14 billion national debt, a bold and unprecedented move that rocked the international financial community and established Peru as a leader in modern South America. (Soon thereafter, both Brazil and Ecuador went into complete default.) Peruvians, long accustomed to mockery from the outside world, were proud of Alan, Raoul especially so. He was a member of Garcia's political party, the Alianza Popular Revolucionaria Americana, which in its sixty-one-year existence had never won a presidential election.

"But I am bothered by our debt," Raoul said. "We should pay, I know, but we cannot pay if we have nothing to pay with. The answer is for you Americans to buy the things we manufacture, instead of stealing our oil and wood."

"Peruvian products are poorly made," Chmielinski said. "There is no market for them. They break."

Raoul sighed. "You are right about that."

"And if you get a lot of American money down here," I said, "Alan will not be president for long."

"You are right about that, too," Raoul said. "We will be like Guatemala, or El Salvador."

We had finished our dinners. We each ordered another.

"There is a joke we tell," Raoul said as he filled our glasses with beer. "You Americans have a machine. You push a black button, you get coffee. You push a white button, you get milk. You pull a handle, you get apple pie. In Peru, we pull on a black udder, we get coffee. We pull on a white udder, we get milk. We pull the tail, we get cowshit. We sell you the coffee and the milk and we eat the shit."

In the morning Raoul brought us fresh bread from the bakery and found a crew of boys to haul our boats down to the river. As we pushed off from the dock, he leaned close. "There is something I have wanted to ask," he whispered. He looked around to see if anyone was eavesdropping. "What do you do for women? I have been married for twenty-five years, and if I did not have my little honey at night . . ."

"After twelve hours on the river," Chmielinski said, "we could have the most beautiful girls in Contamana and we would only fall asleep." This was true.

Two hours later the sky suddenly turned gray, then black, a strong wind blew up, and I heard a rattling sound to my left and saw a field of wild cane flatten along the bank. Seconds later the river erupted in a white, pocked froth and choppy two-foot waves. My kayak bucked wildly and I couldn't see ten feet. The squall passed in minutes, but in its wake, soaked and shivering with cold and fright, I found myself longing for clean, safe Contamana.

But Contamana proved to be an exception. Although I had often envisioned the Amazon as dark and gooey, on the river, at least, the light is immense and the sun shines, if anything, too long. And there are no mountains in the distance, no hills, no skyline—nothing to suggest the possibility of escape. It is flat, forgotten, suffocating country, mucky floodplain with long stretches of mud and sand and toppled trees. And so in the forlorn little river towns there is darkness of another sort, a darkness of the spirit, a giving up, a sense of utter defeat at the hands of the government, the weather, the insects, the river itself.

We paddled late into the night, until we arrived at Orellana, a town about the size of Contamana but not nearly as wealthy. Raoul had given us his card and the name of a friend. The friend wasn't home, but his sister, her arm wrapped in a sling, let us sleep on the back porch of her creaky one-room shack. The porch hung right over the Ucayali, on four skinny stilts, and through the one-inch gaps between the floorboards we could see the river streaming past fifteen feet below.

As we erected our tents two dozen black-toothed men and slack-jawed youths climbed onto the fragile porch.

"You will see!" one of the men yelled. "The rain is coming!"

Another said, "When that first wave hits you, you will fall right out of those silly canoes! The river will eat you!"

Without pausing in his work, Chmielinski asked, "What do experts such as yourselves recommend we do?"

"Jump out of your boats!" a third man yelled. "That is what this asshole did last week!" He pointed to the first man. "He fell out. Now he is afraid of the river!"

The other men laughed, nervously, then fell silent and watched us erect our tents and sponge out our kayaks. No one offered to help. No one asked questions. I had the uneasy feeling that our ambition angered them.

Chmielinski quizzed them. No one could identify the town's namesake, Francisco de Orellana, no one knew where the river ended, no one could tell us the distance to the next town, although this last question did at least generate a discussion. "One day," a man said. "Four hours," another said. "One day and a half." "Half an hour." "Ten hours." "Twelve hours." "Two days."

Such maddening confusion wasn't entirely ignorance. Linear distance means nothing on the river. Travel is measured in time and the number of river bends, or *vueltas*, between one point and another. A lot depends on how well a man paddles, or the strength of his boat's motor, or on where his destination happens to be situated at that time. According to those men, only a few years ago, Orellana had stood on the opposite bank and there had been islands in the river.

The men hung around until we zipped our tents closed and blew out our candles. They returned at dawn. The one who had fallen out of his boat told us to leave the main trunk of the Ucayali and follow a long canal, the Puinahua, that he described as a shortcut to Iquitos. The other men corroborated this, and we made the colossal mistake of trusting them.

We spent four days lost in the Puinahua Canal, and at towns even more desperate than miserable Orellana. At Victoria (thatch huts, one-room schoolhouse, thin frightened men, suspicious women who herded their wormy, scabby-headed children away as we paddled up) we weren't allowed out of our boats. The teacher was gone, and his nervous assistant said, "There are gringo terrorists around here," ran into the schoolhouse, and slammed the door.

In Juancito, a group of men as silent and spooky as vultures shadowed us as we dragged our boats to a falling-down cook shack that had not fallen quite as far as the other dozen or so shacks that made up the village. A crude hand-painted sign declared this the "Hotel Sheraton." An enormous woman was cutting waxed paper into napkins. She tugged at her underwear and screamed at the men to leave. No one moved. She served us plates of stale rice and fish fried in rancid oil. Halfway through the meal a storm descended and the men ran away. We were so anxious to leave Juancito that we did the same, hauling our boats down to the canal as fast as we could and paddling right into the middle of the black tempest.

In the deluge I quickly lost sight of Chmielinski and either bank, but he had taught me a few things after my previous encounter with river rain. I drew my spray skirt around me, tightened my windbreaker, and pointed the boat's nose into the hooking waves. I was warm and dry and far happier than I had been in the Hotel Sheraton.

The storm lasted about twenty minutes, but waves continued to slap the noses of our kayaks for the next few hours, which noticeably reduced our speed. We met a riverboat stuck on a sandbar in the middle of the canal. It had been there two days, its beefy captain, six crewmen, and their wives and children running through the cases of soft drinks, crackers, beer, canned fish, and fruit they had intended to trade along the canal. The captain leaned over the rail and handed us each an Inca Cola.

"Where are we?" Chmielinski asked.

"You are lost!" the captain said. "So are we." He did not know when the water would rise to lift his boat off the bar.

We paddled on. The only other person we saw that afternoon was a man in a suit beating upstream on a motor-driven canoe and broadcasting to the apparently uninhabited banks through a hand-held, amplified megaphone. I heard only, "Tonight's movie, the fabulous Tarzan," before Chmielinski turned to intercept the man, who quickly put down his megaphone and accelerated away from us.

That night we camped in mud and the next day arrived at Bretaña, which in addition to the usual dozen shacks had a bodega. The owner, Emilio Rios Lozano, let us pitch our tents on the wood floor. He had covered the walls with pictures of blond-haired women in various stages of undress.

Here, too, sullen, meek men shuffled into the bodega, lined up against one wall, and stood and stared as Lozano opened two liters of warm beer for us. He had served nine years in the Peruvian navy and seen California, sort of. His boat had sat in port three weeks, but he had not been permitted ashore. In a fit of pique he had quit the navy and settled in Bretaña. Now he was too in debt to leave. "Fuck the navy!" he said.

The silent men stared and swatted mechanically at mosquitoes. Lozano exhibited more flair. When he had a point to make, which was every few seconds, he suspended his monologue and studied the feeding insect until all other eyes were on it. Then he dispatched it with a furious wallop, examined the corpse, and returned to his subject.

"What was I saying? Yes—why do we not have soldiers here? They have soldiers in the mountains, soldiers on the coast, soldiers on the border with Ecuador." *Slap.* "No soldiers down here."

With emphatic gestures he divided my tent top into Peru's mountains, coast, and Ecuadorian border. There were soldiers all over it. The Amazon basin was somewhere down the side of the tent, soldierless and forgotten.

Slap.

"Why do you need soldiers here?" Chmielinski asked Lozano.

"You could be bandits."

"But we are not bandits."

"But you could be."

The other men nodded in agreement and continued to swat.

"And the floods," Lozano said. "They fuck up everything. They come too early, they come too late, we can grow nothing but yucca. *Yucca.* Here in the great jungle. I *puke* on yucca."

But the floods that destroy these people also sustain them, enriching the notoriously poor jungle soil with Andean silt. Of course, when the floods come too early or too late, which is often enough, the corn and rice and plantain crops either drown or wither.

Lozano's wife brought us a plate of fried fish heads and hissed at her husband. I had trouble with the meal—the fish seemed to be staring back at me. I recognized the look. It was the same one the men were wearing.

Lozano pulled three more liters of beer from the shelf. His wife hissed again and disappeared behind a curtain at the back of the shop.

"At least I have my women," he said.

"Your women?"

"Nine. I have nine women. And"—he fumbled with his fingers—"forty-seven children. No, forty-eight. One more last week."

He said this so matter-of-factly I believed him.

We left Bretaña at dawn. Chmielinski propped a magazine on his deck, a four-month-old copy of the international *Time* he had purchased in Pucallpa, and read while he paddled.

"What does this mean," he shouted to me, " 'mob connections'?" That was a story on Frank Sinatra. There was an interview with Paul McCartney, about John Lennon: "What is 'maneuvering swine'?"

As he read, his head down, his boat veered back and forth and he paddled a third again my distance, which about evened us out. My wrists were healing, but I was not yet strong. At night my fingers swelled and my hands curled, and I had to sleep facedown, arms extended at my side.

But Chmielinski did not seem to mind my slow pace. I was thankful for that. Although the towns between Pucallpa and Iquitos were generally awful, the long empty stretches between were wonderful, and I wanted to take time to enjoy them. The green jungle wall was faceless, but not silent. We paddled along it as if eavesdropping. Birds chattered, howler-monkey troops roared loud as jet engines, dolphins breached and blew, and every once in a while a mulelike shrieking sliced the humid air. The day we left Bretaña I asked a man in a dugout canoe about the shrieks. He said they were made by a *ronsoso*, which he described as a wild pig. (I asked him to pronounce the name three times, thinking he may have meant a *ronsoco*, or capybara, which is the world's largest rodent and is sometimes referred to as a water pig.)

Every few miles the bush broke and opened onto a fine white beach. Racks made from driftwood and twine rose from the sand like skeletons, the wood gnarled and bleached like bone, and across them hung layers of fish caked in salt, drying to a marblelike consistency. Plastic sheets stretched from the racks to the sand, and beneath these fishermen hid to keep from baking as dry and hard as their catch. That afternoon, when the sun grew so hot that touching bare skin to the kayak blistered my arms, we stopped and crawled into one of the plastic tents and sat with a quiet man named Rogelio.

He had beached his *lancha*. The fishing was poor that day, he said, and he had chosen instead to read a *fotografía*, a sort of comic book with white bubbles of dialogue superimposed on black-and-white photos, often of men and women in passionate embrace. We broke out crackers and canned fish from the kayaks and read with Rogelio.

"What is this word for?" I asked, pointing to a panel.

Rogelio said, "It is where a woman keeps her melons."

"And this?"

"When you want a woman so bad you are like a dog."

"This?"

"A man hurts you so you hurt him worse."

Rogelio said he had been camped on the beach, alone, for a week, and that he would store half his catch and sell the rest in Pucallpa, where he lived. He was in no hurry to return. This was his secret place, and he had food and the pretty beach and a dozen *fotografías*.

When the sun was lower we readied our boats for the water. Like most river men, Rogelio found our *canoas* strange but *muy lindo*—very pretty. He administered the universal test—a rap on the hull—and nodded approval.

We reached the end of the sad Puinahua Canal near dusk on our fourth day and spent the early evening pursuing the lights of Requena. Glowing on the horizon, they promised a meal, a shower, a bed, but after we grounded our boats in a swamp and storm clouds blacked out the stars, we resigned ourselves to a miserable night sleeping sitting up in the rain, expecting *all the things in which we do not believe.*

Then we heard a motor, Chmielinski yelled, and a flashlight beamed in the dark. A fishing boat was stuck in the muck. We sank to our hips in swamp goo, helped the captain break it loose, and followed him through a hidden channel into the city. But Requena stank of diesel and sewage, derelict hulls and mean-looking deckhands clogged the port, and even in the dead of night, as we sat in the captain's shack trying to sleep, the humidity was stifling. We vowed that from there on, we would make camp at the first dugout canoe we saw after five o'clock.

At 5:19 the next afternoon Chmielinski said, "That one."

As we tied up on shore, intending to follow a path that led from a beached canoe to, we hoped, a dwelling, an old woman paddled up, shuffled on the floor of her canoe, and emerged with two papayas.

"A present," was her only explanation before she continued on her way.

Chmielinski climbed the muddy bank, disappeared into the bush, and found the hut we had expected.

"We heard you were coming," its owner, Antonio Severiano Luna, said when he came down to help drag my boat to his home. He was small, quiet, and old but ageless in the way the river men are if they have a lot of Indian blood. Their faces hardly wrinkle, and they go to their graves with heads of thick black hair.

"How did you know?" I asked.

He shrugged. "A friend of a friend of my brother saw you on the river two days ago."

He shoved my boat under his thatch-covered platform and we climbed the ladder. Chmielinski was already setting up the stove. I wedged pegs in between the floorboards and strung our tents. A young woman who Antonio said was his daughter-in-law watched us, four wide-eyed children clinging to her skirt, and Antonio introduced a second woman, his wife, toothless, bent, and apparently quite a bit older than he.

Antonio sat on the floor and watched Chmielinski cook a pot of chili. Cooking may have been Chmielinski's favorite activity. He made a show of it, passing around spoonfuls of food, asking questions, talking about Poland and the world beyond Peru. Usually he wound up with more food than he gave away, our boats, as we paddled away in the morning, laden with pineapples and papayas and bananas.

I dug in my boat and found a bottle of wine Durrant and Bzdak had given me in Pucallpa. I poured two fingers in my plastic cup and passed it to Antonio. He threw it down like a shot of whiskey.

He said, "Thank you."

I poured another shot. He threw it down. We repeated this until the bottle was empty.

Then the young woman took me aside. Her name was Eravita.

"We have a custom here," she said. "When you sleep in a man's house, he may offer you his woman."

I did not reply.

She said, "What do you think about that?"

I thought that if I slept with her, her husband would kill me when he returned. I also thought that she had fine brown eyes.

"That is an interesting custom," I said.

"You would enjoy that, would you not?"

I gave in. "I would."

"I will ask Antonio."

"Antonio?"

"He owns the land."

"So . . ."

"So you must sleep with his wife."

The old hag!

"Wait!" I said. "I am very tired. We have been on the river all day, and we have a long way to go tomorrow . . ."

High cackling laughter erupted from behind the curtain that shielded the cooking porch from the main room. Then Eravita burst out laughing, and Antonio. A joke on the gringo.

Rain poured down the thatch roof, rolled off, and splattered on the clay outside the house, but not a drop leaked through. Chmielinski and I ate and retired to our tents. The women and children crawled beneath the single mosquito net under which the family slept. I wrote in my diary. The rain stopped and slurping sounds drifted up from the river, punctuated by dolphin blasts. At night, I had noticed, these seemed to be followed by a low moan that sounded something like a man's voice.

Chmielinski blew out his candle and when I had filled my pages I blew out mine. Only then did Antonio stand up and cross the room and slide beneath the netting. I heard giggles and whispers and teasing.

We heard you were coming. We were not sneaking through the jungle alone and unobserved. We were guests.

15 *The Marañón*

Twelve days after leaving Pucallpa we followed the Ucayali into the Marañón entering it from the right, or south. It is at this confluence that the river becomes, in scope if not in name, the Amazon. In fact, it is called both the Marañón and the Amazon for the next four hundred miles, until it crosses the Brazilian border (where Brazilians then call it the Solimões). In any case, at the confluence it is almost two miles wide, or more than three times the width of the Ucayali. It took me thirty-five minutes to paddle to an exposed sandbar in the middle of the river. Chmielinski got there ten minutes ahead of me, and when I arrived he was running up and down the ivory-white sand, hefting his paddle like a spear and shouting "The Amazon!" for no one but me to hear.

A small village, Puerto Franco, sits atop a low bluff of sandstone and clay a few miles below the Ucayali, on the left bank. A dozen bare-chested Indians awaited our landfall there. (Yaguas, I believe, though the differences between *mestizo* and Indian, let alone Indian and Indian, blur so much from that point on down the river as to be meaningless.) A woman descended the bluff. Chmielinski gave her his paddle, and while she played with it in her wood canoe, breaking into an excited whooping, we climbed the bluff.

"Where have you come from?" a squat, muscular man asked when we gained the top. He had broad shoulders, narrow hips, and a sharp, hairless face.

"From where the river starts," Chmielinski said (in Spanish, literally, "from where the river is born").

"Pucallpa?"

"Farther."

The man conferred with his friends. "Atalaya?"

"Arequipa," Chmielinski said.

None of them knew where, or what, Arequipa was, and our conversation faltered. We studied the woman in the canoe, now deftly working the tricky plastic paddle. Behind her, the wind had whipped the tawny river into whitecaps, and I had to strain to see the far bank, a thin green line between water and sky. But for that verdant ribbon I might have been looking at an ocean. *El Río Mar*, as the Amazon is also known: The River Sea.

"How long have you been on the river?" the man asked.

"Three and a half months."

His jaw dropped, revealing a mouth full of fine teeth, and he and his friends jumped up and down and whooped as the woman in the canoe had. At first I thought they were mocking us, but then they clapped our shoulders happily. They lived here, the river came, the river went. That it started so far away, and that we might one day see the place where it ended, delighted them.

We climbed back into our kayaks. As we departed we passed two women poised at the end of the village, silhouetted on the bluff. Three feet in front of them a chunk of earth the size of a small house broke away and fell into the Marañón. Their huts stood a few feet from the lip of the bluff, but the women reacted to the disappearance of their front yards with only a glance.

The river came, the river went, it took their homes with it. Soon the huts would follow that clot of sand and clay. Not long after that, the rest of the village would fall, too, and the families would move on and start again. And Peru would not know where Puerto Franco had gone.

In the roadless bush the Marañón is a kind of country highway packed with river craft, only some of which might properly be called boats. On the Ucayali we had seen perhaps one boat a day, other than our own, but on the Marañón we never saw fewer than three at once, most of them driven by seven-horsepower outboards onomatopoetically called *peque-peques,* with five-foot-long drive-shafts that doubled as rudders. Only the motors on these craft might be considered standard issue. The hulks were wild amalgams of uneven planks, the cabins patchworks of plastic, cardboard, and sheet metal. Often the cabin roofs were thatch, and threatened with ignition by the smoking motors below. Always, in each hull, at least one shirtless man bailed away in a bobbing motion, his dark face bathed in sweat, his water pail rising from the hull and spilling over the side in a rhythm so steady he seemed to be linked to the motor itself.

Passengers, and their pigs and chickens and twine-wrapped crates, were stuffed into the holds of these precarious water taxis well beyond overload, buried in darkness even at noon, as if bound in prison ships. Trapped and helpless, they screamed when the wind picked up and a storm descended and the boats rocked. In those moments I gave thanks that I was in the kayak depending solely on myself, and I worried about Bzdak and Durrant. Though the *Jhuliana* had appeared sturdy on the banks of the Ucayali, she would be dwarfed by the mighty Marañón. But as we paddled among the river traffic there was no word of her.

Rafts also navigated the Marañón floating along at the river's dawdling pace, perhaps one knot. Families drifted slowly to Iquitos with the fruits of a season's labors, one raft carrying a ton of oranges, another a pyramid of coconuts, another bananas ripening too fast for market.

That afternoon we tied up to a raft that struck me as the most ingenious piece of marine engineering I had yet seen. The floor consisted of two dozen fifteen-foot *topa* logs lashed together with liana vines (*topa* is a strong, light, buoyant wood akin to balsa), with a thatch-roofed, bamboo cage on top. The cage held—this amazed me—six cows.

Two huge oars, each about twenty feet long, were fastened fore and aft, and a mahogany blade about two feet square had been lashed to the water end of each oar. The oars were used not for power but to steer the raft away from whirlpools and back eddies. Three young men slumped next to the cage, glazing in the sun.

We ran our boats up onto the raft and woke the men, who were from a village far up the Marañón. Given the one-knot current, they had been afloat . . .

"Three weeks," the tallest of them said. Like his shipmates, he wore only a pair of tight cotton shorts. In fact, the raft appeared to hold little else but the men, their shorts, and the cows, which they would sell by the pound in Iquitos.

"Surely they have lost weight," Chmielinski said.

"Yes," the man said. "But what can you do?" They would sell the raft as well. *Topa* fetched a good price.

"How old are the cows?" I asked.

"Three years."

"How much will you get for them?"

He estimated a price in *soles*. At the current rate of exchange, it came to about a hundred and fifty dollars apiece.

Three men, three years raising the cattle, three weeks on the river watching the cattle waste away. Chmielinski said, "That is a lot of work for not much money."

The man shrugged and said again, "What can you do?"

Iquitos sits on the left bank of the Marañón, on the outside curve of the wide, gradual right turn the river makes before it finally sets its course directly for the Atlantic, twenty-three hundred miles due east. The visitor arriving in Iquitos by boat, even if that boat is a kayak, climbs a rickety wooden stairway from the river and alights on a fading but gracious promenade that runs north along the Marañón for about a mile, or a third the city's length. Looking down into the river from the promenade one sees ocean-going freighters moored to floating concrete docks that rise and fall with the river, which will come up as much as thirty feet during the rainy season. Herons and egrets feed in the marsh below, and, to the east, waves break on the eleven-mile-long island, Padre, that divides the Marañón in two.

One senses immediately that Iquitos is at heart a river town.

Indeed, it is surrounded on three sides by rivers—the Nanay to the north, the Marañón to the east, the Itaya to the south—and to the west, the only road leading out of town ends abruptly in dense jungle after about twenty miles. Consequently, Iquitos is isolated in a way that Pucallpa is not, and has retained a certain grace. The pace is slow (it is too hot to move quickly, and in any case there is nowhere to go) and the fundamental rhythm is not that of the automobile. In fact, the preferred mode of intraurban transport is the motorbike. It is not unusual to see five or six abreast on the city's half dozen main streets, with three people on one machine— daughter at the helm, mother in the stern, grim-faced granny wedged snugly between them, the entire trio outfitted in dresses and heels and hurtling along the waterfront in the humid dusk.

Iquitos is not large as cities go, and it is not old. Though it was founded in the mid-1800s, it did not really grow until the rubber boom at the turn of the century. Still, its core has a colonial, vaguely Mediterranean tone (including a cast-iron building de- signed by Alexandre Gustave Eiffel and shipped from Europe in pieces); until the advent of air travel, Iquitos was closer to Europe than to Lima.

Situated in strategic proximity to two great jungle highways— the Napo River fifty-five miles east and the upper Marañón ninety miles south—Iquitos became the trade capital of the Peruvian jungle. Virtually isolated from outside authority, it developed a scandalous reputation, one not wholly undeserved. There was an oil rush of sorts in the 1970s, but mostly the oil companies came up dry, and turned their attentions farther into the jungle interior. Currently, the zeitgeist is heavily influenced by the cocaine and smuggling industries. One can walk into almost any bar and find the sort of soiled expatriate or local reprobate who enables the travel writer to turn a profit on a cocktail. (I had lunch one day with a Señor Merekike, who played the drunken cook in the film *Fitzcarraldo*. In real life, Merekike—"I slept in Mrs. Herzog's bed!"—is a drunken cook.) For all its reputation, however, and unlike Pucallpa, Iquitos does not seem wicked. If anything, it has simply refused to be influenced by any rhythms but its own, which are as unpredictable as the river itself.

The day after Chmielinski and I arrived, the city's municipal workers went on strike. They demonstrated in the central plaza, the civil guard was called out, and the air quickly filled with tear gas and voices shouting through bullhorns. According to the next day's papers, two people were wounded by gunfire. By the time the first shot was fired, however, I had already escaped around a corner, and the reports sounded flat and harmless.

But I ran anyway, ten blocks east, until I reached the riverfront promenade, which I then followed north, hoping to find the port captain's office. Chmielinski had decided that we could no longer travel the river safely without maps or charts. I walked for about half an hour. The bruised colonial facades gave way to low shacks of wood and plaster, and the streets were thick with people whose faces were surprisingly (to me) cosmopolitan—black, brown, red, yellow. I stopped and had a fine lunch prepared by a Chinese man whose grandfather had come to Iquitos during the rubber boom.

Five blocks farther on I found the port compound, but the guard said I was out of luck. No maps.

I stood outside the chain-link fence and watched a pockmarked naval officer instruct a squad of recruits in the art of saluting the colors. When he had finished his instructions he raised the Peruvian flag. It was upside down, and within seconds the wind had wrapped it around the pole.

A rotund, calmly sweating man had stopped next to me to watch this display. He was smoking a cigarette and he wore a starched white shirt, pressed cotton pants, and polished shoes.

"Poor Peru," he said in Spanish. He nodded toward the flag. "We defeat ourselves."

"Peru cannot find herself," I said.

"What do you mean?"

I told him about the problems we were having on the river, the trouble finding our way, the villages that disappeared.

"You need a map," he said.

"Where do we get one?"

"You don't. There are no maps."

"What do the big boats use? Or the navy?"

"Luck. Prayer. Smell. But they would never try anything as ridiculous as your trip. Why do you do this thing?"

I didn't have a good answer. To stand in Iquitos and say I was looking for adventure seemed trite. Off the top of my head I said I was writing a travel story for a magazine, and mentioned one for which I often worked. His eyes widened. He said he was a professional guide and had once spent three weeks with a writer from that very magazine. I did not believe him until he told me the writer's name, which I recognized.

"Maybe I can help you, too," he said. He led me down the street and into a bar and said, "Wait here." He disappeared in the direction of the port compound.

The bar was little more than a shack, but it had cold beer and a videocassette player. Six blank-faced peasant men dressed in ragged denims and sandals sat before the screen, intent on the one man who seemed to have the potential to unseat Tarzan as Cinema King of the Jungle—Indiana Jones. There was no sound, but they did not react when I joined them. My friend returned while Harrison Ford was suspended above a snake pit.

"Come," he said.

It was dark now. Stumbling, I followed him down the street, through a door, and into a courtyard. Three old women sat in wicker chairs, fanning themselves. They smiled. We walked past them into a room. The man closed and bolted the door, pulled the curtains, and lit a candle, which he placed on the floor. The room had no furniture.

He pulled something that looked like a scroll from beneath his jacket and rolled it partially open on the floor.

The scroll was actually a spool of butcher paper about two feet wide. On it someone had drawn, in pencil, a river chart, at a scale of about 1:100,000. It included towns, islands, and channels, and a trail of arrows showed at precisely which point between the banks the current ran swiftest. The chart began at Iquitos.

"How far does it go?" I asked.

"To Manaus," the man said. "It is new. This is the only copy. The river changes course so much that any chart more than a month old is out of date. Every few weeks the navy sends out a boat with a chart-making team. A friend of mine works on the boat. During the last trip he traced this from the original. Do you want it?"

If the chart was even half as accurate as it appeared to be, it was, at least to us, invaluable.

"How much?" I asked.

"Twenty dollars."

I opened my wallet and began counting out soles.

"Dollars," he said. "American."

I fished out my emergency stash, a U.S. twenty hidden in my shoe, and gave it to him. "Good," he said. "Be careful. The navy considers this chart classified information. If they find you with it, there will be trouble."

I tucked the chart under my shirt. It bulged.

"One more thing," the man said. "If you know anyone who needs my assistance, please send them to me. But do not tell them about the chart." He gave me his card, which I tucked in my shirt pocket unread, and opened the door. I left.

In the dark street every popping motorbike engine sounded like a gunshot, and the half-hour walk back to our hostel seemed interminable.

Durrant and Bzdak had arrived in Iquitos five days before us, their voyage on the *Jhuliana* punctuated by a twenty-four-hour poker game and loud disco music. They had a bundle of mail for me, my first communication from the States in two and a half months, since Cuzco. I sat in a soda fountain with them and drank milk shakes. While they watched television (Tarzan, of course, though this time a color, late-fifties version I didn't recognize), I read my mail. An uncle had died, a favorite aunt had cancer, my girlfriend loved me but was getting lonely, my dog no longer responded to the mention of my name.

When we returned to our hostel Durrant filled my medical kit with malaria tablets, sterile wipes and dressings, packets of rehydration powder, mosquito repellent, antivenin, syringes, and splints. In addition, she had found in Iquitos *sangre de grado,* literally "blood of the grado" tree. It is a kind of resin that when applied to wounds forms an elastic skin. She also outfitted us with a cedar oil said to be excellent for massaging sore joints and muscles (and was to prove particularly effective in combination with a half liter or so of *pisco*). She and Bzdak had sewn up sheets for us to use as bedding in the tropical nights.

I was alone in the hostel courtyard the next morning, packing these supplies into my kayak, when a man approached me. He looked Peruvian (short and dark), but he also looked like something of a pimp—he wore reflecting aviator sunglasses and an expensive watch with a band that was too thick for his thin wrists. As most people did, he inquired about my kayak. After I had explained the rudder and the storage system, he asked, "Are you having trouble with your visa?"

"No," I said, but it was a lie. All four of our Brazilian visas had long since expired, and we were having difficulty renewing them. In addition, the Brazilian consul, whose diplomatic passport had apparently been rejected once in Miami, was getting his revenge at my expense. I had visited his office three times and been told each time to return the next day. But I considered this no one's business but ours.

"Is Piotr Chmielinski here?" the man asked. I was surprised to hear him pronounce the tricky Polish name flawlessly.

"No," I said again. This time it was the truth. In fact, Chmielinski was at that moment running between Peruvian and Brazilian offices trying to negotiate our visas.

The man left, but he returned later that afternoon, while Chmielinski and I were making the last repairs on our boats. The two men spoke in Polish, Chmielinski wearing what I now recognized as his don't-get-in-my-face face.

The man walked over to me and examined the gear laid out around my kayak.

"American tent," he said in Spanish. "No good. A toy. I have a strong Polish tent." He looked at Chmielinski as if for approval, but received only a hard stare.

"Strong like these kayaks," the man continued. "Good Polish craftsmanship."

Chmielinski said, "The kayaks are American."

"That cannot be true," the man said.

"It is true," Chmielinski said. "The best you can get."

The man started to reply, thought better of it, and turned on his heel to leave. At the courtyard gate he said, "I am in the next building if you need me."

Chmielinski said nothing after the man left. We worked in silence until I finished gluing new foam rubber to the seat of my boat. Then I coaxed an explanation from him. He said the man was based in Peru as part of an unofficial wing of the Polish consulate. When Chmielinski's Polish expedition had first come to Peru, the man had shepherded them through the country. "Then we learned that he is spying on us everywhere. Asking questions, scaring our Peruvian friends. We break with him. And then after Solidarity we had the big demonstration in Lima. Now he is always watching."

He would not tell me more.

We left Iquitos four days before Christmas, having arranged to meet Bzdak and Durrant at the Brazilian border. It is Polish custom to keep a Christmas tree through the end of February, and to that end Chmielinski had glued a couple of three-inch, wire-trunk trees to the noses of our boats. "Joe, maybe one day you will find a present under that!"

We dragged the kayaks to the promenade and down the wooden steps, waded knee-deep into the marsh, and shoved off for Brazil, three hundred and thirty miles east.

A strong current sucked us along the waterfront, through a fleet of peeling-paint riverboats, waterlogged *peque-peques*, and rusting ghost freighters. Then we were beyond the city's northern edge, past swamps and rice fields where sad-faced men standing knee-deep in the river watched us as if they had nothing better to do. The city ended abruptly, jamming up against the bush, which rose in giant broccoli-like spears. Over the next ten miles the odd cattle ranch sprawled amid the spears like a neon-green carpet, but otherwise the wide, flat Marañón felt deserted. The bush thickened to a band of black satin, and once, the dim honk and boom of trumpet and drum jumped from it and someone shouted, but we could not see him. After the crowded streets of Iquitos the river seemed a lonely place.

Late the next day we passed, to our left, the mouth of the Napo River. A Spaniard, Francisco de Orellana, sailed down the Napo from Ecuador in 1542 on what would become the first recorded navigation of the Amazon from the Andes to the Atlantic. His looting and killing set the tone for the subsequent conquest of the basin, and his scrivener, Friar Carvajal, inadvertently named the great river through his fanciful account of a conflict with women warriors who sounded suspiciously like the Amazons of Greek myth. They were "very white and tall, and have hair very long and braided and wound about the head, and they are very robust and go about naked, but with their privy parts covered, with their bows and arrows in their hands, doing as much fighting as ten Indian men."

We made camp near the Napo, at the *caserío*, or river hamlet, of Señor Fausto Ramirez, his wife, and their thirteen children. In our honor the Ramirez family hung a transistor radio directly above our tents. Like most Peruvian radios this one had three volume levels—loud, louder, and *amigos norteamericanos.*

Before we retired, we were also treated to a dog fight. As the family gathered around, a black dog and white dog converged in a bloody dynamo in front of the *caserío*, a spectacle that ended with the black sinking its fangs into the white's throat. The white went down with a spooky death rattle.

No one had said a word during the fight, and when it was over they left in silence, all but Fausto's shy wife, who until then had answered our many questions—What is your name? What will the weather be tomorrow? How many children do you have?—with either "*Sí, señor*" or "*No, señor.*"

Now she murmured that the white dog had been hers.

"What did you call it?" Chmielinski asked.

She mumbled something in a small voice. We moved closer, and she repeated it: "Gringo."

By the evening of our third day out of Iquitos we were still a hundred and seventy miles short of the border and in trouble. Chmielinski's Peruvian visa, which he had been unable to extend, would expire at midnight the next night. If we did not reach the border by then, he risked jail.

Knowing this, we had paddled long, hard hours, and I was grumpy and exhausted from the work of it. I was not at all happy at dusk that third day, when, as the three-quarter moon rose to a chorus of frogs, Chmielinski announced that we would paddle through the night. We found a beach and stopped to rest and eat. Silent and petulant, I let Chmielinski do all the cooking.

An hour later we returned to the river. Night had fallen and the moon lit the jungle canopy, but down at water level bush and river had melted into one black, silent belt.

After paddling in near silence for two hours we took a floating break. I fell asleep. I awoke to Chmielinski whistling "Silent Night" and towing my kayak.

"I can paddle myself," I said, and did just that, but at a slow, sulking pace. I wanted to find a beach, bathe, stretch out in my tent, study the moon. I wanted peace and rest. Chmielinski's relentless good cheer only soured me further.

I let him travel a few yards ahead of me and ran through some games devised long ago for this sort of situation. I tried to remember all the lyrics to a favorite record album, but when I got stuck on "Grabbed my coat, put on my hat, made the bus in seconds flat" I decided instead to rebuild my apartment board by board—*These French doors will certainly look nice*—thought about cars (I detest cars), calculated the monthly payments on a new Porsche. Then I contented myself with listening to the *slap . . . slap . . . slap* of paddle on water.

When I woke up Chmielinski was no longer in front of me.

I saw a light to my left and one to my right. I paddled toward the left and yelled. No answer. I paddled right, but that light suddenly disappeared.

I panicked.

I tried to recall what the chart, which Chmielinski carried on his boat, had looked like when we had consulted it back at the beach. There was supposed to be an island coming up, with the main current bearing to the right of it. I aimed for what I guessed was the river's right bank and paddled hard until I heard music and yelling and suddenly realized how alone and vulnerable I was. I retreated to what I guessed was the middle of the river.

"Goddamnit, Piotr!" I shouted, and caught myself.

Something flapped past my head.

In the moonlight I made out the silhouette of what appeared to be an island. I sighed with relief. Surely Chmielinski would be waiting there. But the harder I paddled, the farther away the island seemed to be, as if it were running from me. Then a cloud blotted out the moon and the island disappeared.

In the blackness I couldn't tell whether I was paddling upstream or down, and that paralyzed me. I was afraid to turn my head for fear of losing what little sense of direction I still had. I stopped paddling and drifted. *I do not belong here,* I thought. *I belong at home, in a bar, walking my dog and teaching her my name. I belong somewhere with some LIGHT.* Instead I was stuck in the blackest part of the night in the blackest part of that black hemisphere, only a thin skin of cold plastic separating me from . . .

My kayak bumped something and stopped.

I reached with my paddle and prodded whatever it was.

Sand.

I stepped from my boat and sank to my shins, but two steps farther on it held me. When I looked into the night, however, the night looked back at me, a black plane dissolving into heartless silence. I couldn't tell where the sand began or ended.

I dug in my boat and found my flashlight. The batteries were dead.

Gingerly, I paced off an area large enough to hold my tent and boat. I groped in my boat and found my tent and the candle that was stored in it and set up camp. I had been on the Marañón at least fifteen hours that day and should have collapsed in sleep, but I lay awake worrying that the river would flood, or a storm would hit, or that someone had followed me. I got up and tied my tent to my boat. I opened my pocket knife and lashed it to my wrist.

Then I went out hard.

I woke up with the sun broiling me to a sizzle. My head ached, my mouth was so dry I couldn't swallow, I couldn't move my right arm, and my hands were asleep and swollen into half-moons the circumference of my paddle shaft.

I slithered out of the sweatbox tent and tried to get my bearings. I had camped on a finger of sand about ten yards by five, dead in the middle of the river, the banks more than a mile to either side. The sky held no clouds. It would be a long, hot, brutal day.

A vulture circled, swooped low, appraised me, and landed at the tip of my island. I grabbed my paddle and chased after it, screaming, "No way, asshole!" It jumped in the air and circled slowly a few feet overhead.

Panic boiled in my stomach. *This is the way a crazy man acts*, I thought, and then, *Order. I need order.*

I unpacked my boat, concentrating hard on every movement, as if that might block out my fear. My hands shook. I set everything out to dry, sponged out the boat, scrubbed the cockpit, checked the water bucket. Nearly full. I forced down a liter.

I dove into the river, washed, dried naked in the sun. I inventoried my resources. The lunch bucket held two cans of cooked rice, three chocolate bars, and a can of sardines. Three *comidas plásticas* were crammed into the kayak's nose. I opened a bag of sweet-and-sour pork, mashed it cold with a bag of rice, and made myself eat it.

We had traveled forty miles that first day out of Iquitos, sixty miles each of the next two days, and, I estimated, thirty miles the night before. That left a hundred and forty miles to the border. With luck, two days.

I packed my boat and set off, but I found myself paddling tentatively, as if not fully committed to the task. The circulation had returned to my hands, but I couldn't raise my arms above my chest, and my wrists crackled. The sky, a hot, depressing blue, offered no hint of relief. I longed for the happy gray of clouds and rain.

My intuition said Chmielinski was all right, but I felt like a complete fool. I had set off to chronicle an expedition, and now I was alone on the river. Though I had imagined the journey playing out in dozens of different scenarios, this had never been one of them.

I stopped paddling, drifted, dozed. I woke up when the boat rocked and almost tipped over. Four-foot waves were rolling to my bow and the sky had blackened to something close to night. Here was the storm I had longed for. It scared the bejesus out of me.

I scrambled into my rain suit and secured the spray skirt around my waist and cockpit. Reeds fluttering on the horizon signaled a shallows, with luck a beach. I plowed toward them, punching head-on through the rollers, and hit sand as the sky let loose. I dragged my boat up on the beach, sat in it, and let the storm pound me.

After it had passed I heard voices behind me and turned in my seat to find a leather-faced peasant and a small boy studying me as if I were choice driftwood.

"Where are his legs?" the boy asked the man.

The man said, "He doesn't have any."

"Hello," I said. I stayed in the boat and showed them the compass affixed to my deck.

"Always north," the man said. "A miracle."

"How far to Brazil?" I asked.

"Two hours," the boy said.

"Two days," the man said, "but you must be very careful. Stay to the Peruvian side. The Colombians are all drug runners and hoodlums. They will shoot you."

Before I had come to Peru, of course, that was exactly what I had been told about Peruvians.

But after I thanked them and put back into the river, I could not deny that I was entering strange new country. The river itself had straightened out below Iquitos—there were few of the Ucayali's maddening curves—but it was chocked with islands so long it often took hours to paddle their length. I would forget that the land I saw was an island, until suddenly it fell away, and the true bank appeared a mile or two in the distance. In those moments, my known world abruptly redefined, I felt deceived.

In late afternoon the river narrowed into a long chute perhaps a mile wide, the current increased from one knot to about three, the islands disappeared, and I sped through a no-man's land. On my right, to the south, lay Peru, its bush thick and solid save for an occasional thatch hut and dugout canoe. On the north bank, however, most of the bush had disappeared. Colombia. A procession of sleek powerboats plied the bank, and I saw one sprawling ranch after another, their stately white houses and fat cattle a wealthy contrast to Peru's pitiful huts and ribby beasts. In front of each hacienda stood a large dock. If I were writing a novel and needed a setting for a drug baron's headquarters, I would think: This.

So I was surprised when the bullets flew from the Peruvian side.

At first I heard only the gun's report, to my right. On the bank, a few hundred yards from my boat, a half dozen figures were jumping up and down and waving their arms. *So long, bozos.* I was in no mood to perform for a bunch of trigger-happy Peruvians. I paddled south as hard and fast as I could.

This, of course, was not fast at all.

A bullet hissed across my bow. They were not aiming for my cute little Christmas tree. Past them but still in range, I turned upstream and raised my arms.

"Don't shoot!" I yelled.

They shot again.

They stopped shooting when I put my hands down and began to paddle toward them. When I landed I saw that they were sailors. Boys. The sergeant, who held the only rifle, could not have been nineteen years old.

"Merry Christmas," he said.

He led me to a watchtower. Inside sat a desk and a man, and on the man's shoulder a parrot that had shit down the back of his shirt. As I entered, the man swung around to face me. He wore officer's insignia, mirror sunglasses, a pencil mustache, and greased black hair combed straight back.

"Your friend left this for you," he said.

Sea kayak with Christmas tree, Iquitos.

On the River Sea: Piotr Chmielinski (left)
and the author near the Brazilian border,
two thousand miles from the Atlantic.

Friends in Tabatinga

Piotr Chmielinski and *cabaclo* fisherman
with the author's birthday dinner.

In the storm's wake on the Solimões.

Piotr Chmielinski (foreground)
and the author.

Sea kayak with bushmaster.

The author (left), and Piotr Chmielinski
in sea kayaks; Kate Durrant aboard the
Roberto II.

Downtown Gurupá.

The author (left), Piotr Chmielinski, and *caboclo* fishermen near Marajó Bay.

Oz – the author (left) and Piotr Chmielinski at Belém.

The author (left) and Piotr Chmielinski at
the mouth of the Amazon.

He gave me a paper bag with half a loaf of stale bread, a candle, a hand-drawn map, and a note: "Joe—Meet you at border—Piotr."

There were other uniforms to appease. Civil guard, customs, port captain. One rickety shack corresponded to each. I knocked on the door that said *Guardia Civil.* No answer. A little girl was watching me.

"Where are they?" I asked.

"Drunk," she said. "Make more noise."

I banged again, harder, until a young man opened the door and zipped his pants. Behind him, a half dozen bodies of both sexes lounged on cots, and empty beer bottles littered the floor.

"Kayak Two has arrived!" he announced, and one by one the bodies rose and came to the door and shook my hand. Someone gave me a list of boats that had passed the checkpoint. The last name on the list, written in Chmielinski's hand, was *Kayaka Dos.*

I put my initials next to it, the man gave me a papaya, and I left. I knocked once at customs and once at the port captain's office, received no response, and continued right on down to the bank and my boat. The boy who had shot at me did not ask to see my papers, but he did wish me luck.

"Why did you shoot?" I asked as I untied *Kayaka Dos.*

"Look," he said, and pointed along the bank to a dock and, farther along, to two dugout canoes.

"What?" I asked.

"No boats."

So that was it. Two canoes, but no real boats. The navy, the civil guard, the port captain. Here at the border, in the heart of cocaine country, none of them had boats.

But they had guns.

Not until I was well into the middle of the river did I stop shaking.

At sunset I beached near a big, stinking mangrove log, jumped up and down on it to chase out the snakes (with no proof that the act was more than superstition), dragged my boat behind the log, and erected my tent. I did not build a fire. Later, after dark, I heard voices and a motor idling in the water, but they moved on. I heard shooting all through the night but dismissed this as the unfettered joy of Christmas. I dozed. Twice I woke to a loud scratching sound beneath my tent, but whatever it had been was gone in the morning.

I felt strong and paddled all morning without a break. The river widened slightly. I passed wild, uninhabited islands and heard the wind-over-glacier roars of howler monkeys. I stuck to the Peruvian side until I miscalculated the current and got sucked around an island into what I had come to think of as the Godfather Zone, within shouting distance of one of the Colombian haciendas. I saw a dock with three powerboats and several men, and heard them laughing. I thought I saw one point at me.

Suddenly a motor-powered wooden dory heading upstream veered away from the Colombian bank, directly for me. I froze. But it was a boatload of Indians, and they waved as they passed.

At the island's far end—I could not reach it fast enough—I cut back to the Peruvian side. My Peru! The wind picked up, the river grew choppy. Three men in a canoe drew alongside me. I was glad to see them. Chmielinski's crude map had been useless.

The man in front grabbed my bow.

"Ello meester," he said. "My frin."

"Merry Christmas," I said in Spanish.

He said, also in Spanish, "Do you have any brandy?"

"No."

"Where are you from?"

"The United States."

"Where are you going?"

"Brazil."

"Why?"

As I described my trip it sounded frivolous. I felt sure these peasants would see it only as a rich man's indulgence. When I said that I had been on the river four months, the man turned to his friends and gave a low whistle. He had not let go of my bow. He said, "You are CIA."

"No."

"DEA."

"No."

I was surprised that he was so familiar with the acronyms of U.S. government agencies, but I should not have been. In 1982, under heavy pressure from the Reagan administration and with the assistance of U.S. advisers, the Belaúnde government had instituted several programs intended to curtail the coca industry. Drug barons and peasants had combined to oppose the programs, with predictable results—in one incident, nineteen anti-coca workers were murdered in their sleep. That the government campaign ultimately proved as ineffectual as it was unpopular was, on the whole, a function of economics. In 1985, Peru had an international debt of $14 billion, legal exports of less than $3 billion, and coca exports of $800 million. A peasant could earn about four and a half dollars a day picking coca, or three to four times what he could make any other way, assuming he could find other work. A coca farmer made five times what he would growing the next-most-profitable crop, cacao. And these were the people at the bottom of the drug pyramid. Profits for the *narcotraficantes* themselves were, of course, enormous. "No DEA," I said. "No CIA."

"Tell me," he said. "What do you think of Alan?"

"He is intelligent and brave."

The man smiled. Suddenly he gripped my wrist, hard. My spine stiffened.

"Good luck," he said.

Then he and his friends turned upstream and paddled away.

For the next several hours I cleaved to the Peruvian bank and saw no one until the middle of the afternoon, when the bush broke to reveal a cluster of huts. I asked a couple of kids the distance to Puerto Alegría, the last military checkpoint before the border. I did not want to miss it. I had learned my lesson.

"This is Puerto Alegría," one of them said.

"Joe!"

Chmielinski ran down the bank and hauled my kayak back up before I could disembark. He handed me a cold bottle of beer, and, as sometimes happened when he was excited, he lost the careful discipline of his English.

"I know you are not feeling so happy that night," he said as he put my boat, and me, down. "So I try to leave you alone. You are singing"—he hummed *Grabbed my coat, put on my hat*—"and so I go little bit ahead. I fall asleep, I wake up. Where is that Joe? Nothing! I shine my flash—you are gone! I see lights, I go to this place where the people have the skin falling up."

"A leper colony?"

"Yah, you got it that. Leperds! I wait three hours. I paddle upstrim, downstrim, no Joe. I see a *canoa*, I ask them they see you. This stupid guy grabs my boat. But very quiet-like I am holding *canoa* away with my paddle. Then this stupid guy he says he wants a present. He wants *dinero*. I say no.

"Then I see other *canoa!* Coming fast! I push first stupid guy away, but he will not let it that go, so I take paddle, and"—he made a motion like a man chopping wood—"I break it that stupid guy's hand! He is screaming!

"Here comes other *canoa*. I am pushing on my paddle, and I cut between them. First stupid guy is yelling, 'Grab heem! Grab that guy!' But I am right for front of other boat. He thinks I am going to hit heem, but—ha!—I use rudder. I turn like it that fast to the left. Now I am really pushing, so fast they know nothing. I have twenty-meter lead. I am running for next hour and they cannot follow. Ha!

"When I am safe, I am thinking again, where is that Joe? I think there is not much for you I can do. I leave the map and bread, and then I am going for it. That is the right expression?"

"Yes."

He had, in all, paddled forty hours straight through, taking catnaps in the boat when he could no longer keep his eyes open, and in that time he had traveled about two hundred and thirty miles. He had arrived here at the border at eleven o'clock at night, one hour before his deadline. It had been a terrible pace. Clearly I had had the better end of the deal.

"Joe, you are not making it here tonight, I am hiring motor to find you. I am not going into that Brazil without you!"

Puerto Alegría had barracks for five hundred men built on platforms and stilts and connected by duckwalks, the whole of it winding through the bush like a maze, but only twenty men were in residence, all of them anxious to leave. Most came from Lima and served this isolated jungle duty on one-month rotation. Still, it was Christmas, which meant hot soup and cold beer and snapshots and toasts.

Suddenly, the skies opened up. When the storm ended the soldiers hauled our boats down to the river and waved us toward the border.

"Good luck in Brazil!" the base commander shouted as we left. "All they do is dance and fuck!"

16   *The Solimões*

Night was falling, and paddling away from Puerto Alegría we kept the black wall of a six-mile-long island, Rondina, to our left, blocking us from Leticia, Colombia's only port on the Amazon. By reputation, Leticia's sole industry is smuggling—mainly Peruvian coca paste (in), and processed cocaine (out), but also jewelry, counterfeit money, rare-animal skins, and just about anything else easily transported by boat up or down the Amazon and through the hundreds of local inlets and streams that make detection or pursuit almost impossible.

A mile beyond Rondina we corrected course for the flickering lights of Tabatinga, the Brazilian garrison town that abuts Leticia. An unanticipated reward awaited us. The Brazilian military runs Tabatinga's best hotel (one of three), and Bzdak and Durrant, who had arrived two days earlier on a riverboat from Iquitos, had befriended the general. He in turn had given them the run of the kitchen. At midnight, having taken my first hot shower in five months (as I stood too long under the nozzle, Chmielinski, waiting his turn outside, fumed, "Joe, you are drowning?"), I sat down to a Christmas dinner of Polish sausage, roast chicken, borscht, potato salad, fresh tomatoes, Brazilian wine, and shots of Polish vodka.

In the morning, the four of us walked through dusty Tabatinga, which looked about like any small jungle town, and crossed the border into Leticia, which did not. Smart boutiques sold French dresses and Italian shoes; other shops displayed Jack Daniel's whiskey, Japanese cameras, and American chocolate bars—"Sneekers! The best!" Chmielinski exclaimed, and bought two cases. Down on the waterfront, sleek fiberglass speedboats outnumbered the *peque-peques* and Johnsons, and men in silk shirts, designer blue jeans, and strong cologne strolled the dirt road along the bank or paraded in four-wheel-drive Chevrolets and Jeeps. The rates at the city's one hotel, the Anaconda (built by an American adventurer suspected by the DEA to be a drug trafficker), were five times those in Tabatinga.

We stopped for beer in a waterfront shanty run by a young Brazilian, João, who had been raised in an orphanage in Manaus, nine hundred miles downriver. When he was thirteen he had heard his mother was in Tabatinga, and had come looking for her.

"All I found was this," he said in English, gesturing at the shanty's warped cardboard walls. "I have to get out."

"Why?"

"Too much *matando*," he said, and made a shooting motion.

The next day, Chmielinski worked a lucrative black-market deal with the Brazilian general, who for a pittance in American cash forgot that we had stayed in his hotel. He also let Chmielinski use his telephone, through which we learned that the residents of Casper, Wyoming, the Poles' adopted hometown, were raising money for us to complete the expedition.

With that windfall looming, we decided to invest the bulk of our remaining funds in a small boat for Durrant and Bzdak, so they could accompany us downriver for a few days. They had seen little but towns and cities for the last month, and Bzdak wanted to photograph some wilder sections of river.

Bzdak hired a Johnson captained by a wily, mustachioed man named Felix. I say wily; not until we were twenty miles downriver did Felix admit that his fifteen-foot dory was, in fact, "borrowed." Meanwhile, for a fraction of what Bzdak had paid him, Felix in turn had hired a mechanic and driver named Ramón, a quiet boy who wore rags but could break down and reassemble the seven-horse outboard in an hour. Felix, for his part, was to spend most of the journey honing his own particular river skills, which ran to drinking, smoking, and sleeping. The Johnson shot ahead of the kayaks, stopped, drifted. We caught up and passed it, it passed us and waited again. In this herky-jerky manner we proceeded two days into Brazil.

"You hire me," Felix said that second afternoon, "but you ride in those things." He pointed to the kayaks and shook his head. "While I drink beer." He rummaged on the boat's floor.

"Can I swim here, Felix?" I asked. "Is it safe?"

He threw his cigarette in the river and peered over the side of the boat, looking for I don't know what—the water was far too brown to see anything at all.

"Sure," he said, and opened a beer. "You can swim here."

"Why don't you join me?"

He took a long swallow and thought for a moment. "No thanks," he said. "Who knows what the hell is in there?" He leaned back against the stern and took another swallow. "Why make problems?"

During those two days the four of us regained much of the close-ness we had felt on the raft. That second night, my birthday, we bought a ten-pound catfish from a fisherman (for about a dollar), made camp on a pretty beach, and cooked the fish for dinner. Later, Durrant and Bzdak gave me a machete and a beautifully worked leather scabbard they had purchased in Leticia. It was a gift as practical as it was handsome. After our harrowing Christmas, Chmielinski and I had decided we should carry some sort of weapons.

The next day we reached São Paulo de Olivença, a small town about a hundred and twenty miles from the border. Felix returned to Tabatinga, Durrant and Bzdak checked into São Paulo's two-dollar-a-night hotel to wait for a passenger ship, and we made a rough plan to meet two weeks downriver, in Coari.

At the dock that afternoon, before we left, Durrant took me

aside. "Don't let Piotr push you too hard," she said. "He's setting a mean pace. I'm worried the two of you will burn out."

"You should tell him."

"He won't hear it. So take care of yourself, okay? And keep an eye on him. I think he's more tired than he lets on."

I promised to do that, and Chmielinski and I resumed our routine. The following morning the alarm clock blasted me awake at three thirty—I had been dreaming that one of my brothers and I had been sentenced to prison—and when I tried to make breakfast, I could not get the dirty stove to light. When it finally went off (I did not see the puddle of fuel collecting at its base), it went off like a fireball, followed by my curses, the squawking of terrified birds, and a wild-eyed Chmielinski bolting from his tent and screaming, "Joe, don't kill yourself *now!*"

At the border Brazil shares with Colombia and Peru, the river becomes the Solimões, and from there zigzags east some twelve hundred miles through the state of Amazonas. Brazilians consider Amazonas their Wild West. About the size of Alaska, with fewer people than Philadelphia, it contains some 20 percent of Brazil's land mass but less than 1 percent of its population; aside from the cities of Manaus and Tefé, and a few small towns like Tabatinga, São Paulo, and Coari, it is nearly uninhabited. Given that, the proximity of Iquitos (which has a duty-free port), the influence of Leticia, and the hefty taxes Brazil levies on foreign goods, a comfortable living can be made running contraband boat engines, transistor radios, hand tools, stereos, televisions, clothes, motorcycles, and crates of produce along the Solimões. A smugglers' code governs life on the river.

That morning, seeking directions, Chmielinski overtook a dugout canoe. It raced for the bank and a man jumped out and shouldered a rifle. He relaxed when Chmielinski explained himself, but as we left, he yelled out, "Be careful! The river is full of bandits!"

After that, when we met traffic I hung back in my kayak, secured my paddle, and put my hands under my deck. If Chmielinski felt at all threatened, he mentioned that I was armed and nodded in my direction—a signal for me to squint into the bush as if sighting a target. Though nervous during these charades, at times I had to fight to keep from laughing out loud. I had not touched a gun since I was a kid.

The forest along the Solimões may be the lushest on the Amazon. The trees tend to be tall, well over fifty feet, and the bush thicker than any I had seen in Peru. Our second day below São Paulo we paddled dawn to dusk without spotting a single hut. The river itself was perplexing. In the parlance of the Amazon, the Solimões is a "white" river, thick with Andean silt, which gives it a coffee-and-cream color. The silty deposits have made the *várzea*, as the Amazon floodplain is known, a jigsaw puzzle of natural levees and ditches (variously called *furos, paranás,* and *canals*). Navigation can be confusing, and there are few beaches on which to camp.

That night, New Year's Eve, we traveled until dark before picking up the lights of a cattle ranch, but the frightened owner would not let us stay. We pitched camp on the bank below the ranch, in a fetid puddle of mud and clay. The air reeked of manure and mud stuck like paint to anything it touched. Blackflies competed fiercely with mosquitoes for their pound of flesh.

We took what comfort we could from the routine of making camp. We erected tents, stretched a line between them, hung up life jackets and rainsuits to dry, drew water, brewed tea, sponged out our boats. Chmielinski cooked chili, and the two of us sat on a muddy log and ate it.

"In Poland this is the biggest day of the year," he said. "In Krakow everyone is dancing. The relatives are together eating a big dinner. But never are they eating chili."

"Do you miss them?"

"Yes. And they are missing me. Every year for six years they are leaving one plate empty on the table."

"For you."

"Yes."

"Someday maybe it will not be empty."

"That is something I cannot think about. It will make me crazy."

"Have they ever been able to visit you?"

"No, but they are remembering me."

"I'm sure they are."

"Happy New Year, Joe."

"Happy New Year, Piotr."

After dinner we heard distant gunshots, and that night we slept with machetes at our sides, though I did not know what I would do if I had to use mine. Frogs croaked, nightbirds yawped, bats whirred (Durrant had given me a three-shot rabies prophylaxis against these), and though I dove into my tent as fast as I could, had the netting unzipped for perhaps fifteen seconds, an insect zoo managed to establish itself on the underside of my tent ceiling. By candlelight I saw two enormous red ants, a winged ant that looked like a termite, a squadron of gnats, two black moths, and three fat mosquitoes that became red Rorschach blots on page fifty-two of my third notebook. The disturbed survivors flitted and buzzed until I settled down to sleep.

Late in the night a boat engine idled offshore, and a bright light ran over our camp. Voices argued loudly, but the boat sped away when Chmielinski ran down the bank.

Later still, peering through his mosquito netting, Chmielinski spotted two shadows slouching through the mud right next to our camp. He grabbed his machete, sneaked silently from his tent, and pounced, simultaneously raising his machete and switching on his flashlight to blind our attackers, who proved to be—

"—the life jackets, Joe! They are blowing on the drying line, I am thinking they are trying to get us!"

By eight the next morning a fierce headwind had whipped the river into chop and waves that reduced our speed by a third. Buried in the troughs, I lost sight of Chmielinski, though he paddled only a few feet in front of me. I could not time my stroke. At the moment I pushed hardest, expecting my paddle to bite water, it bit nothing but air. Then, accelerating, it struck the water awkwardly. Executing several thousand such strokes wore me out. When my paddle hit water the shock ran through wrist, up forearm, along shoulder, into neck, and erupted through lips in a frustrated oath.

Meanwhile, five days and two hundred and fifty miles into Amazonas, the clay banks occasionally gave way to low sandstone bluffs, and here and there a sturdy plank-and-frame house sat defiantly on stilts, right over the water. At the mouth of the Içá River we passed a mile-long village, Santo Antônio. The main street ran between houses of brick and wood and ended at either edge of town. As we paddled by, I watched a Volkswagen bug drive slowly along the street, turn around, drive back, turn, and so on, like a plastic duck at a shooting gallery.

Perhaps a dozen settlements dot the six hundred miles of river between São Paulo and Coari, most of them hidden up swamps and small tributaries, and all of them poor. Alan Holman, an Australian who made a solo kayak descent of the flatwater Amazon in 1982, measured these villages according to how many eggs he could purchase. A six-egg village was an oasis.

At the store in no-egg Porto Alfonso three men were leaning against empty shelves, drinking bottles of the raw cane spirit called *cachaça.* One asked Chmielinski where we were going.

"Belém," Chmielinski said.

"Where do you sleep?" another asked.

"In houses, or on a beach."

The third man did not look up from his bottle. "Where are you sleeping tonight?" he asked.

"Maybe Fonte Boa."

"You will not get there today."

"A beach, then."

"That could be dangerous."

"We have big guns," Chmielinski said, "and we are twelve."

"Where are the rest?"

"With the soldiers."

"Soldiers?"

"In the airplane. The one that follows us."

The first man asked, "How do they know where you are?"

"Radio."

As we left the shack we met a distinguished-looking man (he

wore shoes), a Colombian engineer surveying a nearby tributary for a dam. "Three weeks, no eggs!" he said in English. "No food, nothing." He was living on instant rice.

The lepers who inhabited Ilha do Jardim—Garden Island—said that a drought had left them short of food, but they gave us six papayas and three bunches of bananas. The bananas were delicious (in the heat of the day they were often the only food I could keep down), but later, when I tried to eat one of the soft ripe papayas, I thought of those people, the skin dripping off their faces, and though I felt guilty for it threw the fruit in the river.

We paddled eight hours that fourth day below São Paulo, and our chart said we had covered seventy miles. We paddled twelve hours the next day—forty miles. On the sixth day we pulled hard, the banks slid by, the chart said we had gone nowhere. My shoulders developed a sharp, white-hot pain and made popping noises. Our chocolate melted, our bread turned moldy, and we discovered that our *comida plástica,* which I had selected hastily from the crate Bzdak and Durrant had hauled to São Paulo, consisted entirely of chili. After eating it twice a day for six days neither of us could stomach another spoonful.

We paddled long hours in silence, past islands of floating grass and the occasional snake chugging along with its head raised out of the water like a periscope. The wildlife was oblique—a shaking in the bush at night, a tree limb bent by a hornet nest, squawking in a treetop, a dolphin breaching, the zigzagging triangle of a shark's fin. (Several shark species breed in the Atlantic but forage as far upriver as Iquitos.)

Either it rained hard or the sun burned so intensely that in the middle of the day we dove in the river, hung on to the noses of our boats, and drifted downstream with the one-knot current. This was safer than one might think. According to a doctor Durrant had consulted in Iquitos, most Amazonian water snakes swim beneath the surface but are not poisonous, while land snakes, which sometimes are, travel on the surface and are easily spotted. Piranha are overrated—we met no one on the river who had witnessed an attack, much less a death—and the despicable *candiru,* which I have described elsewhere, was thwarted simply by wearing a pair of shorts while swimming.

Several fishermen insisted that a *pirarucú* could eat a man. According to all available scientific evidence the species is incapable of such a feat, but having seen several of the monsters, I cannot blame the fishermen. The *pirarucú* (or *paiche,* as it is known in Peru) is one of the world's largest freshwater fish—it can grow to ten feet and two hundred and fifty pounds—and in addition to gills has a single lung that it must service every few minutes, breaking the water with a loud rolling display not unlike a great scaly red-and-green log. After witnessing this act at close range several times, and being startled half to death, I was willing to believe that such a fish would eat not only a man but a horse.

On our seventh day into Amazonas we stopped at the grassy head of hilly Acarara Island. A big-boned man named Luis paddled a canoe over from the mainland, and we asked permission to camp.

"But of course," he said. "The land is yours."

Like most of the peasants along the Solimões, Luis was a *caboclo*— a person of European and Indian blood who leads a catch-as-catch-can existence dependent mainly on a sunny disposition and traditional forms of fishing, trading, and slash-and-burn agriculture. Minutes later another *caboclo,* Mauricio, arrived on foot, at the head of a parade of goats, and also granted us permission to camp (though with somewhat more authority than Luis, as the land was actually his).

The *caboclos* spoke Portuguese (sufficiently similar to Spanish that we could converse), and while I cooked and we watched a storm approach they taught me the words for knife, fire, rain, and thunder. The English equivalents pulverized them with laughter. *Rain* was hilarious, *fire* induced near-hysteria, and *thunder*—Luis could pronounce it only as "sunder," and collapsed in a fit of snorts and giggles. Later, as he paddled away, his voice carried across the water and up to our bluff. "Sunder!" I heard, followed by his mulish laugh, and I in turn experimented with my new words—*faca, fogo, chuva, trovão*—rolling them around on my tongue like exotic fruit.

Late that night the storm hit with a fury. It would have blown me right off the island and into the river if Chmielinski had not planted my kayak next to my tent as a protective wall. Hearing the commotion, I stuck my head out, shone my flashlight, and spotted Chmielinski running around in the rain stark naked. When I called to him, he yelled back, "I like this being wet!"

Our hosts the next evening, the *caboclo* Francisco Gomez and his family, lived in a thatch-and-palmwood house set well back from the river. Several pocked tin pots hung beside the fire pit in back, next to five huts containing mosquito nets and nothing else. The house itself was a single room with a table along one wall and, against another, a wooden mantel that held two laminated pictures of a blue-eyed Virgin, a hammer, a wind-up cuckoo clock that did not work, and two bottles of antivenin. Below it were five machetes and three beaten cardboard suitcases. That appeared to be the sum of the family's possessions.

We put up our tents in the house, studying the chickens that ran beneath the floor, and Francisco introduced his tough old wife, Fatima, then a young woman with a baby, then another young woman, very pretty, who wore a short skirt, eye shadow, and a jaguar-tooth necklace. Fatima chased her from the room. Three boys came in, and two young men.

"Francisco," I asked, "how many people live here?"

Two more boys entered, a girl, a young mother with a baby.

Francisco thought for a moment. "Thirteen."

In walked an older man, António, who like Francisco appeared middle-aged. He had a small boy with him.

"I count seventeen," I said to Francisco.

He thought for a moment. "Yes," he said. "Seventeen."

"All live here, in this house?"

"All live here."

"All one family?"

He smiled. "Two families."

"Three," António said. "But I am not always here. I have children in other places."

"How many children?" Chmielinski asked.

"Forty-four," António said.

"Forty-four?"

"Yes. I have forty-four children. With ten women." He nodded seriously, and I thought of Emilio Lozano, on the forlorn Puinahua Canal in Peru.

"Where are your children?" Chmielinski asked.

"Everywhere!" António said. "That is why I come to Francisco's home. Only two of them live here."

An hour later all seventeen inhabitants had crowded into the room. The women and children sat along the walls and the men huddled around Chmielinski, who spread open our chart on the table. The men exclaimed when Chmielinski showed them their house, marked by a square. The chart also indicated a canal near Francisco's home, but it was not clear whether the canal cut all the way across a bend in the river. If it did, we would save a day by following it. If the canal petered out too early, however, we would lose two days backtracking.

Did any of the men know about the canal?

"Yes," Francisco said. He pointed knowingly to the chart. "There it is."

Chmielinski sighed. "But does it exist?" he asked. "Is it on the river?"

Francisco shrugged. António, however, said it was, and the other men nodded vigorously.

"Six hours from here," António said.

"Four hours," one of the younger men said.

"One day," Francisco said.

Chmielinski knew that routine. He gave up and cooked our chili, cooked all we had left, and Fatima brought bowls and farinha, the lumpy powder made from toasted manioc that can be, as this was, nutty and delicious. She passed the bowls around and we distributed our chili and everyone sat on the floor and ate. She gave me a Portuguese lesson: knife, spoon, stove, rain, yesterday, today, tomorrow.

I read my Portuguese Berlitz: "Waiter, my fish is cold."

"Your fish is cold," Francisco said. "But you have no fish."

"My fish never gets cold!" António said. The young men laughed.

I read on. "Are you alone tonight?"

"Stupid question," António said.

After dinner Chmielinski continued to work with the map, but I was tired and said good night. I crawled into my tent and wrote in my notebook. I woke up with my nose on the page. When I rolled over on my back four tiny faces were staring down at me through the netting. I closed my eyes and sometime later woke to António and Francisco arguing about, I think, a calf. Then the young men got into it, and the women, and the place was in an uproar. Finally, Chmielinski called out from his tent, in slow, precise Spanish, "Excuse me. I know this is your house, but you have invited us to stay, and we have much work tomorrow. So please."

The Gomez family retired. I fell asleep. When I woke again, an hour before dawn, they were sitting along the walls.

Chmielinski and I spent all of the next day searching for the canal, and all of the next two days backtracking. Perhaps we had misunderstood the Gomezes, lost something in the cracks between Portuguese and Spanish. Perhaps the canal had simply dried up. Or perhaps in their generosity the Gomezes had given us completely false information, because it was what they had thought we wanted to hear.

The next night, our tenth on the Solimões, we stayed with a thirty-two-year-old *caboclo* named Eduardo. He had silver-blue eyes and strong square features, and he lived in a stilt house right on the river, at the mouth of a lake the color of his eyes. Six other houses along the water made up Cabo Azul, or Blue Cape. Eduardo's wife had gone away somewhere, and in both celebration and sorrow he was drinking rum.

A monkey troop of young boys stuffed our boats into Eduardo's house and fetched water from the river while Eduardo cooked *bodó,* a fish with a lobsterlike exoskeleton. The meat flopped out in a steaming hunk, redolent of peppers. When we finished, the boys washed the plates in the river. Then, as one, they demanded "A song!"

Eduardo pulled a guitar from beneath a pile of rags and badly but loudly played four-chord ballads of romance, drink, and fishing. We unloaded the kayaks and the boys turned them over and set to a fierce drumming, six to a boat, building a mellifluous, smoothly syncopated whole. Eduardo played until my fingers hurt for watching him, but the boys pleaded for more.

After an hour or so I walked out to wash myself in the Solimões, then strolled along the duckwalk that connected the six houses. The drumming and Eduardo's earnest crooning filled the cool night air. *This,* I thought, *is Brazil.*

I returned to the house. The boys made room at my kayak, and I pounded and banged in honky time and drank rum until dawn painted the river.

Later, as we packed to leave, two men paddled up in a long canoe. One held a rifle, and in the floor of the canoe, bathed in blood, were a dead fifteen-foot caiman, green and scaly, and a shorter, baby caiman, also dead. I might have felt bad for the critters or happy for Cabo Azul, for this would be community meat, but as I stared at the lifeless eyes frozen open in horror I could think only, *That is the face of my hangover.*

We paddled right past Tefé, hidden a couple of miles up a tributary of the same name, and on to Coari, which after our twelve days on the Solimões looked like Paris. The village sits on a black, silt-free lake that is cool and perfect for swimming, ringed with white sand and green jungle, and so big it would take an entire day to navigate the shore by motorboat, but so empty that you might see one fisherman, or a woman doing wash, or no one at all.

The port held two dozen small boats, and people on foot and bicycle crowded Coari's score of mud streets. Sensuous *forro* music gushed from shops and homes, and the air was rich with the aromas of meat roasting in the town's *churrascaria.* We met Durrant and Bzdak at the clean, quiet, and nearly empty Palace Hotel, unpacked· the boats, and then sat in the *churrascaria* and ate barbecued chicken and drank vicious rum-and-lime *batidas*.

Coari was a pleasant place in which to suffer a nervous breakdown. Despite Durrant's cautions, I had not noticed Chmielinski's exhaustion, had not understood that he reacted to stress much differently than I did. I flat-out collapsed, without grace. But the wearier Chmielinski grew, the harder he drove himself. He had slept little on the river, working late into the night on his maps or rigging some new apparatus for the kayaks, and during the days he delivered an endless stream of chatter—on the twelve-day run from Tabatinga I had heard, in detail, the history of Poland since the Huns.

Nor did Chmielinski rest in Coari. Though isolated, the town had a radar dish and a public phone, and Chmielinski spent two long, fruitless days trying to contact the international wire services in Rio de Janeiro and São Paulo. He had gambled heavily on the Amazon expedition—had quit his job, invested most of his savings, jeopardized his marriage, and obligated himself to half a dozen sponsors who had donated food, equipment, and money. Our journey, if completed and publicized, would both fulfill those obligations and promote the New York travel company Chmielinski had started with two Polish partners the year before.

Durrant and Bzdak, too, were showing the strain of five months of river travel. They were locked into our kayaking schedule, forced to travel from port to port in suffocating, often hazardous riverboats, and had constantly to find ways to stretch our little money. Worst of all, Durrant said after the four of us had climbed to the hotel roof and sat beneath a black, overcast night sky, Chmielinski and I were excluding them, acting as if the expedition were only the two of us.

She was right. My excuse was that I was so worn out that whenever we met up with them I could do little but eat and sleep. I felt bad that they interpreted this as an attempt to exclude them. Though Durrant, Bzdak, and Chmielinski had been strangers to me when I had arrived in Peru, in the five months since then we had shared what was the most intense experience of my life, and, as far as I could tell, of theirs as well. Yet we had stuck together through it all, and until then I had not doubted that if the skyline of Belém ever rose up before us, we would see it together.

As best I could, I told them that.

The situation was harder for Chmielinski. He was our motor, but to operate at the pace he did, he needed Bzdak's undivided loyalty. That need, and the enormous mutual trust that went with it, had been demonstrated dramatically on the Apurimac. If Chmielinski now asked Bzdak to perform more mundane duties—finding supplies, changing money, hustling shelter in advance of our arrivals—that underlying need had not lessened.

Chmielinski couldn't run without Bzdak, but Bzdak had fallen in love. There was only one graceful solution: Chmielinski had to trust Durrant as he did Bzdak. Her work was impeccable, her courage demonstrated beyond doubt. She deserved that trust.

"Guys," Chmielinski said to them, "I am sorry. Now is the hardest time. We cannot make it without you. We are in the kayaks, you are in the boats, but it is all the same. We are not here if you are not here."

He also had a card up his sleeve. He had phoned Casper, and learned that the "Save the Amazon Expedition" committee had raised enough funds for us to finish our trip. The money would be waiting in Manaus. Meanwhile, we would use what remained to hire a boat, and make the three-day run to Manaus as a team.

When we heard that we exchanged hugs all around. Bzdak rummaged in the hotel kitchen, emerged with a transistor radio, and tuned it to a station in Tefé broadcasting the infectious *forro*. And then, there on the darkened rooftop, in the middle of wild Amazonas, we danced.

At dawn Bzdak and Durrant went to the port to hire a boat and buy supplies. Having arranged to meet them downstream, and half asleep, Chmielinski and I departed Coari. By midday, under a hot blue sky, I was still paddling dreamily along the gently rolling river. Then a soft wind picked up and waves began to build so slowly I barely noticed them. I stroked, crested each wave, and as it passed beneath me slapped the paddle down.

All at once I realized the waves were over my head.

I looked up. The sky turned bright red, then purple, then so black the river, whipped into whitecaps, glowed against it.

An air horn honked to my right and I saw a cargo boat twenty feet abeam and lurching wildly. The *Coronel Brandão*, according to the lettering on its hull. A blue tarp hung amidships. A hand drew the tarp back. Bzdak thrust his head out and waved to me. As best I could I returned the gesture. He waved again.

But he wasn't waving—he was signaling frantically for me to head for the bank, which, as I crested the next wave, I saw a mile to my left. He disappeared behind the tarp and the *Brandão* swung hard to port. Pitching in the waves, it broke for land.

At the top of the next wave I looked for Chmielinski, and spotted his long white kayak far away, near the left bank.

Mesmerized, I watched the storm finish its approach. To my left, treetops bent and flattened at the foot of the black sky, and seconds later the bank disappeared behind a frothy white wall. Then the storm hit me—my face felt as if it were being stung by a swarm of bees—and the wind gusted so hard I had to fight to hold on to my paddle. Everything went white around me, then gray. Blinking rapidly against the driven rain, I focused on the tip of my kayak. My little coat-hanger tree was now bent as severely as the trees on shore.

Thinking I would try to follow the *Brandão*, I turned left, broadside to the waves, and felt my boat begin to roll. My stomach tightened. Reflexively, I braced as Chmielinski had taught me, extending my paddle to my left, like a pontoon, and leaning away from the wave, down its face. When the wave had passed beneath me I righted myself in the trough and paddled toward shore, until the next wave forced me to brace again.

Brace, paddle, brace, paddle. To say I proceeded in this manner for the next twenty minutes sounds as if I were in command. Actually, as I went up and over each wave I heard, as if it belonged to someone else, my own quavering voice shouting "no . . . No . . . NO!"

A cargo boat suddenly appeared and was within five feet of running me down when I turned my stern to a wave and surfed its face. I was proud of that maneuver until the boat's wake caught me. Moving at right angles to the river waves, it tipped me sideways, and I surfed the next wave with my boat almost on its side and me hung far out to my right, bracing with my paddle.

Though scared silly, I did manage over the next hour to pull within sight of the left bank, where I saw waves pounding the shore, long stretches of bank and trees collapsing into the river, and five or six big boats pitching about. One looked like the *Brandão*. Trembling, I paddled back out, then turned my nose downstream and held on there for an hour or so, waves breaking over my bow, until the storm abated.

Another hour and I saw Chmielinski silhouetted against the skyline, waving his paddle in an arc. "Hey!" he yelled as I approached. "Now you are a big kayaker!"

I wouldn't have said that, but I did feel as if I'd undergone a kind of baptism. I had new confidence in my ship. She'd held her own in the waves and the wind, and I had never felt, as I had with the white-water kayak, that I was fighting her. We were one tight little unit.

Chmielinski shouted, and pointed behind me. I turned to see not one but two spectacular rainbows lighting up the south bank of the Solimões for miles.

The *Coronel Brandão* found us at sunset. Bzdak motioned us to follow, and after the boat was tied up to a sturdy tree on the right bank we went aboard. The captain, Edison, and his first mate, Miguel, were large, swarthy, middle-aged *caboclos,* and, like most I'd met, confident and imperturbable.

A trio of young boys scrambled about the legs of these giants, mopping the *Brandão's* deck, cleaning the galley, greasing the engine. When they had finished, Edison fired up a generator that roared so loudly we could not hear one another even when we shouted. The generator's sole function was to power a television. Though we were too far from anywhere to pick up a signal, the boys sat before the set transfixed, as if desire alone could pull an image from the snow-white screen.

The crew's last member, and the *Brandão's* jewel, was Maria, a dark beauty who claimed to be eighteen but looked a mature fifteen. On her small shelf in the stern she kept a tidy collection of cheap jewelry, dolls, perfume bottles, deck shoes, and a pair of shiny cobalt-blue pumps, and beneath the shelf a hamper of skirts and blouses. I took her to be Edison's daughter, until that evening, when the charged grunts issuing from the stern quarters she shared with Edison suggested otherwise.

Not dissimilar grunts rose from the *mosquiteiro* Miguel shared with the three boys.

The three-day run to Manaus was a kind of holiday, although Chmielinski, adamant that he and I travel entirely under our own power, refused to let me set foot on the *Brandão* until she came to a dead stop. But at night we slept aboard. Freed of the burden of making camp, we put in long days on the water, from an hour before sunrise to an hour after sunset. My shoulders ached, and Durrant had to outfit me with elastic wrist braces, but we ate fresh fish every night and drank cold beer.

That third night, long after dark, we met the *Brandão* in the port of Manacapuru, the last town on the river before the metropolis of Manaus. Edison, by authority of his physical bulk, had simply bulled his way between two other boats, one of them empty, the other occupied by a frail old woman whose skin hung from her head in loose folds. Her boat had probably not been on the river in years—the hull was so covered with muck I could not see wood—and she stared at us for only a moment before she crawled into her hammock, shattered by the blast of the *Brandão's* generator. The boys had picked up a Manaus station and were immersed in *Os Flintstones.*

This being a Sunday night, Edison and Miguel dressed for

church. They donned bright yachting caps, clean polo shirts with reptilian insignia (*"Caiman!"* Maria squealed), bleached white trousers, and white tennis shoes. Maria dressed up, too, in a white cotton dress and her blue pumps, but Edison would not allow her to leave the boat. She stamped her feet and pouted, but in the end settled in with the boys and Fred and Wilma.

We four gringos followed Edison and Miguel through the old woman's boat, passing her hammock without a word, then descended a gangplank to the waterfront and climbed a set of stairs into town. Dozens of young couples were strolling Manacapuru's one small plaza. Illuminated by a single streetlamp, two ancient Chevrolets circled the plaza, chased by several new Volkswagen bugs (which are still manufactured in Brazil). The churchgoers went to seek their god. We four expeditioneers went in search of beer. We found a bar overlooking the river, but a band was playing loud disco music, and I returned alone to the *Brandão*.

Maria, still in her fancy clothes, stood atop the boat and stared up at the bar. The music rushed down as clearly as the stars shone overhead.

"You do not dance?" she asked, though I did not understand her until she placed one hand over her stomach and the other in the air and executed a hip-wiggling circle.

"Yes," I said, "but I am too tired to stay in there."

She sighed. To be here in Manacapuru was for her quite an occasion, but, however unwillingly, she had outgrown dancing and courting. Her mate was in church and she was at home where she belonged.

I put up my tent in the boat. To my surprise and gratitude, the boys turned off the television and silenced the generator. Maria lit a candle. The four of us talked for a while. They did not attend school, and they could neither read nor write. They did, however, have an intimate knowledge of the television show *Dallas*, which I had never seen. Unable to answer their questions about J.R., I felt as if I had broken an agreement I had not known I had made.

I crawled into my tent. Music continued to pulse down from

the bar. When they thought I had gone to sleep, Maria and the boys began to dance.

The next day we slid left off the Solimões, north, into a canal we hoped would drop us into the Negro River a few miles downstream from Manaus. The *Brandão* took the lead, Chmielinski followed her, and I followed him.

Entering the canal was like leaving a freeway for a narrow green alley. For weeks the jungle wall had seemed hard and solid, but now, not ten feet to either side, it looked porous and revealing. Here and there I spotted ratty huts, tilted and ajar, thatch full of holes, stilts splintered and collapsing, and once I saw a pair of glittering eyes and, as I drew closer, a dark, naked man frozen in place.

"*Bom dia,*" I said, but he did not respond.

When I paddled still closer, he turned and fled.

In front of me, the canal appeared to end abruptly. A solid gray wall stretched across its mouth like a dam. When our little fleet left the canal and entered the broad, ink-black Negro River, however, the wall revealed itself to be the hull of a supertanker, the *Evros,* anchored a thousand miles from the Atlantic. At six stories, it was the tallest man-made thing I had seen since Lima.

A sleek powerboat glided past us. Three very fat but elegantly barbered men sat in the cockpit, holding drinks, and four young women in tiny bikinis were sunning themselves on the deck. One of the women blew Chmielinski a kiss. The man at the wheel scowled, the boat sped away, and soon it was nothing but a cloud of white foam swallowed by the skyline of Manaus.

17 *The Amazon*

The Manaus waterfront differs from other tropical water-fronts only in that it is bigger than most, a broader anarchy of mud and garbage, thicker rivulets of refuse flowing down the bank and over one's bare feet, a louder cacophony of unmuffled engines, more house-of-cards shacks serving bowls of starchy stew the ingredients of which you do not want to know.

We did not linger there. Dragging the kayaks, Chmielinski, Durrant, Bzdak, and I ascended the stairs into the city, absorbing the cool night air fragrant with the stuff of the next dawn's market, the cilantro and garlic and onions and lemons stacked in vague mounds next to other vague mounds which upon close inspection proved to be sleeping *caboclos*. Chmielinski rousted one of the men, who in turn rousted several others. We struck a deal, they hoisted our boats to their shoulders, and we followed them into the gray-black streets.

Half an hour later, standing in the handsome lobby of the Hotel Tropical in downtown Manaus, we could as well have been on Rodeo Drive, or Fifth Avenue. Dripping river slime onto the rich red carpet, we contemplated what a room would cost for the night, then returned to the street and spoke with the *caboclos*. They took us to a hotel near the waterfront that did not have carpets anywhere.

When we arrived we thanked the men for their wisdom and

climbed to our room, hauling the kayaks behind us. I took a cold shower, soaping up several times over, and studied the infections in my crotch and arms and legs, the swollen arthritic middle finger of my left hand, and, in the mirror, the face burned to leather. I speculated about the lingering numbness in toes and heels.

Then I put on the clean clothes stored so carefully in the nose of my boat and walked back to the Tropical. I sat at a table on the sidewalk out front and had a beer, and another. At the next table a woman with coal-black skin, dressed head to toe in a body-hugging leopard-skin leotard, her eyes wide and bloodshot, flung a slurred oath at a groomed, silver-haired man in a white linen suit. He left. The fine-boned young woman began to cry, then approached me with an offer of "Something from Bolivia or Peru." I declined.

I hailed a cab from the fleet of yellow Volkswagen bugs that are the city's ball bearings and proceeded northwest along the Negro River, trying to make sense of the architectural chaos, the skyscrapers and shacks, the suburban homes, the prefab warehouses, the Victorian mansions that early in the twentieth century were considered among the finest in the world. I tried to picture Manaus in 1910, at the height of the rubber boom, the third city in the Western Hemisphere to have electricity. Her population of ninety thousand spent $8 million a year on jewelry. They shipped their laundry to London, their children to school in France.

In 1912 rubber trees smuggled out of Brazil by an English botanist began to thrive in the Far East. Manaus died, then rose back up. Nineteen sixty-six: The Brazilian government declares the city a free port. Foreign manufacturers bring in component parts free of the stiff import taxes in effect throughout the rest of the country and assemble them at the hundreds of boxlike instant factories that soon ring the city. Sony, Sharp, Honda—the principal exports of "The Capital of the Jungle" are stereos, televisions, motorcycles. From all over Brazil people fly into the jungle to shop. Manaus becomes a giant flea market. In ten years her population quadruples to eight hundred thousand.

My driver ignored the cab's meter and pulled a rate card from the glove box. With inflation running at 200 percent per annum, it was impractical to continue to adjust the meters. New rate cards were issued weekly.

In the morning I chose to live dangerously. I went shopping for a pair of shoes. The "free zone" was a mob scene of Manhattanesque proportions. In street after street, in stall after stall the size and shape of a one-car garage, people were jammed shoulder to shoulder, tearing at bins of cheap goods. Overwhelmed, afraid to dawdle and judge, I found myself sweating harder than I ever had on the river. I panicked and bought the first pair of shoes I saw, only to discover as I fled that they were not shoes at all but slippers, the sort of thing my grandfather wore padding around his house.

Distracted, shoved into another stall, this one offering German tennis rackets, Chinese shoes, French shirts, American computers, Japanese motorcycles, and Italian espresso machines, I was confronted by a clerk who tried to sell me a plastic hat with a built-in solar-powered radio. At first it seemed the perfect thing for those long days in the kayak—it would help my Portuguese—but the only station I could find was playing Lionel Richie.

Back in the street I was quickly trapped again, blocked by a crowd watching a television on which Moses was speaking to a wig-haired American Indian maiden wearing a fringed buckskin dress. She had long black hair and blue eyes. Pointing at Moses, someone in the crowd shouted "Ronald Reagan," but the man on the screen was Charlton Heston, and he was playing not Moses but an Indian fighter. The Indian maiden in his arms was an American housewife, Donna Reed. War raged around them. A blond Indian on horseback plugged Moses with an arrow. The man standing next to me yelled the Portuguese equivalent of "Fucking Indian."

The jungle life.

I bought the shoes (the slippers) because I had been asked to speak at a radio station, the most popular in Manaus. To reach the station, situated on the top floor of the city's tallest building, I first passed the famous opera house, built in 1896. With its golden dome, its Florentine facade of Italian stone, and, inside, its plush overstuffed chairs, velvet opera boxes, ornate balconies, florid murals, and gilded columns, it is a fitting testament to the city's halcyon days. It looks, as the writer Catherine Caufield so aptly described it, "like an oversized Italian biscuit tin."

The radio station, by contrast, looked as if it had been built in a hurry—bare walls, uncarpeted floors, cracked glass windows. Twenty stories below, Manaus was drenched in a smoggy yellow haze. The engineer who led me to the broadcast booth was a very pretty young woman wearing what seemed to be the uniform of the pretty young women of Manaus, a tight neck-to-ankle body stocking. She blew the disc jockey a kiss and closed the door behind me. The disc jockey was on the far side of middle age, big-bellied and bald save for long gray sideburns. Most of the records stacked in front of him were American (Willie Nelson, the Beach Boys, Michael Jackson), but the one on top was Brazilian. When it began to play I recognized the tune as "Sunny," a pop hit in the United States twenty years ago. This version was called "Sonia," and the lyrics were Portuguese. The disc jockey translated:

> Sonia, I would like to have anal intercourse with you.
> Sonia, I would be very happy if you masturbated me.
> Sonia, please place your tongue upon my rectum.

And so on. He said "Sonia" was the most-requested song in Manaus, and offered it as evidence that a "new" Brazil was emerging with the recent ending of military government.

I spoke with the disc jockey until a different tightly clothed young woman entered the booth. She leaned over and stuck her tongue in his ear. Time to leave.

As I did the pretty young engineer asked me who I was. *A rock musician on a concert tour,* I wanted to say, *and I love you.* Instead, I tried to explain, in my idiot Portuguese, that I was paddling a kayak down the Amazon. She looked disappointed, and, rejected, I suffered a moment of painful epiphany. For weeks, for months, I had reveled in the role of the sophisticate. I had brought news of the modern world to wide-eyed primitives. But there in Manaus, standing in that high-rise, dressed in my grubby khaki pants and those *goddamned granddaddy shoes,* I understood that I belonged on the river, something with which Manaus had very little to do.

The Amazon proper begins about five miles below Manaus, at the confluence of the Negro and Solimões rivers. In volume the Negro is not only the Amazon's largest tributary but the sixth-largest river in the world, with a discharge four times that of the Mississippi. Where it collides with the Solimões the water boils with whirlpools and reflected waves. The silt-rich Solimões is tawny, the Negro coal black; the two rivers roll along side by side for almost six miles before their waters mix.

This spectacle, known as "The Meeting of the Waters," may well be the most impressive natural display in the Amazon basin. Yet recently, on its left bank, the Brazilian government began construction of a cement plant. The project typifies what is happening to the Amazon. Like the Solimões, the Amazon courses through a flood plain, or *várzea,* but the growth along the banks of the Amazon is grassier, lower, and less dense. To a limited degree this is natural; to a larger degree it is the work of man. Between Manaus and the sea, a distance of over a thousand miles, there is no virgin jungle along the water. Every foot of riverbank foliage has been cut down or burned at least once.

The bush that one does see along the Amazon is what biologists call "modified" growth. Some 25 percent of the entire Amazon basin now consists of such modified forest, with the destruction heaviest along the rivers. "Destruction" is the right word—modified forest harbors but a fraction of the species found in primary forest. In the Amazon, the dimensions of this loss are staggering. Though man has identified some 1.5 million species on the entire planet, there may be three times that many undiscovered in the Amazon basin alone.

This destruction has many roots, but in recent years the main one has been cattle ranching, which is now the most important agricultural activity in the basin. Converting rain forest to pasture-land is deceptively pernicious. The forest's fertility is in its canopy and its floodwaters, not its soil, which tends to be poor. Once denuded of forest cover, the soil quickly bakes hard. Virtually every cattle ranch established in the basin prior to 1978 had been abandoned by 1983. In the eastern half of the state of Pará, which begins about three hundred miles downriver from Manaus, thousands of acres that were once rich rain forest are now uninhabitable desert.

It is difficult to determine how much of the Amazonian rain forest has already been destroyed, but it is generally believed that 15 to 20 percent has disappeared in the last twenty years alone. And there seems to be agreement on another point: The rate at which the forest is being destroyed is increasing exponentially. Philip Fearnside, an American-born ecologist who since the early 1970s has studied the Amazon basin from a station near Manaus, has predicted that if the destruction continues to increase at its present rate the rain forest will be gone by the turn of the century.

As Chmielinski and I worked our way down from Manaus, we witnessed a disconcerting irony. In the heart of a basin estimated to contain some five thousand species of fish (there are less than two hundred species in all of North America), it was often difficult to find fish to eat. Beef was more readily available. This might seem a blessing for the heavily exploited local fisheries, but consider the *tambaqui,* whose sweet flesh comprised nearly half the fish sold in Manaus and its environs in the 1970s.

Like much of the rest of the Amazon basin's commercial catch, the *tambaqui* survives not on insects and worms but on the fruits and seeds of the forest itself. According to the Amazonian biologist Michael Goulding, one of the *tambaqui*'s primary food sources is the Spruce rubber tree, which produces seed capsules that mature at the onset of flood season. About a month later, on hot days, the capsules begin to burst open, ejaculating their seed for distances of up to twenty yards. The seed lands in the flooding river, where much of it is gobbled up by the voracious *tambaqui.* The explosions continue for two to three months, during which time a thirty-five-pound *tambaqui* may carry up to a pound and a half of seed in its stomach.

But as the rain forest disappears, torn down for pasture that bakes to death in a few short years, the Spruce rubber tree goes with it. As goes the Spruce, so goes the *tambaqui*. So it is not all that farfetched to stare at a plate of tough Amazonian beef and see dead fish, and, in turn, a diminished chance of the forest regenerating itself: In the Amazon, it is fish, not birds, that are the primary dispersers of plant seed.

As I paddled out of Manaus that first day, singing deliriously into a cyclopean sun, the destruction of the rain forest was for me a horror more conceptual than real. The bush looked different from what I had become accustomed to—there was less of it, and it was lower—but the idea of land quickly became an abstraction. I could barely see the banks. Where we crossed the Meeting of the Waters and turned east into the Amazon, our kayaks rocking on the chop like hobby horses, the river was five miles wide and the waves were head high, which meant I spent most of my time buried in troughs.

Suddenly, I was overcome by chills and vomiting. In a doctor's office in Manaus I had seen a map of the Amazon basin. Along the river it was peppered with dozens of colored pushpins denoting outbreaks of disease. There in the kayak, puking over the side, I envisioned the pins as so many bumpers on a pinball machine, Chmielinski and I bouncing among them.

The range of disease along the Amazon proper, always extraordinary, has grown dramatically as the rain forest has been cut down. Host insects once content to ply their business in the canopy have come in closer contact with human prey, and standing water trapped behind large new dams provides fertile breeding grounds. Malaria is epidemic. The next-most-common affliction, leishmaniasis, can kill, but it is more widely feared for the leprosy-like disfigurement its worst form can cause—victims eventually lose nose and ears. "Leish" can be controlled with antimony, but it can't be cured. The first Brazilian case of dengue fever was discovered in 1982; the virus has since moved into urban areas, as has yellow fever, which once was contracted only deep in the forest. (Tefé had suffered a violent outbreak the year before.) Oropouche fever, virtually unheard of before 1980, infected more than a quarter million people between 1980 and 1984. Something called Mayaro fever, only recently discovered, has torn through Indian populations with terrible force, killing almost 60 percent of those who contract it. Over the last decade there has been a huge increase in infectious hepatitis, one form of which often leads to cirrhosis of the liver among children and adolescents.

Botflies bury larvae in the skin that erupt months later as inchlong maggots. Mosquito-injected worms work their way into the eyes, causing blindness. Chagas' disease, spread by beetles, causes a victim's internal organs to atrophy so slowly that he can live twenty years without knowing he is infected; then suddenly he drops dead. As for the usual suspects, the intestinal worms, the doctor in Manaus had said, "Don't concern yourself with avoiding them. You cannot. They are everywhere."

On our second day out of Manaus we arrived after dark in Itacoatiara, a brooding shantytown huddled around a jute mill. While I slumped in my kayak Chmielinski persuaded a bald, wall-eyed man with boot-black skin to let us sleep on his wooden fishing boat, one of perhaps a hundred nuzzling the port. As Chmielinski pitched our tents the man hurried into town and returned with a pot of scrambled eggs, onions, and bread. He and Chmielinski worried over me and urged me to eat, but I couldn't hold food. I fell asleep on the galley table.

In the morning, to save time, Chmielinski packed my kayak and put me on the river while he scoured Itacoatiara for supplies. I paddled my boat into one of the floating grass islands that clog the river below Manaus, hoping it would pull me along faster than I could drift against the headwind.

After I had settled in and propped my feet up on my deck, I looked back toward Itacoatiara and picked up the steady white flashing of Chmielinski's paddle. White dots rose and fell quickly—he was racing to catch me. He drew within shouting distance, forty yards to my port side, still without seeing me. When I started to yell I vomited. I retched uncontrollably for three or four minutes. By the time I regained my voice Chmielinski had sped past me and was nearly out of sight.

It was hopeless to think I could catch him. I spotted a fishing boat and paddled out of the grass island as quickly as I could and hailed it. The driver looked at me, gunned his motor, and raced away.

"STOP, YOU SON OF A BITCH!" I screamed, but that had absolutely no effect on anything save my already burning throat. I watched Chmielinski's flashing blades shrink.

I did not know what to do. Desperate, I tried telepathy.

I formed one thought and concentrated on it as hard as I could: *Piotr, this is Joe. If you cannot see me in front of you, I must be behind you. Piotr, this is Joe. If you cannot see me in front of you, I must be behind you. Piotr, this is Joe. If you cannot see me in front of you, I must be . . .*

After two or three minutes of this I saw the white flashing of his blades slow down, then stop.

Piotr, this is Joe. If you cannot see me in front of you, I must be behind you . . .

Then a yellow line appeared beneath the place where I had last seen his blades. He had turned his boat broadside. The line disappeared; he had turned around to face me. The flashing began again, slowly. By and by, the blades grew.

The next two days passed in a roller coaster of chills and sweat and blinding headache. Chmielinski paddled beside me and spoke to me all day long. I heard his voice, but few words. I do know that he asked me if I wanted to stop and that I said no. By now I was obsessed by the idea of paddling to the Atlantic. In that way the fever helped me—I was too far gone to think.

Each day, all day long, either the sun flashed off the river and seared the eyes and skin, or cold, slashing rainstorms flew across the sun and blocked out the light. The river-sea straightened its course and lumbered east unimpeded by islands or curves, as if in its lust for the Atlantic it had wiped all obstacles from its path. With nearly a thousand miles of straight fetch the wind roared up the river and raked it into a choppy mess. We had nowhere to hide. Our world was nothing but water and sky and the thin band of green that bonded the two.

The third afternoon below Manaus I watched the waves toss, willy-nilly, a passenger ship the size of an ocean liner. By then the river was thick with such boats, and each one, it seemed, had a dark urge to run us down. The big boats would veer sharply toward us, their props throwing four- and five-foot waves, their passengers leaning over the rail and shouting at us. As the ships blew by and we desperately surfed their wakes, their Portuguese names appeared like Blakean visions: *Under the Shield of the Lord, Faith in God, Ship of the Angels.*

For hours on end it seemed the wind would never cease or the sun set. The sound of my paddle hitting water hypnotized me. Once, awakened by a sharp pain behind my left ear, I slapped at it and came away with a dead bee. My ear hurt like hell, but I was relieved to have been attacked by a single bee. Killer bees travel in swarms.

Sometime late in the day I found myself chattering wildly at Chmielinski, who was chattering wildly right back at me. It took me a couple of minutes to figure out where I was, having blocked out the *slap . . . slap . . . slap* of paddle on water as if some other being were making that sound. Then I was forced once again to confront the endless brown flood before me. I picked out a landmark, a far-off hut, but we seemed to paddle for hours without drawing any closer to it.

The sun had set when we landed in Urucurituba. The dot on the map suggested a sizeable town; in reality, Urucurituba was a wretched hole that merited its dot only because there were no other candidates for miles. A ragged crowd gathered at the foot of the mud bank—stooped old men, three young toughs in pointy leather boots, a dozen children with bloated stomachs. Chmielinski climbed the bank to search for lodging. No one spoke as he muscled through the crowd, but when he disappeared the three hoods slid down the bank and stood over me. One of them flicked a cigarette on the nose of my kayak. The other two laughed.

I did not know how to react. Finally, I offered the smoker my paddle, and said, "Why don't you try the boat?"

A hard rain began to fall. It was dark and cold. He rubbed his boot in the muck. The people on the bank watched, waiting for a reaction. Then a deep voice boomed, "Bring those boats up here!"

The owner of the voice was tall and broad, his thick gray hair cut short and combed straight back. The hoods did not hesitate. They hauled the boats one after the other up the slippery bank and along the town's one muddy street into a cement shell that might once have been a house.

The shell belonged to the gray-haired man. As he watched us unpack he said it was a good thing we'd brought our own food, because there was none in the town. Then he returned to Urucurituba's one bar.

The clouds lifted and the half-moon revealed Urucurituba to be poor even by the Amazon's meager standards. No cars, no mill, no harbor. Canoes and launches were simply tied up along the bank, there to be pounded to splinters in a storm.

Rain continued to fall, but the big-bellied children stood outside the shell most of the night, staring at us through its cracks. At dawn, before anyone was awake, we slipped down the streets and put our boats on the river.

Slap . . . slap . . . slap: The next day was another with the world askew. I forgot that I was on the Amazon. I lost myself in dreams. When I came around late in the afternoon, Chmielinski informed me that we were well short of the ninety miles we had planned to paddle. So, beneath a moon waxing full, we continued into the night, hoping the current would increase and drag us into Parintins, some three hundred miles from Manaus. We had told Durrant and Bzdak we would try to meet them there.

Instead, we got lost in a swamp and washed up on a clean, mosquito-free beach tended by a chorus of gently croaking frogs. We unpacked the boats and scrubbed them out. Chmielinski brewed tea. I sat against a log and tried to write in my notebook.

"Joe, what are you thinking about today?" Chmielinski asked when he brought the tea.

"I don't know," I said. "I can't remember." I couldn't recall a damn thing about the day—my notebook page was blank.

He returned to the stove to cook dinner. I put down the notebook, fetched a bucket of water, and listened to the frogs.

"Cars," I said when I brought him the water. "Cars and motorcycles."

He stirred the cookpot. Tonight we would eat the last of the *comida plástica* we had carried all the way from Arequipa. He poured chicken cacciatore into our little bowls.

"What were you thinking about, Piotr?"

"That big hole on the Apurimac. The one where Zbyszek pulled Jack out. Do you remember this?"

It seemed long ago, another river altogether. How far we had come since then: the lower Apurimac, the Ene, the Tambo, the Ucayali, the Marañón, the Solimões. Three thousand miles of river. Though I had paddled every foot of it, it didn't seem quite real.

And though it had been three months since we had navigated the Acobamba Abyss, I had a recurring nightmare about it. A green monster surrounded me, threw me head over heels, and would not release me. The curious part was that I did not get wet, but neither did I escape. Not, that is, until I woke up in a cold sweat, not an easy feat in the tropics.

"We are lucky to make it through that place," Chmielinski said. "I think it is lucky even that we are here now."

"I suppose you're right," I said, but I didn't feel it.

The next afternoon, as we drew near to Parintins, the banks narowed and the constricted river rebelled with such strength that it ripped the rudder off my kayak. The boat developed a head of its own, bucking like a spooked horse. I was not surprised to see that Parintins had a seawall, a protected harbor, and a cement ramp that descended from the wall like a castle drawbridge.

Despite that ominous entrance, the town appeared to be pleasantly and agreeably unspectacular, with the easy feeling of rumpled harmony that comes with age; the Parintins church, an immense red-brick affair built in the eighteenth century, is the oldest in the state of Amazonas. A graceful, tree-lined promenade runs along the river, and leafy palms ring the plaza. On the street surrounding the plaza I counted seven mules, three of them pulling carts; nine rickety three-speed bicycles; four Volkswagen bugs; and one dusty Mercedes-Benz sedan. That, in a nutshell, seemed to sum up not only Parintins but the Amazon itself.

The only hotel was a cool, cinder-block affair built around a garden. We found Bzdak and Durrant waiting for us, and with them a new addition to our troupe—Jacek Bogucki, who had left Poland with Chmielinski and Bzdak in 1979. Bogucki and his Peruvian wife, Teresa, now lived in Casper, Wyoming. He had brought Polish sausages, chocolate, a motion-picture camera, and what was left of the bank loan he had taken out to purchase his plane ticket.

He had also brought the money the people of Casper had raised for us and which they had requested we invest in a support boat, so that we would all reach the sea together. There were hundreds of cargo boats in port in Parintins, all but one of them wood, and by the time Chmielinski and I arrived, Durrant, Bzdak, and Bogucki had hired the eighteen-meter *Roberto II.*

The captain was a tall, wide, placid sixty-year-old *caboclo* named Deomedio, who, depending on the light, could have passed for Indian, Portuguese, or Asian. Bzdak had quickly dubbed him "Capitan-Almirante," the Captain-Admiral of our fleet. Until I shook hands with him, Capitan had never met a North American. In fact, he had made the sixteen-hundred-mile round trip from Parintins to Belém only once, in 1951. His first and only mate, Afrain, a shy, skinny fifteen-year-old and the youngest of Capitan's twenty-one grandchildren, had never been more than ten miles from Parintins.

We would have left port that day, but a dream had revealed to Capitan a leak in the *Roberto II.* He hauled the boat out and spent the day repairing the leak, which as it turned out was right under the wheel.

While Capitan worked on the boat, Chmielinski discussed the

voyage with him. Capitan said he knew the river as far as Santarém but from there would have to rely on his nose and eyes.

"This will help," Chmielinski said, and handed him a river chart he had purchased in Manaus.

Capitan studied the chart, nodding his head and grunting, then returned it.

"I cannot read that," he said.

"Why not?" Chmielinski asked.

"I cannot read," Capitan said. "But it does not matter. A pilot who needs such a thing does not belong on the Amazon."

That night the members of the Amazon Source-to-Sea Expedition were honored guests at a dance kicking off the *carnaval* season. It was held at Club Knapp, a patio and bar overlooking the river. The quartet (saxophone, conga, bass, drums) specialized in *forro,* which in Parintins is danced with the torso held rigid, the hips gyrating wildly, and the partners clinched so tightly they seem, as Durrant described it, "as if they are attached at the groin." Each chorus is quicker and more frenzied than the last, and a single dance can last up to an hour.

To the crowd's delight, Durrant was the best *forro*ist among us. Bzdak made up in enthusiasm what he lacked in grace. The dapper Chmielinski was the favorite of the Parintins women, but, raised on waltzes and minuets, he found the *forro* on the lewd side. "What is this they are doing?" he asked me during a break, and made a grinding motion with his hips.

I tried my best. My fever had passed; I was ready for anything. Isabella, a buxom, dark-skinned woman a head taller than I, wanted to trade dance lessons for English lessons. She hoped to move to Manaus and become a guide for American tourists: "The Spanish talkers gots more pipples, but da Englitch talkers gots more monies!"

The first few dances went all right, but during one particularly long round I found myself suffocating in Isabella's considerable cleavage. This distracted me from our delicate thigh-beneath-groin connection, which, given the high speed at which the *forro* is danced, all at once caused me great pain.

I escorted Isabella off the dance floor slowly. We sat at a table and ordered beer. She smiled and said, "The pipples of de Amazonas eats menly fitches en maniocs. In Chenuar da ribber he floods and da island she sinks. I like da Ford Escort wit da stick ships."

I excused myself and wandered out to the river. Chmielinski was sitting on a bench, studying the water. For the sixth time on our journey the moon was coming full. It cast a rippling bronze path across the river, a path that dissolved into darkness—even by the moon's strong light the far bank was invisible. In bronze and black the Amazon looked as beautiful as she did powerful, but Chmielinski seemed sad, an emotion rare for him. I asked if everything was okay.

"It is a nice town here," he said, "but it does not feel right."

"What do you mean?"

"Even one day off the water and I am not comfortable. *That* is my home." He pointed to the river. "I feel like now I know this Amazon. I do not want to be away from it."

To my surprise, I found myself agreeing with him.

In the morning Capitan invested the whole of our first payment to him in a shiny new Formica-topped table for the ship's galley. When the table was in place, Chmielinski and I climbed into our kayaks, Durrant and her two Polish escorts boarded the *Roberto II*, Afrain undid the mooring lines, and the Capitan-Almirante guided his fleet out of the harbor and into the Amazon. Then he sniffed the wind and set course for the Atlantic, still some eight hundred miles to the east.

While the *Roberto II* hugged the right bank, Chmielinski and I paddled into the middle of the Amazon, where the current ran swiftest. Though the sky was clear, I had to squint to see the thin green strips of land two miles to either side of us. Then the sky fogged over and settled on the river, and I could not see land at all. We met no one on the river until late that afternoon, when, pitching on the oceanlike swells, the *Roberto II* lurched into our gray cocoon. As she took form in the mist voices broke the day-long silence and arms waved from atop her high white hull. When she pulled abeam a can of cold beer dropped in my lap.

Then Afrain shouted—he had spotted a bushmaster snake, or *surucucú* as they are called, wriggling toward my bow. Afrain jumped onto my boat and slid my kayak paddle under the critter and lifted it from the water. It was about two feet long, small as bushmasters go. Bogucki, a pack rat by reputation, dumped the contents from a jar of mayonnaise and filled the jar partially with *cachaça,* figuring the alcohol would both drown the snake and preserve it. Afrain grabbed the bushmaster behind the head and dropped it into the jar, which Bogucki quickly capped.

Capitan recoiled from this effort. "That is grotesque," he said. "In Brazil we do not eat snakes with mayonnaise."

The sunset, an hour later, was one of those Amazonian spectacles that I had been taking too much for granted. Turning to scan the horizon behind me, I saw the yellow ball of the sun, small and distant in the equatorial sky, sneak from beneath a bank of purple clouds. It lit up the now-placid river like a silver sheet, flashed crimson against the black front of a northerly storm, and glazed the marshy *várzea* a deep mustard green. A light wind rose and died, stirring the river into wavelets that chinked the silver with painterly brown splotches.

In front of me, to the southeast, the moon rose full and yellow, then as she climbed above the blanket of humidity turned a fierce white. Our last full moon, if all went according to plan. We hoped to reach the sea in less than a month. In memory, at least, my first full moon south of the equator, the one that had risen over the frozen *puna* the night we had descended from the source of the Amazon, was twice the size of this tropical one. But I had been lonely then, and short of hope.

Now I paddled in the moonlight bone tired, but also peaceful and happy. For the first time in the six long months since I had arrived in Peru I found myself daring to believe that we would actually make it all the way to the Atlantic.

The *Roberto II* hummed along beside me, her powerful diesel low and barely audible. On the bow, silhouetted by the moon, Bzdak sat with his arms around Durrant. In hiring Capitan and the *Roberto II* we had drained some of the adventure from our trip—no longer would Chmielinski and I bang on strange doors seeking shelter—but that was a small loss compared to the enormous gain of traveling with such boon companions as the photographer and the good doctor.

Capitan led us into a black-water lagoon set below a high, gladed bluff. The lagoon was alive with the sounds of insects and night birds and splashing fish, and ringed with thick bush. Intending to tie up my boat, I stood in my cockpit and leaned into a ceiba tree. I heard a branch snap and felt it droop over my right arm. When I finished securing the kayak I reached with my left hand to remove the branch and found a pair of tiny eyes rising up to meet mine. I jerked involuntarily and flung the snake far into the night. Then I fell out of my kayak, into the shallow lagoon, which only scared me more.

Capitan witnessed this fiasco from start to finish. "Yo," he shouted to me as I climbed out of the water, "do you want some mayonnaise?"

18 *The Pará*

Thirty miles below Parintins the Amazon entered the state of Pará and day by day grew more oceanic. Although a procession of freighters plied the river between Manaus and Belém, we seldom saw more than a silhouette on the horizon, suspended in a seamless gray wall of river and cool rainy-season sky. The birdlife was pelagic—terns and gulls—and, though still nearly eight hundred miles from the Atlantic, we noticed an eerie tidal change of some ten feet a day. Eerie because the tide had no current. The river rose and fell like a bathtub filling with water. Or, as I began to think of it, like a snake slowly filling and emptying its air sacs.

In navigating the two hundred and twenty miles from Parintins to Santarém, Chmielinski and I traveled with the *Roberto II* as we had with the *Coronel Brandão* from Coari to Manaus. We hit the water before dawn, coffee thermos strapped to my boat, and paddled alone through the day except in a storm, when Capitan would crisscross the river to find us and ride alongside until the bad weather passed. This was far more dangerous for him than for us. Our little boats handled the storms well, but the shallow-keeled *Roberto II* pitched wildly in the waves, and more than once seemed close to capsizing.

At night, after Capitan had moored the *Roberto II* in a lagoon or creek and we had washed ourselves and settled down for a meal, he held court around his shiny new galley table, speaking slowly but constantly in even-toned Portuguese. He did not mind if we only half understood his stories, for they delighted him no end. He told the same ones every night. His favorites were Portuguese jokes: "*Caboclo* finishes his dinner and says, 'Thank you.' Portuguese finishes his dinner and says, 'I want more.'" He also told scarifying tales, and seemed all the more satisfied when we did not believe them. Like the one about the anaconda that only the month before had risen up and squeezed the life out of a boat the size of the *Roberto II* itself.

While we set up tents and hammocks after dinner Capitan would sip from a glass of wine and talk with Afrain, instructing him in the river's way. Afrain listened, nodded, said little. Capitan never raised his voice with Afrain. One day, however, while Afrain kneeled on the afterdeck scrubbing a batch of exceptionally dirty dishes, the river reached up and hauled two burnt pots overboard.

When Afrain informed his grandfather of this, Capitan said nothing, but a while later, as the *Roberto II* passed a row of wretched huts along the south bank, Capitan swung the boat's nose to shore and pointed. "Work hard," he said quietly to Afrain, "or you will end up in one of those."

Afrain did not attend school, but he had a searching intelligence. He was amused to find that my Berlitz lacked the Portuguese words for sex, penis, vagina, and breast, and taught me several ways to refer to each. He also had what may have been, after a gut understanding of the river's moods, the talent most critical to a budding *caboclo* river captain: the ability to repair anything on this boat with little more than spit, sweat, and a meager tool kit, in Afrain's case two screwdrivers and a spanner wrench.

On Afrain's sixteenth birthday Durrant gave him a thing akin to jewelry—her multi-bladed Swiss Army knife. Afrain sharpened the blades and oiled the knife and hung it from a string, which he tied around his neck. The knife remained either there or in his hand for the remainder of our voyage.

Admiring this gift, Capitan said, "It is my birthday in four days."

Bzdak said, "Prove it," but Bogucki gave him his spare sunglasses, and I donated my San Francisco Giants baseball hat. That the hat had traveled all the way from the source of the Amazon meant as much to Capitan as the idea of baseball, which is to say nothing at all. But hat and glasses somehow invested him with great power when dealing with the river locals, and from that moment neither one left his head when the sun was in the sky.

In return Capitan tried to give Bzdak his watch. By then, however, we all knew about the watch.

"What time is it, Capitan-Almirante?" Bzdak would ask each night at dinner. Solemnly, Capitan would consult the broad silver orb on his wrist and wait for silence before reporting what he had found there. These reports, though accurate according to his watch, were seldom within two hours of the actual time. When Bzdak would point this out, which he never failed to do, Capitan would only shrug and say, "Portuguese watch."

Then he would carefully wind the watch, as if to confirm that in this part of the universe, our notions of time did not apply.

When Chmielinski woke me before dawn on our fourth day out of Parintins I could hear rain beating on the roof of the *Roberto II*. Serious rain. Eye-stinging, monster-wave rain. The previous afternoon something had snapped in my back. As I rolled over to take the cup of coffee Chmielinski offered, a bolt of pain tore through my left side. I did not want to get in the kayak.

Procrastinating, I asked, "What kind of day is it?"

"It is a beautiful day."

"That is Polish bullshit."

"There you go. Start the day talking about my nationality." Immediately he climbed into his kayak and left the *Roberto II* without me. I got going as quickly as I could, but he would not let me catch him. During the entire day we did not speak. Finally, at sunset, he slowed down, and I drew alongside. We paddled in silence for several minutes, until he asked, "Why did you say that?"

"Say what?" The incident had not stuck with me.

" 'Polish bullshit,' " he said, imitating my own wise-guy tone perfectly.

"I'm sorry. I thought you were joking with me about the beautiful day. It was raining."

"I was not joking. All day I am *furious.* Maybe I am too sensitive. But that is the way I am."

I apologized again and promised to exercise more care in my choice of language. I felt terrible about my gaffe, and I was also worried. Chmielinski and I had disagreed about things before, but most of those disputes had concerned strategy—how far to try to paddle on a particular day, how much food to carry. They had never been personal. Despite the long months we had spent together, we had never really argued about anything. Usually I simply deferred to his judgment.

I suspected that his reaction was symptomatic of a much deeper problem. He, Bzdak, Durrant, and I had been traveling together for six months, and though we were still at least three weeks short of our goal, each of us, in his own way, was cringing in anticipation of the psychological jolt our arrival at the Atlantic was sure to deliver. The river had demanded so much from us, every day, that we could no longer quite imagine the world outside it.

That question loomed largest for Chmielinski. He carried the expedition's heaviest emotional burden, and not only as leader. He was also our publicist, a talent he had demonstrated dramatically in Manaus. We had entered the city penniless, caked in mud, and with barely a pair of shoes among the four of us. Over the next few days, in a country whose language he could hardly speak, Chmielinski had mounted a whirlwind public-relations campaign, playing the national tourist board against the state tourist board against the city media against the local politicians. We had left Manaus not only as the toast of the city but with guarantees of free hotels and meals in Santarém, Belém, and Rio de Janeiro and a free ride home. Given our fiscal condition, which despite the help from Casper continued to be shaky, that assistance was substantial. But the effort had drained Chmielinski.

At the same time, he still had to keep his rendezvous with his wife, Joanna. It had been six months since he had last been able to telephone Poland. As far as he knew, Joanna was due in the United States within a matter of weeks. He had not only to meet her there but to find a way to support them both. Joanna had earned master of science degrees in both pharmacology and clinical chemistry, but it would be months, at least, before she could expect to find work in the States.

As we drew closer to the Atlantic Chmielinski drove himself harder and pushed the rest of us to keep pace. We did not always react well. Now that we were traveling together, there was less room in which to release the expedition's mounting internal pressures.

I probably had the easiest time of it. If Chmielinski and I had not learned by then to forgive each other's transgressions, we would long since have parted. So we dismissed this latest outburst as a mere contretemps. For Durrant and Bzdak, however, life within the confines of the expedition had become increasingly difficult. For them, too, our incipient finish was unsettling. Bzdak had no choice but to return to Casper after we reached the sea. He had a job there, and, like Chmielinski, he was in the last year of his residency requirement for U.S. citizenship. It had been risky to depart the United States for the Amazon, but moving to London would be a step almost as bold as leaving Poland.

Durrant's situation was no easier. What kind of life could she expect in Casper? Getting licensed to practice medicine in the United States would require another year of medical school, and with a recent drop in world oil prices, Casper, an oil town, was suffering an economic depression. In all probability, she would have to return to London.

The next day we crossed the sharp line, almost as spectacular as that at Manaus, where the translucent blue Tapajós collides with the silty brown Amazon. No sooner had we glided into Santarém and checked into our hotel room (Capitan and Afrain, unwilling to leave the *Roberto II*, chose to sleep aboard) than Chmielinski began to pepper Bzdak with demands for photographs to distribute to the local papers, instructions for purchasing maps and supplies, and requests for food.

This was not unusual, except that his tone had a curt edge. When he announced a plan to send Bzdak ahead to Belém to do advance work, rather than all of us arriving there together as we had planned, the usually unflappable Bzdak exploded. His anger shocked Chmielinski, who, in turn, was indignant. Durrant tried to keep out of the confrontation, but in the end she, too, lashed out at Chmielinski, telling him that his hunger for publicity threatened to ruin us.

I was left out of this, our worst crisis since Luisiana. While they argued around me I sat and worked on my notes. I felt guilty about that, for I was only then beginning to understand what the expedition's end would mean for them.

We left Santarém the next day under a hot blue sky. Chmielinski and I paddled far ahead of the *Roberto II*, cruised north along the Tapajós, bounced across the *encontro das águas* and into the Amazon, and took aim on Belém, five hundred miles downstream.

"It is that woman," Chmielinski said. "We have never had this kind of problem on an expedition. A woman has never come between Zbyszek and me in that way."

I tried to explain what I saw as the root of the conflict, the strain each of us was under. Chmielinski listened and did not disagree, but that night and all of the next day he refused to speak to either Durrant or Bzdak. Bogucki told me he had never seen such hard feelings between his countrymen. Bzdak was quiet, his expression vacant, and Durrant spent long hours sitting alone atop the *Roberto II*.

The next night, as if something had snapped inside him, Chmielinski was wracked with chills, fever, violent shakes, and bouts of severe vomiting that left him too weak to climb out of his tent. In the morning he looked pallid and confused. Durrant's preliminary diagnosis was malaria, although she could not be certain until the symptoms had established a pattern.

Chmielinski insisted on trying to kayak. After we put our boats in the water I paddled next to him, keeping close watch. His eyes were bloodshot, he could not sit up straight, and his boat veered erratically. Twenty minutes later I convinced him to return to the *Roberto II*. Capitan moored in a lagoon and we put Chmielinski in a hammock, where he quickly fell asleep.

When he woke up after lunch he again insisted on kayaking, an exercise that yielded the results it had earlier. He went back to sleep. If he had malaria, or any of the half dozen other afflictions that matched his symptoms, we had to get him to a medical facility soon.

It was too late in the day to begin a return to Santarém, however, and as the light of dusk is the photographer's favorite, I agreed to accompany Bzdak on a kayak exploration of the lagoon. He had hoped to shoot jungle plants, but we found only marsh grass, low shrubs, and the occasional lonesome ceiba tree. A herd of water buffalo stood belly deep at the far end of the lagoon. Behind them, six emaciated white zebu cattle were squeezed onto a receding rise, slowly starving to death as the flooding river drowned their grazing land.

We paddled up to a ten-foot-square shack planted on thin stilts in the middle of the lagoon. Four toothless adults and eight bony children spilled out of it, their clothing gone to rags, their expressions listless. They said they had neither fruit nor fish to sell, and that the animals and the land that surrounded them belonged to a man in Santarém.

When we returned to the *Roberto II* Chmielinski was still asleep. Capitan was worried. He did not know the Amazon below Santarém, and he had come to rely on Chmielinski to help him decipher the river. Capitan, too, was in pain. It took Bzdak and me a couple of hours and a bottle of wine to convince him to submit to an examination by Durrant, but when he did, the reason for his reticence was clear—he did not want a woman poking around his infected, painfully swollen testicles.

After Durrant had supplied Capitan with a course of antibiotics she turned her attentions to me. I had new lesions on my legs,

ankles, and jaw, and behind my right ear. Durrant suspected botfly
larvae. She lanced the boils and cleansed them. Then I put up my
tent and went to sleep.

In the dead of night I awoke to the sensation of the *Roberto II*
rocking in an unfamiliar way. I climbed onto the deck. The air was
thick with the sound of chirping crickets and the smell of musk,
and I saw shadows rubbing up against the hull—the water buffalo
had surrounded us. There was nothing aquatic about their rocking.
It was an alien rhythm, thumping and irregular, and each knock
seemed to shake the equanimity from my soul. The peace I had
felt that first night out of Parintins was being overwhelmed by
dissension and disease. In that sad lagoon the Atlantic seemed as
far away, as unreal, as it had on the desolate *puna* five months
before.

Dawn brought a good sign: Though not yet himself, Chmielinski
felt stronger, and before the sun had risen he summoned us to the
galley table and spread out charts bought in Santarém. We faced a
critical decision. At the mouth of the Amazon an island larger than
Switzerland divides the river. Some seven-eighths of the river's volume
flows north around the island, called Marajó. Many hydrographers
say that only this course can be considered the Amazon, and that the
system flowing to the south is another river altogether, the Pará.

However, it can be said—*is* said, particularly by Brazilian hydrographers—that because some Amazon water flows to the south
of Marajó, through the Gurupá Canal, and joins the Tocantins
and several lesser rivers to form the Pará, that this, too, is the
Amazon.

At stake is the question of supremacy. Measured by the northern route, the Amazon is the planet's second-longest river, seventy
miles shorter than the Nile. Measured by the southern route, it is
fifty miles longer than the Nile (and, as Brazilians are quick to
point out, in either case carries some ten times the Nile's volume
of water).

Which route should we follow? Given the maze of canals and
tidal currents in the Gurupá Canal, the northern route might

deliver us to the sea as much as two weeks earlier than the southern. We discussed the question for an hour or so, but in the end decided as I suspected we knew all along we would. We had started from the river's farthest source; it was only right that we also follow her longest course to the sea.

Although I believed this decision was the right one, I was not overjoyed at the prospect of spending an extra two or three weeks on the river. My muscles were strong now, but my joints ached. The popping sound my shoulders made with each stroke worried me despite Durrant's assurance that I was causing no permanent damage.

Marajó Bay worried me, too. According to what little information we managed to glean from fishermen, we could expect severe storms, breaking waves, and gale-force winds blowing straight from the Atlantic into the bay's broad, unprotected mouth.

But the next day, when we slid south, then northeast into the Gurupá Canal, we were rewarded in ways that I had not anticipated. The Gurupá is actually the first in a webwork of canals weaving through a type of floodplain we had not yet encountered, an estuarine *várzea* governed by tidal currents rather than rainfall. Unlike the main trunk of the river, which floods five months out of the year, the estuarine *várzea* floods twice a day, backing up and releasing in response to ocean tides three hundred miles east. Instead of running through well-defined banks, the river floods into the forest. The vegetation, denser than any we had seen in the eight hundred miles of river below the Solimões and dominated by palm trees (at least a dozen species grow along the canals), looked like a herd of giant houseplants set free. Sounds that we had not heard in too long—howler-monkey roars, parrot screeches—ricocheted through the bush like greetings from old friends.

Chmielinski's health seemed to improve with the scenery. Shortly before we entered the Gurupá he broke his silence with Bzdak. The exchange was in Polish, but Bogucki told me later that Chmielinski had simply requested that Bzdak take a series of photos in the canals. That had been enough. Bzdak was soon scrambling about the *Roberto II*, shooting film at a rapid clip.

Meanwhile Chmielinski kayaked into a side canal and returned with his deck festooned with orchids, trumpet vines, and irises. These he presented to Durrant, along with a shy apology. That night the flowers sat brightly on the galley table in a plastic vase.

As we pushed deeper into the humid estuary, we passed a handful of small logging towns all of a pattern: one tiny, gas-powered, belt-saw lumber mill flanked by ten or twenty austere shanties. Food was scarce. In the shanty towns we found farinha, or, more often, nothing. We ate the last of our oatmeal, our last rusty can of Peruvian sardines.

Three days into the estuary and a few miles short of the Pará we met a parade of dugout canoes and funky motor-driven heaps that were not so much boats as collages of twine, rotting plywood, pieces of tin, and scraps of leather and cloth. Always a man at the tiller and a man bailing, and between them a dozen worried black heads or a load of palm wood or a heap of red clay. The names painted ornately on these leaky hulks were the wildest of boasts: *Queen of Belém, Grace of God, Princess of the Sea*, the word *Princesa* all but obliterated by soot from her farting engine.

The dugout canoes now bore crude triangular sails for negotiating gusty Marajó Bay. Chmielinski stopped to ask one intrepid navigator how his dugout, which had neither keel nor centerboard, remained upright in the bay's notorious winds.

The man shrugged. "Canoe blows over, I fall out, wind stops. I climb back in."

This was new country for Capitan, and he was baffled not only by the tides and the canals but by the fact that Chmielinski always knew in advance that we were approaching a town. However, once Capitan had determined that what he saw on the charts corresponded to what he later saw on land, he undertook a vigorous program to master map reading. (His unfamiliarity with nautical charts was easily explained: The ten Chmielinski had purchased in Santarém would have cost Capitan a month's earnings.) He tacked the charts above the wheel and often spent an hour at a time gazing at them.

One day I gave him my compass. He held it in his palm and

turned slowly in a circle, his eyes fixed on the dial. When he finished his experiment he nodded solemnly and said, "It works." Then, after my too-brief lesson in the instrument's use, he tacked it up next to the charts. I never did see him employ the compass, but several times I noticed him staring at it intently, as if wondering what strange demon drove it.

We had hoped to run the estuary's spiderweb of canals in three days, pick up the Pará River, follow it into Marajó Bay, and then paddle down the bay to Belém. But we had not figured on the tide, which now that we were within two hundred miles of the Atlantic ran three to four knots at its peak. From one canal to the next the currents never flowed in the same direction. We would navigate one canal and find the tide running with us, turn into a second and find the tide against us, turn into a third and meet water standing dead still. Though we had planned to travel fifty miles a day, we were lucky to make twenty. Ten days after leaving Santarém we were out of food, tempers were short, and it seemed we might never reach the sea. In Breves, the largest town in the canals, we could rustle up only one scrawny chicken.

We had worse luck when we left the canals and entered the five-mile-wide Pará River. That first night we stopped at Curralinho. Aside from its smart red-brick church it was a dingy town, with dozens of dilapidated thatch huts, a loud, joyless bar, a garbage-choked port, and, other than a hearts-of-palm cannery, no food anywhere.

But we arrived on the first weekend of *carnaval*, and that night all of us but Capitan walked into town and tried not to think about our stomachs. A trash fire burned in the middle of the flat clay plaza. A wiry, shirtless black man beat fiercely on a big drum. His pants were ripped off at the thigh and his right foot was bare, but his prosthetic left leg bore a spanking new orange sock and a neon-blue tennis shoe, the only shoe I had seen since we had cruised into the Gurupá.

Several lesser percussionists, playing tambourines and congas, surrounded the drummer. The troupe's personnel changed constantly.

Someone arrived with the family drum, sat in for an hour, left. Two lithe young women danced in skirts torn to mid-thigh, shaking, as Durrant described it, "things where other people don't have things."

The pounding drums, the sweaty, kinetic women: Distracted, I forgot my hunger. Which, days later, and on a full belly, I decided had been precisely the idea.

From Curralinho we traveled forty miles along the left bank of the east-running Pará, arriving after two days at the point where the broad Tocantins River enters the Pará from the south. There, the river widens abruptly to about ten miles and a little further on is known as Marajó Bay. We temporarily parted with the *Roberto II*, which could not handle the bay's swells and sudden storms. Capitan would work his way back upstream, descend through a system of canals on the right bank, and rendezvous with us in the port of Abaetetuba, tucked safely behind an island.

Late that afternoon, with storm clouds hovering in the east, Chmielinski and I sprinted across Marajó Bay. Luck was with us. The bay threw high rolling waves but no breakers and the skies darkened but did not storm. Yet when we reached Abaetetuba my jaws ached—my teeth had been clenched during the entire crossing.

The *Roberto II* met us as planned and moored for the night in Abaetetuba. Shortly after dark, drumbeats drifted down from town. *Carnaval* was the year's high point for Afrain. He grabbed his whistle and hurried to the plaza but returned an hour later profoundly disappointed. *Carnaval* in Abaetetuba meant a solitary drummer, drunks passed out in the street, and a handful of dazed locals walking in circles. Most of the townspeople were gathered in a bar, watching a television broadcast of festivities in Rio de Janeiro. That night the lights of Belém reflected off the dark sky, as did those of a passing jet, something I had not seen since Lima. While we slept, Durrant's windbreaker was stolen from the *Roberto II*'s clothesline. It was our first theft in Brazil.

The next day Chmielinski and I paddled twenty miles along the right side of the bay and, just as a storm hit, ducked into a canal, the Furo do Arrozal. (Rather than risk the bay, Capitan had motored up the Tocantins and then east through a system of small rivers, arranging to meet us in Belém.)

Had I not known from our maps that we were within fifteen miles of the largest and, I presumed, most civilized city on the Amazon, I would not have had the slightest clue, based on what I saw in the Furo do Arrozal. The faces that now and then peered from behind a palm or mangrove were desperate and frightened—a consequence, I decided, of the estuarine rain forest, which was damp, dark, and suffocating. The only light drifted down from the thin opening in the canopy directly above the canals, and even at midday no direct sun reached the forest floor. The few people I saw appeared torpid and inert, save four men cutting chunks of clay from a bank exposed at low tide. Alerted by the slapping of our paddles, they turned to look at us. Their backs were broad and muscular, but their eyes were flat and dead. They stared but did not speak.

We turned into the Furo do Cavado, a canal so narrow we had to kayak in single file. The shacks were little more than rotting trash piles, the people few and spiritless. No birds sang, no fish jumped. From time to time herds of two-inch opaque-yellow salamander-like creatures would burst from the shadows in a ghostly cloud, inflate themselves as they leaped, float for a few seconds when they hit the water, then sink from sight. Those ten miles struck me as the most primitive of our entire journey. The only suggestion that we were in the twentieth century was a rusting yellow Volkswagen bug propped on a small, decaying pier. But the car had no tires, no doors, and no engine.

The canal twisted, turned, and shrank until it was but a paddle length wide, while growing ever darker and spookier. We rounded a bend and then—boom—the skyscrapers of Belém rose up before us, two miles and centuries across the choppy Canal da Das Oncas.

19 *The Atlantic*

Belém, Portuguese for Bethlehem: Unbelieving, we slouch toward our goal of six months, four thousand miles, three million paddle strokes. "Where are you going?" I have been asked hundreds of times by people who will never see what I am seeing now. My reply has been unvarying: *"A Belém!"* Dulled with use, the words have lost all meaning.

The *Roberto II* awaits us in port. While Capitan fills his hold with onions (he will sell them on his return voyage, in the produce-starved hamlets between here and Parintins), we take Afrain into town and buy him dinner and a pair of rakish sunglasses. He is stupefied by the city's size, as am I—its population of a million and a half is probably ten times the number of people living along the entire two thousand miles of river between here and the Peruvian border. (With the exception of Manaus, which, in fact, is on the Negro.)

After dinner we return to the *Roberto II* with a bottle of ersatz Brazilian champagne. Under the influence of this and, I will realize days later, the onions now stored in the ship's hold, Capitan breaks into tears. At first we fear that we have somehow offended him, although we have paid him considerably more than contracted for (and he has delivered considerably more than promised). As it turns out, he is upset only that he cannot accompany us to the sea, still seventy hard miles north and east. But the *Roberto II*, so mighty in tiny Parintins, is dwarfed by even the smallest fishing boats in Belém, all of which sport high, defiant, wave-cutting bows.

We finish the champagne and exchange hugs and farewells. Then the good ship *Roberto II* sets course for the west, where she belongs. I will miss her crew, and remember them fondly.

We climb back into the city. Bogucki has already left on a jet bound for freezing Wyoming and his worried wife. As if born to them, Durrant and Bzdak have settled into the five-star hotel rooms arranged for us by Embratur, the Brazilian office of tourism.

Chmielinski and I, however, have work ahead of us. After embarrassing myself in the hotel sauna—for no reason I can explain other than homesickness, a Frank Sinatra song piped over the loudspeaker reduced me to tears—I climb to my room nervously clutching a cold bottle of beer. I am not looking forward to the last leg of our journey, the passage through Marajó Bay into the Atlantic. I have no confidence in my ability to handle the open sea, a fear reinforced by the size of the boats in port here.

But there is no question of quitting now. Tomorrow, as I have for months, I will simply plow along behind my good friend Piotr Chmielinski.

February 17

At first light we descend to the port. Surrounded by shouting fishermen and the smell of fresh coffee, we slip our little plastic boats into the flat gray Das Oncas and paddle north.

Bzdak and Durrant escort us through the morning in a small power launch provided by the Brazilian navy, Bzdak snapping the last of the seven thousand slides he has taken on this journey. Once, turning at his shout, I lose my sunglasses, which slip into the deep without a sound. Over the last week the river has snatched my knife, my thermos, a hat, two pens, and the silly slippers. It is as if she wants to purify me, wants to send me to the sea stripped of all but thought and memory and the bonds of friendship.

"When we first come west," Bzdak tells me, "we learn that every river must take something. Better some thing than some body."

Soon, after wishing us luck and promising champagne and

muita festa in three days, half our team turns back for Belém. Chmielinski and I turn into Marajó Bay, and east.

The water is flat and the horizon clear. To take advantage of the strong outgoing tide we paddle far into the bay, until land drops away on all sides.

Here the bay, the river—in my mind they are the same—is over fifteen miles wide. In one way the Amazon basin recalls the high Andes: Its immensity encourages contraction. So often my universe has been defined entirely by the Polish fellow who is stopping to share coffee with me as I write these notes. Back at Atalaya, when we were first setting out in two kayaks, I had feared the intimacy the river would force upon us. Since then Chmielinski has seen me at my worst, sick and afraid and despairing, and has not abandoned me. I hope I have been half as good a companion. It is true that our days pass with long silences, but it is the silence of brothers. (He is one of nine children, I one of six.)

After all this time Chmielinski's enthusiasm remains undimmed. When we resume our paddling he launches into one of his Polish marches, straining his lungs. By now I know the words and sing along, though I have no idea what the words mean, and no inclination to ask. The paddling is easier than anticipated, the bay rocking us on gentle swells, the sky a thin gray, and by dusk we have covered almost forty miles. My confidence soars, giving rise to a guarded optimism—soon I will step from my little boat for the last time. I will be in California for the start of baseball season. I will sleep in one place for more than two nights in a row. I will kiss the woman I love.

We decide to attempt a landfall at the small port of Vigia. A band of grizzled roughnecks, all Popeye forearms and missing teeth, stares down at us from the seawall. Assessing that gallery of tough faces, I am pleased to discover that I am not intimidated. I think: I am as much the riverman as any one of them. Then I employ one of Chmielinski's tricks. I take five hard strokes and drive my kayak far up into the sand at the wall's base. It is a cocky display, one that identifies me as either one tough *homem* or a complete idiot. In either case, not to be messed with.

My hairy-chested bravado is unnecessary. These rogues are fishermen, brothers of the sea. When Chmielinski explains our mission they shoulder our boats and we march in a long line to Vigia's one hotel, where we are feted with beans and fried fish and cold beer.

Out of the kayak, endlessly rocking. As I drift off to sleep on a cool patio near the kitchen my body vibrates with the rhythm of ocean swells.

February 18

Whatever hubris possessed me yesterday Marajó Bay beats out of me today. In mid-morning the skies darken and a storm descends, throwing breakers that rise up and curl and crack over our heads. Though we travel parallel with, and a mile off, the bay's right-hand shore, it would be pointless to run there for shelter—the waves are rolling right into a mangrove swamp and would crush us against the exposed roots of the foul-smelling trees.

So, following Chmielinski's example, I turn the nose of my boat into the waves and hang on until mid-afternoon, when the storm finally abates and the sea calms.

After holding in the waves for half the day, paddling hard but standing still, we are drained of energy. Yet the shoreline is a tangle of thick bush and there is nowhere to put in and pitch camp. We continue to paddle.

Two hours later reeds fluttering on the horizon signal a shallow island. We drag our boats through knee-deep mud and up into a sandy clearing. Two dark, bony men huddle around a bed of coals. A pig nuzzles a discarded meat tin, and a scabby dog and two cats, the first I have seen in Brazil, negotiate over a fish head. One of the men rolls a cigarette and lights it off the embers. Studying us from the corners of his eyes, he says that we are welcome to make camp on his sleeping platform. This consists of twelve warped planks and four stilts held together, as near as I can determine in the fading light, solely by *a graça de Deus.*

The air reeks of pig, everything is damp, and six neighbors who seem to have materialized from the sand itself sit on their haunches and stare at us, nodding in mute incomprehension as Chmielinski tries to explain our purpose. One, a pregnant girl, has a head swollen like a hydrocephalic's.

Why am I disappointed with this reception? After four thousand one hundred and fifty miles I should know that to come from the source of the Amazon is to come from Mars. I should expect no more than the pig that burrows under the platform while we sleep, rooting and snorting the night through.

He is gone in the morning—the clearing has flooded. We paddle away from the platform without waking the owner, curled up in a corner on a piece of cardboard.

February 19

Today Marajó is altogether different from yesterday, undulating easily, like a calm gray lake. We run with the outgoing tide. Shortly after noon, as the tide begins to turn against us, we are about a mile short of Taipu Point. Marajó Bay runs almost due northeast and, on its north bank, meets the Atlantic at Cape Maguari. On its south bank, it ends roughly at Dos Guarás Island, thirty-five miles southeast of Cape Maguari and ten miles northeast of Taipu. If we paddle due north from Taipu, in thirteen miles we will intersect an imaginary line drawn between Maguari and Dos Guarás.

We take shelter in a nearby lagoon and find a small gaff-rigged schooner anchored there. The *God Judges You* is twenty-five feet of sturdy wooden boat, sail only, no engine save the muscle of a sleepy crew of three: the leathery captain, Juarez; the first mate, Edinor; and Manol— *"Marinheiro!"* he says, and thumps his thin, hairless chest. They have been swinging to anchor for two days, waiting out the storm that hit yesterday. Though the storm has passed their *cachaça* supply has not, and so, for the time being, the fish of Marajó Bay are safe.

The lagoon is a fine place to stop for a drink. Palms and mangroves rise thick on all sides, and a row of aristocratic, long-legged ibis stand along an exposed sandbar. As the tide begins to turn in our favor I paddle toward them, but they explode into the gray sky like an orange cloud.

Then we bid good-bye to the crew of the *God Judges You*, Chmielinski sets course due north, and we paddle out of the lagoon in search of the Atlantic.

A mist descends on Marajó Bay and slowly thickens to fog. The source of the Amazon, too, had been shrouded by fog, but in my memory it seems another world altogether. I have been a tropical man for so long now that I can hardly remember what it means to be cold. What had the Polish stranger and I said as we staggered across the continental divide? "All downhill from here." For six months I have chased an idea that I now understand was only an excuse to move.

Three hours later the bay begins to rock us with gentle waves that arrive in long, slow sets. Foot by foot, stroke by stroke, the turbid waters thin to a translucent green. A hundred yards ahead of us a shadow creaks in the fog. As we paddle closer the frayed canvas sails of an ancient cutter take shape in the still air. The *Jesus of Galilee:* Rough jute rigging, splintered wood, absence of brass and plastic. A vessel not of this century.

We ship our paddles. Chmielinski shouts. No response. The fog grows thicker yet, sealing us in a gray envelope with the ghost cutter. We sit quietly and listen to the slap of rigging on wood, watch the old boat rock ever so easily, going nowhere.

Chmielinski leans over and scoops a handful of water to his lips.

"Salt," he says.

Afterword

Eight years after we ran the Amazon, five years after this book was first published, I still get questions. Two, mainly. One is: What happened to everybody?

Well, no, Kate and Zbyszek did not stay together. The differences—geographic, cultural, emotional—were simply too vast. After the expedition Kate lived in London for a year and worked for the national health service. Then, bored out of her mind, she lit out once again for South America. For the Bolivian Andes, to be precise, where she spent three years directing a health-education project for Aymara Indians. I visited her there in 1990. It turned out to be the end of her stay: That same week she came down with typhoid and her joints swelled up like balloons. She moved back to England.

Zbyszek, for his part, became an American citizen and married a fourth-generation Wyomingite. (I went to the wedding, at which Zbyszek delivered one of the great matrimonial vows: Trying to wrap his lips around "With this ring, I thee wed, and bestow upon thee . . . " he somehow came up with, "With this ring, I be wed, and be still upon you!") He has published two books of photography, and his photos often appear in major magazines. He and his wife, Lauren, now live near Chicago, where he is staff photographer for a local newspaper. I talk to them about once a week, because Zbyszek and I have continued to travel and work together.

I'm in close contact with Piotr, too. After we finished the Amazon, he managed to get his wife, Joanna, out of Poland and into the United States, where both now have citizenship. They live outside Washington, D.C.; Piotr owns an environmental engineering firm, HP Environmental, that is, by all accounts, one of the best in the country. Let me put it this way: When the World Trade Center was bombed, Piotr was the man called in to investigate potential chemical contamination. He and Joanna have a three-year-old son, Maximilian, who, the story has it, was born running.

Jerome Truran took that last shot at an international title, didn't win but did well, retired, and married a Canadian, Morna Fraser, herself once ranked among the world's top ten female kayakers. They have settled in Vancouver, British Columbia, and one way or another I see them about once a year. They live quietly and happily, and they still spend a lot of time on the water. In 1991 they were the lead kayakers on a *National Geographic* expedition that ran Peru's Colca Canyon. It was an expedition that, in its way, said something about the bonds of friendship formed during the running of the Amazon—once again, Piotr was the leader, Zbyszek the photographer, and I the author, this time of an article that appeared in *National Geographic* in January 1993.

I have no contact with the other principal characters in this book. From what I hear, Jack Jourgensen had a bitter split with François Odendaal and later fell on hard times. As for Odendaal, I have neither seen nor spoken with him since the day he fled the Amazon. I do know that at about the same time that he was in London telling the Royal Geographical Society that he led the first source-to-sea navigation of the Amazon, I was ducking bullets along the Peruvian border, still twenty-two hundred miles short of the Atlantic. Tim Biggs, meanwhile, is in South Africa, raising a family. Sergio Leon is back in Costa Rica. I shared good times with Sergio, and I hope our paths cross again.

Me, I married the girl I left behind, Elyse Axell, and we have a two-year-old daughter, Clare. Running the Amazon was frightening, but I didn't know real fear until I had a child. After Clare was born we lived for a while in Ecuador, where I was on assignment for *The New Yorker* and researching my next book (*Savages*, to be published in 1995). We have since returned to California, and I have taken up adventure gardening—I grow these *killer* tomatoes.

The second question I'm asked is, would you do it again?

Let me be absolutely clear about this: I think so. Maybe. Who knows?

Without a doubt, running the Amazon was the looniest thing I've ever done. That I survived was a matter of luck as much as anything else. I felt relieved when we finished and was happy to get home. I own a house and a car. I like books, movies, good food, cold beer. In short, I enjoy the distractions of modern life, and I'm thankful to be in a culture that readily provides them. But the Amazon taught me something about the true cost of such comfort: Basically, it's insulation. Direct experience is our best teacher, but it is exactly what we are most bent on obliterating, because it is so often painful. We grow more comfortable at the price of knowing the world, and therefore ourselves.

So all I can say is this: For a while, at least, the Amazon sucked me out of my cocoon, and my life has been the better for it. To anyone seriously considering a flying leap into the void, I say: Go.

Joe Kane
Oakland, California
October 1994

A NOTE ABOUT THE AUTHOR

Joe Kane has written for *The New Yorker, National Geographic,* and many other publications. His first book, *Running the Amazon,* was a national bestseller and is now in print in ten languages. His second book, *Savages,* will be published by Alfred A. Knopf in 1995. He lives in Oakland, California, with his wife, Elyse, and their daughter, Clare.

Alex Shoumatoff is the author of ten books, including four about Brazil: *In Southern Light, The Rivers Amazon, The Capital of Hope,* and *The World Is Burning.* He lives in Keene, New York.